| DATE DUE | | | |
|---|---|---|---|
| JUN 0 4 1990 | | | |
| DEC 1 8 1995 | | | |
| APR 0 6 1998 | | | |
| APR 0 6 1998 | | | |
| | | | |
| | | | |
| | | | |
| | | | |
| | | | |
| | | | |

# The Ambiguous Relationship

# The Ambiguous Relationship

## THEODORE ROOSEVELT AND ALFRED THAYER MAHAN

Richard W. Turk

CONTRIBUTIONS IN MILITARY STUDIES, NUMBER 63

Greenwood Press
NEW YORK • WESTPORT, CONNECTICUT • LONDON

**Library of Congress Cataloging-in-Publication Data**

Turk, Richard W.
  The ambiguous relationship.

  (Contributions in military studies, ISSN 0883-6884 ;
no. 63)
  Bibliography: p.
  Includes index.
  1. Roosevelt, Theodore, 1858-1919—Friends and
associates.   2. Mahan, A. T. (Alfred Thayer), 1840-1914—
Friends and associates.   3. Sea-power—United States.
4. United States—Foreign relations—1865-1921.
5. Geopolitics—United States.   I. Title.   II. Series.
E757.T87   1987      973.91'1'0924      87-222
ISBN 0-313-25644-6 (lib. bdg. : alk. paper)

British Library Cataloguing in Publication Data is available.

Library of Congress Catalog Card Number: 87-222
ISBN: 0-313-25644-6
ISSN: 0883-6884

First published in 1987

Greenwood Press, Inc.
88 Post Road West, Westport, Connecticut 06881

Printed in the United States of America

The paper used in this book complies with the
Permanent Paper Standard issued by the National
Information Standards Organization (Z39.48-1984).

10   9   8   7   6   5   4   3   2   1

**Copyright Acknowledgments**

The author and publisher gratefully acknowledge permission to use portions of the
following:

Mahan to Roosevelt letters:
From *Letters and Papers of Alfred Thayer Mahan*, edited by Robert Seager II and
Doris D. Maguire. Copyright © 1975, U. S. Naval Institute, Annapolis, Maryland.

Roosevelt to Mahan letters:
From *Letters of Theodore Roosevelt*, edited by Elting E. Morison and John M. Blum. 8
vols. Cambridge: Harvard University Press, 1951–1954. Copyright © 1951, 1952,
1954 by the President and Fellows of Harvard College; © 1979, 1980, 1982 by Elting
E. Morison. Reprinted by permission.

# Contents

To my mother, Marjorie Gamble Turk,
who would have been proud to see this
project completed, and to my father,
Kenney Wellington Turk, who is.

# Acknowledgments

There are many contributors to this work; more than I can possibly acknowledge here. I am indebted to Dr. John A. Gable, Executive Director of the Theodore Roosevelt Association, and to Wallace F. Dailey, Curator of the Theodore Roosevelt Collection at Harvard. Thanks are also due to the staffs of the Massachusetts Historical Society, the Manuscript Division of the Library of Congress, and particularly to Anthony Nicolosi and Evelyn Cherpak, archivists at the Naval War College. Tony was instrumental in encouraging me to undertake this project, and in helping me to obtain a research grant from the Naval War College.

I owe an enormous debt to Elting Morison, John M. Blum, and John J. Buckley, editors of the eight-volume work *The Letters of Theodore Roosevelt*, and to Robert Seager II and Doris D. Maguire, editors of the three-volume work *Letters and Papers of Alfred Thayer Mahan*. Without their efforts, this project would have been immeasurably more difficult, if indeed possible.

Special thanks are also due my friends and fellow naval historians K. Jack Bauer of Rensselaer Polytechnic Institute and Kenneth J. Hagan of the U.S. Naval Academy, for reading the manuscript in its entirety and making a number of valuable suggestions which have, I trust, improved the final product.

I must also acknowledge the assistance of Provost Andrew T. Ford of Allegheny College, who approved a timely sabbatic leave; my colleagues in the History Department—particularly Bruce L. Clayton and Jonathan E. Helmreich, scholars in their own right—for their advice and encouragement; Dorothy Jean Smith and Don Vrabel, reference librarians at Allegheny's Pelletier Library, for patiently enduring my many requests for assistance in tracking down sources; and my typist, Audrey Onspaugh, for her unstinting care with the manuscript.

My teenage sons Rob and Geoff have tolerated my disappearances on campus and my preoccupation with Mahan and Roosevelt far more than I would have expected. Anne, with the multiple responsibilities of wife, mother, jobholder, and handholder, has my humble gratitude for having done far more than she will ever know.

# 1 Roosevelt and Mahan: Retrospect and Prospect

A casual perusal of the standard works dealing with Roosevelt, Mahan and sea power suggests that most historians believe, in varying degrees, that Mahan "exerted a powerful and unique influence over Roosevelt."[1] Henry Pringle refers to Mahan as "the naval authority whose views influenced Roosevelt profoundly."[2] William D. Puleston is positively hagiographic. "These two vigorous men," he states, "were not only in accord upon naval matters but upon the larger aspects of national life. They entertained almost identical views on foreign policy, expansion, naval administration, armaments and arbitration."[3] William R. Braisted, in more restrained fashion, echoes Puleston by crediting Roosevelt, "already a convinced follower of Mahan," with building the New Navy and shaping it into an effective instrument of war and diplomacy.[4] William E. Livezey doesn't discuss the Mahan-Roosevelt relationship in detail but implies that a substantial degree of consensus existed between the two men.[5] Richard Challener contends that most U.S. naval officers were receptive to Mahan's ideas and outlook.[6] Peter Karsten likewise maintains that "expansionists" in the 1890s, Roosevelt among them, "avidly received the Captain into their midst, and proclaimed him their spokesman."[7]

Some historians, recently, have been a bit more cautious. William Harbaugh, for instance, though agreeing that certain policies of Theodore Roosevelt "reflected the influence of Mahan," maintains that the "controlling intelligence" was Roosevelt's.[8] William C. Widenor's perceptive study of Henry Cabot Lodge discusses Mahan's impact upon Lodge and Roosevelt, particularly during the 1895–1900 period. Although Mahan and Lodge "were not personally close," Lodge held "Mahan's opinions in high regard." Lodge and Roosevelt "were much indebted to Mahan's suggestions" on matters of naval construction and strategy. "But to say that Lodge followed Mahan closely on those matters does not mean that reading Mahan led him to support a larger navy and expansion. . . . He used Mahan's ideas to supplement his own, and . . . would have opted for a powerful navy and for the annexation of Hawaii with or without Mahan."[9]

Frederick W. Marks barely mentions Mahan, except to note that Roosevelt used Mahan to mislead the public regarding the real purpose of the around-the-world cruise of the fleet in 1908–1909.[10] And, in a recent article, Peter Karsten suggests: "Rather than continuing to argue that Mahan 'influenced' Roosevelt, it would be more meaningful to say that Roosevelt 'used' Mahan. The distinction is real, and the shift in emphasis important."[11] But he is on less firm ground when he speculates that "Roosevelt may in some way have stimulated this outburst"—i.e., Mahan's literary outpourings in the 1890s.[12] Robert Seager avoids passing judgment on the Mahan-Roosevelt relationship in his recent biography of Mahan, although the overall effect of his portrayal is to diminish Mahan's importance where Roosevelt was concerned.

In the ebb and flow of historical writing, the revisionists currently appear to have the upper hand. Yet if it is clear by now that Mahan did not "enter the White House in the person of Roosevelt,"[13] neither was the apostle of sea power without influence. Roosevelt, fittingly, wrote an obituary entitled "A Great Public Servant," which appeared in the *Outlook* six weeks after Mahan's death. In this Roosevelt made several salient points. Mahan was, Roosevelt noted, "merely one among a number of first-class" naval officers "working for the navy from within the navy"—and many of the others were better than he in the "practical handling" of the "instruments of modern war." Yet in the task of educating the public to a "true understanding of naval needs, Mahan stood alone. There was no one else in his class, or anywhere near it." Significantly, also, Mahan was the "only great naval writer who also possessed in international matters the mind of a statesman of the first class." Roosevelt went on to specifically cite *The Interest of America in International Conditions*, calling it "of really capital importance today," and possessing "extraordinary insight" into the "tendencies at work" which produced the First World War.[14] This is a fair assessment; who better than Roosevelt could have made it?

It is fashionable in some circles to consider both Mahan and Roosevelt hopelessly outdated, victims of technological change and different strategic requirements. The former, clearly more at home in the seventeenth and eighteenth centuries, fell victim in his own lifetime to technological change and the introduction of new weapons systems and new dimensions of naval warfare. The continued preeminence of the battleship for a quarter century after his death bears testimony, however, to his influence. Roosevelt, for his part, becomes a comic figure on the world stage: charging up San Juan Hill, seeking war with Germany or Japan or Mexico or even Great Britain, wielding the "Big Stick" over yet another cowering misbehaving American republic, "taking" Panama.... The list could go on and on. Although there is some truth to this caricature, Roosevelt—like Mahan—was a keen student of international relations and a proponent of the balance of power. He strove to secure American preeminence in the Western Hemisphere and its seaborne approaches, yet showed a concern for and knowledge of great power relations exhibited by no president before— and few since.[15]

During the period covered by this study, Germany and Japan emerged as the powers with whom a clash was most likely. It is no coincidence that the period of the Roosevelt administration's greatest activism in the Western Hemisphere (1902–1905) coincided with the time when a German attack was something more than a theoretical possibility. As an added measure of security, Roosevelt and Mahan saw the British navy as our first line of defense against the Kaiser's high-seas fleet, and so supported continued Anglo-American understanding. Yet both also realized this understanding had its limits.

Japan required more delicate handling. The empire of the rising sun had become the premier East Asian power as a result of her victories over China and Russia. The Philippines had become even more vulnerable, and American strategic planners sought in vain to ensure the archipelago's safety in the face of a Japanese attack, knowing that it would take several months for the United States fleet to steam to their rescue. Roosevelt sought accommodation with Japan and tried to deflect her ambitions westward, at the expense of China and Russia, rather than south and east. Yet neither he nor Mahan was certain that a clash between the United States and Japan could be avoided. The need to develop a two-ocean navy capable of meeting Germany in the Atlantic and Japan in the Pacific seemed essential.

Mahan not only predicted the outbreak of World War I but accurately foresaw its course at sea as well. The British navy would blockade the high seas fleet in its ports and strangle German maritime commerce. This sooner or later would bring the German navy out, enabling the British to triumph in a decisive battle.[16] What Mahan did *not* foresee was that Jutland would not be decisive. Nor did he foresee that the submarine would bring the fondest hopes of the nineteenth-century French navy's *jeune école* (new school) near to realization; it would return the *guerre de course* (commerce warfare) to a position of prominence in naval warfare. It also would become evident that the United States Navy, like the Royal Navy, was not really prepared to fight this kind of war.

Yet in fairness to Mahan, he was a consistent advocate of the convoy system as the proper response to commerce warfare. It was British reluctance to adopt convoying which helped to make the German submarine onslaught effective.

In the main, however, Mahanian doctrine emerged intact from the Great War. Sea power ultimately had proved decisive. So, at least, it seemed to the naval powers, who faced a new set of problems. The Washington Treaties of 1921 managed simultaneously to head off a potentially bankrupting naval arms race, ensure the continued preeminence of the battleship for another two decades, and defuse the potential for conflict in the Western Pacific. Sea power had become three-dimensional, although the submarine and the airplane were viewed by most strategists as useful adjuncts to the main battle fleet rather than possessing independent striking power.

Nowhere was Mahanian strategic doctrine pursued in purer form than in the Imperial Japanese Navy.[17] It was in some respects fortunate that the Japanese navy had absorbed Mahan's theories so completely. The principal target of *Kido butai* in December 1941 was the American battleships at Pearl Harbor. Their destruction forced the United States Navy to rely on aircraft carriers. The emergence of the carrier as the *new* capital ship dates back to 7 December 1941. As Mahan had foreseen, the Japanese ran wild in the Pacific in the early stages of the conflict. Yet the counterthrust across the central Pacific in 1943 and 1944 followed a route recommended years before by Mahan.[18] Simultaneously, submarine warfare against Japanese sea lanes proved how deadly the *guerre de course* could be—aided, it is true, by Japanese neglect of both antisubmarine measures and commerce protection.

In the European theatre, the lessons of the First World War had to be slowly and painfully relearned. Americans discovered the importance of convoys in the first six months of 1942. The British adopted convoying almost from the outset of the war, but the submarine threat was not finally countered until the convoys were provided with sufficient escorts throughout the voyage and could be protected in mid-ocean by carrier aircraft as well. For the Allies to lose the Battle of the Atlantic would have been tantamount to losing the war in Europe. Amphibious operations became an increasingly important component of Allied strategy in the European theatre, as they had been in the Pacific.

The Mahan-Roosevelt legacy reaches into the post–World War II era as well. Just as in Roosevelt's day, the nation has reacted to challenges to American preeminence in this hemisphere, particularly in the Caribbean and Central America. The roll call stretches from Guatemala in 1954 to the Bay of Pigs and the Cuban missile crisis during the Kennedy administration; from Johnson's intervention in the Dominican Republic to Chile during the Nixon-Kissinger era; from Grenada to El Salvador and Nicaragua under the Reagan administration. Both Korea and Vietnam represented attempts to counter Soviet expansion-by-proxy on the East Asian perimeter where we could bring our sea power to bear. The Inchon landing during the Korean War was a notably successful example. Mahan at the turn of the century saw Russia as the major antagonist of the maritime powers (Great Britain, Germany, the United States, and Japan) and projected a struggle between land power and sea power across the "debatable ground" of Asia— Turkey, Iran, Afghanistan, and northern China. The American naval presence in the Persian Gulf and the Indian Ocean, and the utilization of the Rapid Deployment Force in this region bears continued testimony to this legacy. As will be seen, Roosevelt agreed with Mahan's analysis but did not believe American public opinion would support an enhanced presence in Asia; Vietnam, in some ways, proved him to have been correct.

The strategic problem in Europe is similar to what it was in both 1914–1918 and 1939–1945: to prevent an opponent from overrunning western Europe (including Great Britain) and to keep the trans-Atlantic sealanes open to mount a counteroffensive. The American navy will attempt to maintain control of the Pacific (including Japan, Okinawa, the Philippines and Indonesia), the Indian Ocean, the Mediterranean, and the North Atlantic. The carrier task force is the nucleus of American naval strength, as was the battleship earlier in the century. The decisive battle, if there is to be one, is projected to be fought in the Norwegian Sea, to prevent the Soviet navy from breaking out in strength into the Atlantic.[19]

Despite the technological and international political changes of the past half century, both Roosevelt and Mahan would understand and approve of contemporary American naval strategy. Their legacy is an enduring one, and it is in tribute to their vision that this study has been undertaken.

## NOTES

1. Guy Cane, "Sea Power—Teddy's 'Big Stick,'" *United States Naval Institute Proceedings*, 102 (August 1976): 48.

2. Henry F. Pringle, *Theodore Roosevelt: A Biography* (New York: Harcourt, Brace, 1931), p. 171.

3. William D. Puleston, *Mahan: The Life and Work of Captain Alfred Thayer Mahan* (New Haven: Yale University Press, 1939), p. 290.

4. William R. Braisted, *The United States Navy in the Pacific, 1897–1909* (Austin: University of Texas Press, 1971), p. 10.

5. William E. Livezey, *Mahan on Sea Power* (Norman: University of Oklahoma Press, 1947), pp. 230–31.

6. Richard Challener, *Admirals, Generals, and American Foreign Policy, 1898–1914* (Princeton: Princeton University Press, 1973), pp. 12–15.

7. Peter Karsten, *The Naval Aristocracy: The Golden Age of Annapolis and the Emergence of Modern American Navalism* (New York: Free Press, 1972), pp. 341–42.

8. William H. Harbaugh, *Power and Responsibility: The Life and Times of Theodore Roosevelt* (New York: Farrar, Straus and Cudahy, 1961), p. 181.

9. William C. Widenor, *Henry Cabot Lodge and the Search for an American Foreign Policy* (Berkeley: University of California Press, 1980), pp. 88–89.

10. Frederick W. Marks III, *Velvet on Iron: The Diplomacy of Theodore Roosevelt* (Lincoln: University of Nebraska Press, 1979), p. 57.

11. Peter Karsten, "The Nature of 'Influence': Roosevelt, Mahan, and the Concept of Sea Power," *American Quarterly* 23 (October 1971): 598.

12. Ibid., 599.

13. Harold and Margaret Sprout, *The Rise of American Naval Power, 1776–1938* (Princeton: Princeton University Press, 1939), p. 250.

14. Theodore Roosevelt, "A Great Public Servant," *Outlook* 109 (13 January 1915): 86.

15. See Richard H. Collin, *Theodore Roosevelt, Culture, Diplomacy, and Expansion: A New View of American Imperialism* (Baton Rouge: Louisiana State University Press, 1985).

16. Robert Seager II, *Alfred Thayer Mahan: The Man and His Letters* (Annapolis: U.S. Naval Institute Press, 1977), p. 598.

17. Asada Sadao, "The Japanese Navy and the United States," in *Pearl Harbor as History: Japanese-American Relations, 1931–1941*, ed. Dorothy Borg and Shumpei Okamoto (New York: Columbia University Press, 1973), pp. 225–60.

18. Alfred Thayer Mahan to Raymond P. Rodgers, 22 February 1911 and 4 March 1911, Robert Seager II and Doris D. Maguire, eds., *The Letters and Papers of Alfred Thayer Mahan*, 3 vols. (Annapolis: U.S. Naval Institute Press, 1975), 3: 380–88, 389–94.

19. "The United States Navy," *Economist* 299 (19 April 1986): 57–69.

# 2 Like Father, Like Son

Alfred Thayer Mahan and Theodore Roosevelt had much in common. Both were elder sons in families where the father's influence was considerable. Both had outstanding minds and were omnivorous readers. Both became recognized as historians of national (indeed, international) renown. They shared an interest in the nation's maritime heritage, and they moved in the vanguard of the expansionistic thrust of the late nineteenth century. It was a common interest in naval history (as well as the active intervention of the founder of the Naval War College, Rear Admiral Stephen B. Luce) that brought the two men together in 1888.

Alfred Thayer Mahan, eighteen years senior to Theodore Roosevelt, was, to use Robert Seager's felicitous phrase, "truly Government Issue."[1] The oldest of six children, Mahan was born 27 September 1840 to Professor and Mrs. Dennis Hart Mahan of the U.S. Military Academy's faculty. Dennis Hart Mahan had graduated from West Point in 1824, first in his class. Assigned to the Army Corps of Engineers, he was appointed by Superintendent of the Academy Sylvanus Thayer as Assistant Professor of Mathematics. From 1825 to 1830 Dennis Hart Mahan studied military engineering and fortifications in France, then returned to West Point as an instructor and remained a member of the faculty until his death in 1871. Not only did he exert a significant influence on an entire generation of American army officers, but he also helped through his writings to shape the strategic thinking of the United States Army—as his son was to do for the navy a half century later.[2] His influence on his oldest son must have been considerable.

The few surviving letters to his father, written while Alfred Thayer

Mahan was serving in East Asian waters aboard the *U.S.S. Iroquois* read like travelogue excerpts. In Mahan's autobiographical reminiscences, *From Sail to Steam*, the portrait of his father shows a man of Irish antecedents with a "profound dislike" of England, attributable partly to his ancestry and partly to his recollections of British depredations in the Chesapeake during the War of 1812. Raised in Norfolk, Virginia, he assumed the attitudes and views of the South. His years in France contributed to "a fondness for the French." He apparently disliked public speaking, and in the presence of others was diffident rather than gregarious and outgoing. Significantly, the son noted, "the spirit of the profession [of arms] was strong in him . . . ; the Academy was his life."[3]

Mahan recalled that his father did not want him to enter the navy, believing him more fit for a "civil profession."[4] This account must be taken with a grain of salt. Mahan's younger brothers also became career officers. Surely, therefore, Dennis Hart Mahan had no bias *per se* against a military career. Yet, caring little for the "pride, pomp, and circumstance" of the military, he must have tried to disabuse his fifteen-year-old son of his youthful enthusiasm for the navy, gleaned largely from the pages of James Fennimore Cooper, Frederick Marryat, and Henry Colburn's *United Service Magazine*. He was wise enough to realize, however, that the son must be allowed to find out for himself. Mahan's closest friend from Academy days, Samuel Ashe, recalled that Mahan had told him in 1858 that "the day of traditional naval heroes, men like Stephen Decatur, was over, that distinction through personal daring would be difficult if not impossible to achieve, and that he 'proposed to win renown in his profession through intellectual performance.' "[5]

Unfortunately for Midshipman Mahan, he did little to conceal his admitted intellectual superiority from his classmates. This created a serious problem for him when, flouting tradition, he put fellow first-classmen on report for disobeying orders, and very quickly found most of them ranged against him.[6] Here, too, Dennis Hart Mahan's influence is evident. Writing to Sam Ashe later in the year, the son mused:

In the whole affair one thing gives me the greatest pleasure and that is my father's delight at my course. A man of the sternest honor and principle himself, utterly devoid of moral cowardice, and that to an extent rare in even determined men, he appreciates such a quality in others, and values it above most others, and although he says little I know he feels a great deal.[7]

Alfred Thayer Mahan recalled that his father earlier that year had undergone a court-martial at West Point arising from charges preferred against him by another member of the engineering department faculty.

This individual, Lieutenant James Morton, had accused Dennis Hart Mahan of incompetence in his field—and made it appear that this charge was endorsed by the academy's Board of Visitors, which in fact was not the case. The Mahan became aware of the charge and, in the course of soliciting favorable testimony from former students, revealed Lieutenant Morton's deception—thus leading Morton to bring charges of defamation of character against Mahan. Dennis Hart Mahan was acquitted, but the episode suggests again that Alfred's own prickliness of disposition when wronged owes much to his father.[8] It appears, therefore, that Dennis Hart Mahan, whom his son very much resembled, served as a model in terms of disposition, raw intellect, and ultimately choice of career.[9]

Mahan possessed a highly selective memory; he made no mention of the unpleasantness at Annapolis in his reminiscences. Most of his recollections relate to the period from 1859 to 1869, from Mahan's graduation from the Naval Academy through his Civil War experiences (which confirmed, for Mahan at least, that the day of the traditional naval hero was indeed over) and his cruise in East Asian waters aboard the U.S.S. Iroquois. Only one chapter deals with the years from 1870 to 1888—the years which were crucial to the emergence from the chrysalis of the advocate of sea power. "In America," Mahan noted, "the naval stagnation of that period [the 1870s] was something now almost incredible."[10] It was never quite as bad as he suggested.[11]

Returning from a two-year tour of duty as commander of the U.S.S. Wasp on the South Atlantic station (February 1873–May 1875), Commander Mahan became involved in a variety of reform issues. He became a member of the United States Naval Institute, a haven for those officers who sought change, and involved himself in the line-staff controversy which would continue to plague the officer corps throughout the remainder of the century. On this issue, he remained with the traditionalists, intent to preserve his own perquisites as a line officer rather than extend them to engineers, doctors, and the like who were converts to science and steam engineering and its application afloat. More importantly, he urged that the Department of the Navy establish a "Board of Admiralty." This agency would supplant the all-powerful bureaus in the department and possess the power "to recommend the classes, designs, sizes, numbers, armament, construction, operational life spans, and ultimate disposition of all the vessels of the U.S. Navy."[12] This was a cause which Mahan would pursue for the remainder of his life, and one which finally was to achieve partial fruition with the creation shortly after his death of the Office of the Chief of Naval Operations.

The acknowledged leader of the naval reformers at the time—the late 1870s and early 1880s—was not Mahan but rather Commodore

Stephen Bleeker Luce.[13] Luce, years earlier, had served briefly as Mahan's commanding officer, but it was the fact that Mahan had established his credentials as a naval historian with the publication in 1883 of *The Gulf and Inland Waters* which led Luce to urge Mahan to join the staff of the newly constituted Naval War College to teach naval history and tactics. Mahan's first book contained "no suggestion or hint of his later sea-power hypothesis," but it did bring Mahan a renewed appreciation of the importance of the U.S. Navy's role in the Civil War, as well as a realization that naval control of the Gulf of Mexico and the rivers debouching into it brought the Confederacy measurably closer to defeat.[14]

Luce had a great respect for the "science" of history and its utility. The report of the "Luce Board" to Secretary of the Navy William Chandler in June 1884 envisioned students at the proposed Naval War College studying "the great naval battles of history, even from the earliest times, which illustrate and enforce many of the most important and immutable principles of war."[15] Mahan thus was one of the few officers of the United States Navy at that time qualified to teach at the kind of institution Luce envisioned—a writer of naval history, an officer associated (like Luce himself) with naval reform and possessing the competence to deal with tactical evolutions of modern warships (although in this latter expectation Luce erred).[16]

Luce's invitation reached Mahan at what could truthfully be described as the nadir of his professional career. The *U.S.S. Wachusett*, with Mahan in command, was stationed at Callao, Peru, protecting American interests during the final stages of the War of the Pacific. Mahan was thoroughly disgusted with his ship, his crew, and his assignment. The United States, he felt, had "the fewest interests and fewest people to protect" of all the powers; any policy which smacked of imperialism was "hateful," and Mahan abhorred the notion of "outlying colonies or interests, to maintain which large military establishments are necessary."[17] These words a decade later would have sounded strange indeed; the truth of the matter is that Mahan was feeling sorry for himself, doubtless ruing the day that he decided to make the navy a career.

Luce's letter changed all this. Mahan, though obviously intrigued by the offer, had mixed feelings. "I believe I have the capacity and perhaps some inherited aptitude for the particular study," he replied to Luce, but the scope and magnitude of the task was daunting. "In fact, but that experience has shown me that my self-distrust is usually more than need be, I should at once say no." Mahan nevertheless accepted, assuming that Luce still felt him qualified for the position. Meanwhile, awaiting final word from his mentor, he would get to work, using "what is at hand."[18]

What was at hand, in the library of the English Club in Lima, was Theodore Mommsen's *History of Rome*. Mahan began to envision the sea as both a commercial highway and an avenue for one power to launch an attack upon another. He next began to consider sources of "maritime power or weakness": material, personnel, national aptitude, harbors, coastlines, control of commercial routes.

> I proposed after to bring forward instances, from ancient and modern history, of the effect of navies and the control of the sea upon great or small campaigns. Hannibal for instance had to make that frightful passage of the Alps, in which he lost the quarter part of his original army, because he did not control the sea.... I read 2-1/2 volumes of Mommsen in this one view. Having elucidated the value of navies in this way, I proposed next to study great campaigns.... Of course I should introduce, which I have so far omitted, a study of the great naval campaigns.[19]

The following year was truly an *annus mirabilis* for Mahan. Luce's invitation, and Mahan's acceptance, served as the catalyst to bring together the ideas which were to form the nucleus of his lectures at the Naval War College and the book-to-be, *The Influence of Sea Power Upon History, 1660–1783*.[20] Of equal significance, the *Wachusett* participated in the United States government's intervention on the Isthmus of Panama in 1885. This marked the beginning of an alteration of Mahan's anti-imperialist stance, and of his view that the country needed nothing more than "a fleet of swift cruisers" and adequate coastal defenses. He admitted to Ashe that his previous views assumed the absence of vital interests outside the country's borders. "If we are going in for an Isthmian policy we must have nothing short of a numerous and thoroughly first class iron clad navy—equal to either England or France."[21]

Mahan's arrival at Newport was delayed until the fall of 1886, Luce having granted him the intervening year to work up his material for his lectures on naval tactics and naval history. The former, mercifully, never saw the light of day: Mahan already was rapidly losing touch with technological advances that would revolutionize naval warfare. The presidency of the Naval War College fell into his lap due to Luce's detachment to command the North Atlantic Squadron. It was fortunate that Mahan had completed his lectures, for he almost immediately found himself involved in a struggle to define the college's mission and, indeed, to defend its separate existence. The root of the problem was an initial failure to delineate the college's purpose to everyone's satisfaction. Was it to be the teaching of naval history and grand strategy, diplomacy, and international law? Or was it to be sharply focused on the significance of technical and technological advances? Added to this problem was the nearly inevitable struggle to exert control over the fledgling institution, waged within the navy between the Bureau of Navigation, the Bureau of Equipment, and the Bureau of Ordnance. The resulting conflict nearly destroyed the college; its second president was to be temporarily exiled to the shores of Puget Sound.

Yet the college was not without its defenders, foremost among whom was its founder, Rear Admiral Stephen B. Luce. Luce some years before, while serving as senior member of a board inspecting the New York City reform-school ship *Mercury*, had become acquainted with Theodore Roosevelt, Sr. The elder Roosevelt introduced Luce to his son Theodore, Jr., then a student at Harvard. Luce also was aware that the younger Roosevelt had published a book in 1883, *The Naval War of 1812*, and was achieving a degree of prominence in Republican party circles. Luce early in 1888 wrote to tell the young author, "there is no question in my mind that your work must be accepted as the very highest authority we have on the subject," noting that it would be used as a textbook at the Naval War College. "May we not hope that the study you have given to the early history of the Navy will lead you to take some interest in a naval institution now struggling through the ills of infancy?" Would young Roosevelt, in short, visit the college and make the acquaintance of Mahan?[22]

Theodore Roosevelt did not at first glance appear to be a likely candidate to write books, let alone one in the field of naval history—which in due course would prove to be the link that put him in contact with Mahan. The Roosevelts for generations had been solid, respectable New York merchants. His father, the youngest of five brothers, dutifully followed the family hardware business but became far more interested in charitable works in the city. He also had an amazing rapport with children. Young Theodore called his father "the best man I ever knew," and clearly his influence on the boy was considerable.

Yet his mother, Martha Bulloch, was equally significant. A member of the Georgia plantation aristocracy, she was famous for her story-telling ability. She brought the Old South alive and could draw upon her own extensive family ties for some of the tales of adventure, heroism and derring-do. Young Theodore early developed a taste for reading such literature, including the works of Frederick Marryat (whom Mahan also had enjoyed) and Thomas Mayne Reid.[23]

The Civil War caused strains in many American households; that of the Roosevelts was no exception. Theodore Roosevelt, senior, by all accounts, regretted having not served his country in uniform. His decision to remain a noncombatant was understandable. First, married to a Southern wife, there was a very real prospect of involvement in battle with his in-laws in Confederate gray. Second, it was common practice for men of his class to purchase substitutes. Finally, his actual contribution in enrolling thousands of soldiers to send portions of their pay home to their families during the conflict was considerable. Nevertheless, the tensions of the war would have been felt by young Theodore, who must have developed qualms about the correctness of his father's decision.[24]

Martha Bulloch Roosevelt would have told her son of the exploits of those members of her family who served the Southern cause. Her brother Irvine left college at the outbreak of war, received an ensign's commission in the Confederate navy, and served on board the *C.S.S. Alabama*, and later the *C.S.S. Shenandoah*. Her half-brother James, a former U.S. naval officer and subsequently a packet captain, was responsible for the construction of the *Alabama* and the equally famous Laird rams. His efforts to build and equip commerce-raiders not only led to extensive losses of Northern merchant shipping, but also brought the United States and Great Britain dangerously close to war. The *Alabama* claims afterward were to poison Anglo-American relations for the better part of a decade.

When after the war the Roosevelts decided to undertake the Grand Tour through Europe, Theodore, then 11, must have been in awe of his "Uncle Jimmy" when he met him in Liverpool in 1869. Significantly, he called him "as valiant and simple and upright a soul as ever lived. . . . My uncle was one of the best men I have ever known."[25] It may be true that the disparaging remarks of a British historian concerning the American naval effort in the War of 1812 goaded Roosevelt to begin his own study of the conflict while a senior at Harvard, but it may equally have represented an opportunity to do homage to James Dunwody Bulloch, a product of the old navy and its traditions. Finally, the emphasis upon naval actions at sea—of courage and heroism under fire—could serve as a partial catharsis for Roosevelt's feelings of guilt with respect to his father's noncombatant status. Roosevelt continued to work on the manuscript while attending classes at New York University law school and becoming involved in politics, and he took it with him while travelling with his first wife, Alice, in Europe in the summer of 1882. When they visited their uncles in Liverpool, Roosevelt wrote that

. . . I spend almost the entire time with the blessed old sea-captain, talking over naval history, and helping him arrange his papers, of which he has literally thousands. I have persuaded him to publish a work which only he possesses the material to write, about the naval operations during the last war, which were conducted and managed by him—including the cruise in the Fingal. I enjoyed talking to the dear old fellow more than I can tell; he is such a modest high souled old fellow that I just love and respect him. And I think he enjoys having some one to talk to who really enjoys listening. Of course, had I been old enough, I would have served on the Northern side; but I am none the less interested in his history on account of that, as I do not think partisanship should ever obscure the truth.[26]

The Roosevelts returned to America early in October. Two months later, the completed manuscript was sent to the publisher. A detailed analysis of the book belongs to a later chapter; suffice it to say here that it remains one of the standard works on the conflict it portrays.

The succeeding years were eventful ones in Roosevelt's life. If Mahan in the early 1880s was experiencing a "career in stays," for Roosevelt the period was anything but. His years as an Assemblyman in Albany (1881–1884) not only brought an education in practical politics, but developed a reputation for the young man as a comer in the reform wing of the Republican party. These were the years, also, of his involvement in cattle ranching in the Badlands. The weeks and months at the Elkhorn ranch helped him to cope with the tragic deaths of his wife and mother in 1884, and brought about his growing acceptance by as hard-bitten a group of individuals as could be found anywhere. The acceptance of an eastern patrician by these cowboys was, if not unique, certainly a tribute to his ability to inspire respect and loyalty. These years also saw the beginnings of the lifelong friendship between Roosevelt and Henry Cabot Lodge, a rising figure in Massachusetts Republican political circles. This friendship, born in the fires of the 1884 Republican convention in Chicago, was to be solidified as both men experienced the fury of the reformers who bolted party ranks to vote for Grover Cleveland over the Republican nominee, James G. Blaine. Lodge and Roosevelt refused to join them—a decision that cost them dearly among the patriciate but gained them the grudging admiration of the party regulars, thus in retrospect assuring illustrious political careers for both men.

Lodge was elected to Congress in 1886, serving three terms in the House and gaining one of the Massachusetts Senate seats in 1892, which he was to hold until his death in 1924. Roosevelt's path was not nearly so smooth. He answered the Republican party's call to run for mayor of New York in 1886. His loss was attributable to numerous Republicans' bolting the ticket to vote for the Democratic nominee, Abram S. Hewitt—a "safe" candidate by comparison to the independent challenger, Henry George, a man of dangerously radical ideas so far as the Republican establishment was concerned. Roosevelt sailed for Europe believing his political career was at an end. His marriage in London to Edith Kermit Carow was to bring about some much-needed stability in his personal life. Theirs was to be an enormously successful marriage. So, too, was Mahan's to Ellen Lyle Evans in June 1872.

Roosevelt and his bride returned from an extended honeymoon on the Continent late in March 1887. In order to augment his income, strained from the debacle of his ranching investment (overgrazing, followed by an exceptionally severe winter in 1886/87, had wiped out the herds), he entered into a period of enormous literary productivity. A biography of Gouverneur Morris was written in the summer of 1887 for the American Statesmen series which his friend Henry Cabot Lodge was editing. With avenues of political advancement closed for the time being, Roosevelt began to conceive of a major historical project, the multivolume study which was to be titled *The Winning of the West*. When Rear Admiral Luce's letter requesting support of the Naval War College caught up with Roosevelt, he was in Washington, D.C., researching his *magnum opus*. As his reply indicated:

I doubt if I have ever received any letter which gave me more genuine pleasure than yours did; it gave me a real pride in my work [*The Naval War of 1812*]. Praise coming from you is praise which may indeed be appreciated. I certainly did try to make the work as full and impartial as possible. In fact I felt that the deeds were themselves altogether too creditable to our navy to be spoiled by any exaggeration.

I know Captain Mahan by reputation very well; it is needless to say that I shall be delighted to do anything in my power to help along the Naval college.[27]

Roosevelt had little time, in all conscience, for naval affairs. In February 1888 *Century Magazine* carried the first of a series of six articles, published in book form the following December under the title, *Ranch Life and the Hunting Trail*. Two other books (*Gouverneur Morris* and *Essays on Practical Politics*) appeared in that same year, as did articles in the *North American* and *Murray's Magazine*. Roosevelt headed west to hunt in Idaho's Kootenai range in late August and early September, returned to campaign in the Middle West for Republican nominee Benjamin Harrison, and through it all managed to complete volume 1 of *The Winning of the West* in December. Sometime in August, before leaving for Idaho, he hurried up to Newport, Rhode Island, lectured on "The True Conditions of the War of 1812" to the officers assembled there, and met Alfred Thayer Mahan. What either man thought of the other on the basis of this initial contact remains a mystery to this day.[28]

The apparent absence of contact between Roosevelt and Mahan during the next eighteen months (September 1888–May 1890) is understandable. Roosevelt, thanks to Henry Cabot Lodge's efforts on his behalf, was offered a position as civil service commissioner by President Harrison (his salary of $3,500 matching exactly that of Mahan's as a navy captain). He threw himself into the job, and into Washington life, with typical ebullience. Mahan, for his part, was doing what he could to ensure the survival of the Naval War College, while simultaneously researching his second sea power book, and trying to find a publisher for *The Influence of Sea Power Upon History, 1660–1783*. Little, Brown and Company of Boston brought it out on 6 May 1890. Theodore Roosevelt read the book during the weekend of May 11–12 and immediately dashed off a congratulatory letter to the author. "I can say with perfect sincerity that I think it very much the clearest and most instructive general work of the kind with which I am acquainted. It is a *very* good book—admirable; and I am greatly in error if it does not become a naval classic."[29] He reviewed it in the October 1890 issue of the *Atlantic Monthly*.

Roosevelt subsequently read and reviewed Mahan's *The Influence of Sea Power Upon the French Revolution and Empire, 1793–1812*. This book, which appeared in 1892, though not covering so wide a range as the first, was a "thoroughly fit companion piece" for its predecessor.[30] In both reviews, Roosevelt stressed "the folly of trying to rely upon privateering or commerce-destroying of any kind as a method for crippling, or even disheartening, a resolute and powerful enemy."[31] Nevertheless, commerce-destroying, although a "secondary" factor, could be of "very considerable importance." In one of the few criticisms, Roosevelt chided Mahan for his failure while discussing the American Revolution to "give sufficient weight to the military operations on land, and to the effect produced by the American privateers."[32]

There was no ambiguity in either review on the need for preparedness. Coastal fortifications and a mere passive defense—waiting for the enemy to strike when and where it wished—would not do. The United States needed ships "of the best kind, . . . and plenty of them."[33] Roosevelt considered it "sheer folly" for a government to believe it could improvise an efficient navy "in the face of a trained, hostile navy of superior force." Only sea power could make headway against sea power.[34]

One sentence in Roosevelt's first review may, in retrospect, be extremely important in understanding the evolving relationship with Mahan.

Hitherto, historians of naval matters, at least so far as English and American writers are concerned, have completely ignored the general strategic bearing of the struggles which they chronicle; they have been for the most part mere annalists, who limited themselves to describing the actual battles and the forces on each side.[35]

Could Roosevelt, in a rare moment of self-abnegation, have included his own *Naval War of 1812* in this assessment?[36] Is it possible that Roosevelt, who was justifiably proud of his own literary accomplishments, was awarding Mahan pride of place among the ranks of naval historians? If so, whether Mahan viewed it as other than his due is doubtful. After all, Roosevelt's voice was but one among the chorus of reviewers who praised both sea power books. With a touch of complacency, Mahan noted: "I saw Roosevelt today, and understand he has finished his notice. I was glad to know he thought the 2d book equal to the former."[37]

If Roosevelt was willing to consider Mahan's accomplishments as a naval historian superior to his own, Mahan was equally willing to trade on this approbation. On two separate occasions in the mid–1890s he sought Roosevelt's assistance: once to avoid assignment to sea duty, and the second time when he became embroiled in controversy with Admiral Henry Erben. Mahan already was overdue by two years in being posted to sea, thanks partly to his growing reputation as a naval historian, and also to his skillful lobbying on behalf of his continued association with the Naval War College. With the support of Secretary of the Navy Benjamin F. Tracy, Senator Nelson Aldrich of Rhode Island, and Rear Admiral Luce, Mahan was reappointed president of the Naval War College in 1892. In the process, he earned the enmity of the chief of the Bureau of Navigation, Francis M. Ramsay. This might have been manageable had not the election of Grover Cleveland to a second term in the White House brought with it the elevation of Hilary Abner Herbert of Alabama, a long-time chairman of the House Naval Affairs Committee, to the post of secretary of the navy. Herbert had shown himself to be a consistent foe of naval appropriations in general and of continued funding of the Naval War College in particular.

Mahan recognized the danger at once; he went to Washington, D.C., to plead his case in person, enlisting the support of Senator Henry Cabot Lodge, Rear Admiral Charles H. Davis (Lodge's father-in-law), Stephen B. Luce, and Civil Service Commissioner Theodore Roosevelt. Roosevelt asked Mahan to put in writing the reasons why continued shore duty was advisable. Mahan did so. He told Roosevelt that he had planned to write a "Systematic Treatise on Naval Strategy" for the Naval War College and a study of the War of 1812 "upon the same general lines" as his other works; finally, he noted that a New York publisher had requested him to write a naval history of the Civil War. Although Mahan had little interest in such a project—then or later— its inclusion was designed to appeal to Roosevelt, who had made no secret of his wish that Mahan would do a study of sea power in that sanguinary conflict. Mahan argued to Roosevelt as from one historian to another: the interruption which a tour at sea posed would probably end his writing once and for all. Noting that magazine editors were seeking articles from him on current "questions of naval policy," Mahan felt that his role as a publicist would enable him "to contribute to the intelligent comprehension of naval necessities by the country at large."[38] Once accept the premise, as Roosevelt clearly did, that the United States needed to continue to expand the navy, then Mahan's argument as to his value as polemicist was both irresistible and irrefutable.

Roosevelt did what he could. He called personally on Secretary of the Navy Herbert, and although he could not obtain a firm promise—no doubt he read more into Herbert's remarks than was there—he did assure Mahan that Herbert was taking a favorable view of the request. Mahan was effusive in his thanks. He thought it particularly fortunate, he told Roosevelt, that the civil service commissioner would take up his case, "prohibited as you are by your reputation from seeking to further it on any other grounds than the merits."[39]

None of this, in the final analysis, did any good. Ironically, it was Mahan's own pen which did him in.[40] A letter to the editor of the *New York Times*, and a subsequent article in the *Forum*, both advocating the annexation of Hawaii and the augmentation of American naval power, struck a sour note with the Cleveland administration, which for its own reasons did not wish to push Hawaiian annexation at that moment, and very much resented naval officers' urging them to do so. This injudicious action on Mahan's part gave Ramsay his opportunity. On 3 May 1893, Mahan was posted to the *U.S.S. Chicago*, destined for European waters. When the axe fell, Mahan informed Roosevelt that he would continue his writing after all—but his next project would not be on the War of 1812, but a biography of Admiral Horatio Nelson. "Well," Roosevelt replied, "I hate to have you abandon our own war-history, even temporarily; but you are the one man to write a history of Nelson, and such a history we ought to have. Good luck go with you!"[41] It certainly did.

Mahan took command of the *Chicago* and steamed straight into glory. The vessel, as flagship of the European squadron, performed duties of a largely ceremonial nature. She wintered on the French Riviera and based herself at northern European ports during the summer and fall. This, coincidentally, gave British admirers of Mahan the opportunity to lionize the apostle of sea power. Captain Mahan was wined, dined, and generally feted by the nobility, members of Parliament, and brother officers in the Royal Navy—and even was presented to Queen Victoria and Kaiser Wilhelm II of Germany. This attention and flattery would have turned the head of many a lesser individual, and the British obtained in return Mahan's lifelong devotion to them, their navy and their empire. Mahan's triumphal passage was marred by only one incident: a quarrel with his commanding officer, Rear Admiral Henry C. Erben.

Erben, a career officer, had been raised in the old school. He could hand, reef and steer (which came hard to Mahan), he had a distinguished Civil War record (which Mahan did not), and he expected, logically enough, that command of the European squadron was a fitting climax to his career. It took him some time to realize that the entertainments staged were not in his honor, but in Mahan's. Erben reacted as any mortal would: first he became irritated, then he became angry, and finally his wrath exploded in the text of a fitness report he prepared on Mahan. Commenting on the captain's professional ability, he noted that "... his interests are entirely outside the service, for which, I am satisfied, he cares but little, and is therefore not a good naval officer. ... Capt. Mahan's interests lie wholly in the direction of literary work and [are] in no other way connected with the [Navy]."[42] Erben's judgment had an element of truth in it, but it was no easier for Mahan to swallow on that account. As he had on prior occasions, he enlisted the aid of his friends in the service and out of it—notably Theodore Roosevelt and Henry Cabot Lodge.

Mahan wanted one individual in Washington to control the efforts made on his behalf and asked Roosevelt if he would be willing to do so. He later wrote to his wife that he had experienced "much trouble" from the erratic and ill-concerted efforts of others during the campaign to save the Naval War College, and he thought it best to let Roosevelt coordinate the campaign. He asked the civil service commissioner to talk to Secretary of the Navy Herbert and to explore the issue of whether or not a formal investigation of the fitness report written by Erben should be ordered—in the form of a Court of Inquiry. If not, he requested that he be allowed to bring the *Chicago* home rather than be relieved of command abroad, so that a board of inspection could pass on her condition.[43]

Roosevelt considered it advisable that he not see Herbert himself to plead Mahan's case (perhaps some investigations of civil service violations had touched upon Herbert's domain), and instead asked Lodge to do so. Lodge willingly complied and wrote Mahan an account of the interview. Herbert, Lodge said, had not been aware of the problem, since Ramsay had pigeonholed the file of the case. After reading over the papers, Herbert thought the whole thing a tempest in a teapot and did not think a court of inquiry and the resulting publicity would help matters at all.

He said Erben's report merely amounted to saying that in E's opinion you gave more attention to literature than to the ship. I said, "Yes, and it amounts also to saying that too much attention has been paid to Captain Mahan abroad." The secretary smiled & assented & Ramsay looked very solemn.[44]

Lodge told Mahan that Herbert had read Mahan's books the past summer and "greatly admired them." The senator agreed with the secretary of the navy that the best course for Mahan would be to await an inspection of the vessel when she went out of commission, and thereby "receive vindication." Lodge also passed on the substance of the meeting to Roosevelt, who immediately wrote to Mahan's wife that Herbert's suggested course of action was "a practical victory for Captain Mahan."[45]

Roosevelt advised Mahan to take "extreme care" that the *Chicago* was in excellent shape when he brought her home. Mahan assured Roosevelt that he would do so: "I fully recognize both the spirit and wisdom of your advice...." Yet he couldn't resist a note of self-congratulation:

I confess to have derived great satisfaction from the lavish expressions of appreciation given to me personally—that is, to my work. To have an ex-first lord say he never had understood how they downed Napoleon, and a veteran admiral that he had never before comprehended the first of June, gave me ground to hope that I might yet be of some use to a navy, despite adverse reports.[46]

It may have been some small consolation to Erben that Mahan did, indeed, suspend his literary efforts for the remainder of the cruise.

It was their shared interest in naval history, therefore, that brought Mahan and Roosevelt together and was to be the underlying bond of their relationship until the mid–1890s. It was Roosevelt's recognition of Mahan's value as a writer and polemicist which induced him to intervene on Mahan's behalf when the latter faced sea duty aboard the *Chicago* in 1893. It would be tempting to portray the younger man deferring to the elder, but such was not the case. Roosevelt respected Mahan and his work but did so with an appreciation of his own credentials as a historian. Theirs was a relationship of equals; it was to become even closer as the conflict with Spain loomed—with strategic planning as the common denominator.

## NOTES

1. Robert Seager II, *Alfred Thayer Mahan: The Man and His Letters* (Annapolis: Naval Institute Press, 1977), p. 2.

2. See, for example, the account in Russell F. Weigley, *The American Way of War: A History of United States Military Strategy and Policy* (Bloomington: Indiana University Press, 1977), pp. 81–88.

3. Alfred Thayer Mahan, *From Sail to Steam* (New York: Harper & Brothers, 1907), pp. ix–xiii. Officers serving overseas typically wrote narrative accounts of their experiences to family members. Mahan merely followed suit in this instance.

4. Ibid., p. xiv.

5. Seager, *Alfred Thayer Mahan*, p. 14. See also Samuel A. Ashe, "Memories of Annapolis," *South Atlantic Quarterly* 17 (July 1919): 203.

6. The episode, which scarred Mahan indelibly, is discussed in Seager, *Alfred Thayer Mahan*, pp. 21–24.

7. Alfred Thayer Mahan to Samuel A. Ashe, 8 March 1859, Robert Seager II and Doris D. Maguire, eds., *The Letters and Papers of Alfred Thayer Mahan*, 3 vols. (Annapolis: Naval Institute Press, 1975), 1: 67.

8. See Mahan to Ashe, 1 January 1859, Seager and Maguire, *Letters and Papers*, 1:43–44.

9. Suggestive on many of these points are chapters 1 and 2 in William E. Livezey, *Mahan on Sea Power* (Norman: University of Oklahoma Press, 1947).

10. Mahan, *From Sail to Steam*, p. 267.

11 See Kenneth J. Hagan, *American Gunboat Diplomacy and the Old Navy, 1877–1889* (Westport, Conn.: Greenwood Press, 1973), and Lance C. Buhl, "Maintaining 'An American Navy,' 1865–1889," in *In Peace and War: Interpretations of American Naval History, 1775–1978*, ed. Kenneth J. Hagan (Westport, Conn.: Greenwood Press, 1978), pp. 145–73.

12. Seager, *Alfred Thayer Mahan*, p. 112.

13. A thorough study of the life and career of this fine officer is long overdue. See John D. Hayes and John B. Hattendorf, eds., *The Writings of Stephen B. Luce* (Newport, R.I.: Naval War College Press, 1975), and Ronald D. Spector, *Professors of War: The Naval War College and the Development of the Naval Profession* (Newport, R.I.: Naval War College Press, 1977), chap. 2. Albert Gleaves's *Life and Letters of Rear Admiral Stephen B. Luce, U.S. Navy* (New York: Putnam, 1925) is outdated.

14. Seager, *Alfred Thayer Mahan*, p. 135.

15. Ibid., p. 161. The Luce Board, composed of Luce, Commander William T. Sampson, and Lieutenant Commander Caspar F. Goodrich, was appointed in May 1884 by Secretary of the Navy William E. Chandler to consider Luce's proposal for a naval war college.

16. Mahan never mastered seamanship in the Old Navy, as a perusal of his tours of duty aboard the *Iroquois*, the *Wasp*, and the *Wachusett* reveals. See Seager, *Alfred Thayer Mahan*, chapters 3, 4, and 6. Nor was he any more comfortable with the vessels and technology of the New Navy. This was at least partially why he resisted appointment to the command of the *Chicago* in 1893.

17. Mahan to Ashe, 26 July 1884, Seager and Maguire, *Letters and Papers*, 1:574.

18. Mahan to Stephen B. Luce, 4 September 1884, Seager and Maguire, *Letters and Papers*, 1:577–78. Apropos the subject of "inherited aptitude," Mahan recalled that "at the Military Academy my father . . . had of his own motion introduced a course of strategy and grand tactics, which had commended itself to observers." Mahan, *From Sail to Steam*, p. 273.

19. Mahan to Luce, 16 May 1885, Seager and Maguire, *Letters and Papers*, 1:606–07.

20. Seager argues persuasively that many of Mahan's ideas had been expressed by other writers—both military and civilian—in one form or another in the decade prior to publication of *The Influence of Sea Power Upon History*.

See Seager, *Alfred Thayer Mahan*, pp. 199–209, and also Lawrence C. Allin, "The Naval Institute, Mahan, and the Naval Profession," *Naval War College Review* 31 (Summer 1978): 29–48.

21. Mahan to Ashe, 11 March 1885, Seager and Maguire, *Letters and Papers*, 1:593.

22. Spector, *Professors of War*, pp. 54–55; Hayes and Hattendorf, *Writings of Stephen B. Luce*, p. 33.

23. Frederick Marryat (1792–1848) served in the Royal Navy from 1806 to 1830, rising to the rank of captain. He wrote fifteen novels and six children's books, drawing upon his professional experience and knowledge for much of his material. Thomas Mayne Reid (1818–1883), born in Ireland, lived much of his life in America and England. His novels—nearly seventy in number—were predominantly adventure stories or romances, and included a number of books for boys.

24. David McCullough, *Mornings on Horseback* (New York: Simon and Schuster, 1981), p. 57; Edmund Morris, *The Rise of Theodore Roosevelt* (New York: Coward, McCann & Geoghegan, 1979), pp. 39–40.

25. Theodore Roosevelt, *An Autobiography* (New York: MacMillan, 1913), pp. 15–16.

26. Theodore Roosevelt to Martha Bulloch Roosevelt, 14 September 1881; Elting E. Morison and John M. Blum, eds., *Letters of Theodore Roosevelt*, 8 vols. (Cambridge: Harvard University Press, 1951–1954), 1:52.

27. Theodore Roosevelt to Stephen B. Luce, 5 March 1888, Luce MSS, Library of Congress Manuscript Division (hereafter cited as LCMD), Container #9.

28. Peter Karsten contends that Roosevelt's study of the War of 1812 had given him an awareness of the importance of "command of the sea" on the Great Lakes and Lake Champlain during that conflict and, by inference, its absence upon the ocean as the British gradually exerted their strength along the eastern seaboard. He thus had an equal appreciation of sea power by the time of his initial meeting with Mahan. Karsten is on less firm ground when he infers that Roosevelt may have sparked Mahan's interest in sea power at this time. See Peter Karsten, "The Nature of 'Influence': Roosevelt, Mahan and the Concept of Sea Power," *American Quarterly* 23 (October 1971): 586–88, 598–99.

29. Theodore Roosevelt to Alfred Thayer Mahan, 12 May 1890, Mahan MSS, LCMD, Container #6.

30. Review of *The Influence of Sea Power Upon the French Revolution and Empire, 1793–1812* by Alfred Thayer Mahan, *Atlantic Monthly* 71 (April 1893):556.

31. Ibid., p. 559; review of *The Influence of Sea Power Upon History, 1660–1783* by Alfred Thayer Mahan, *Atlantic Monthly* 66 (October 1890): 567.

32. Review of *The Influence of Sea Power Upon History, 1660–1783*, p. 566.

33. Ibid., p. 567.

34. Review of *The Influence of Sea Power Upon the French Revolution and Empire, 1793–1812*, pp. 558–59.

35. Review of *The Influence of Sea Power Upon History, 1660–1783*, p. 564.

36. Probably not. There were annalists, there were "a few excellent histories

dealing with naval strategy and tactics, or detailing the actual deeds accomplished by the fleets of some given power...," and there was Mahan. Review of *The Influence of Sea Power Upon History, 1660–1783* and *The Influence of Sea Power Upon the French Revolution and Empire, 1793–1812* by Alfred Thayer Mahan, *Political Science Quarterly* 9 (December 1894): 171. In this review of a two-volume edition of Mahan's works, Roosevelt called it "the best book that has ever been written upon naval history."

37. Mahan to Horace E. Scudder, 3 February 1893, Seager and Maguire, *Letters and Papers*, 2: 94.

38. Mahan to Theodore Roosevelt, 1 March 1893, Seager and Maguire, *Letters and Papers*, 2: 96–97.

39. Mahan to Roosevelt, 26 March 1893, Seager and Maguire, *Letters and Papers*, 2: 100–101.

40. See the account in Seager, *Alfred Thayer Mahan*, pp. 247–53.

41. Roosevelt to Mahan, 13 June 1893, Mahan MSS, LCMD, Container #6.

42. Seager, *Alfred Thayer Mahan*, p. 282.

43. Mahan to Ellen Evans Mahan, 14 February 1894, Seager and Maguire, *Letters and Papers* 2: 225; see also Mahan to Hilary A. Herbert, 25 January 1894, ibid., 2: 212–15. Roosevelt was given a copy of Mahan's letter to Herbert.

44. Henry Cabot Lodge to Mahan, 10 February 1894, Mahan MSS, LCMD, Container #6. See also Roosevelt to Ellen Evans Mahan, 12 February 1894 and Roosevelt to David B. Ogden, 12 February 1894, Mahan MSS, LCMD, Container #6. Ogden was Mahan's lawyer.

45. Roosevelt to Ellen Evans Mahan, 10 February 1894, Mahan MSS, LCMD, Container #6.

46. Mahan to Roosevelt, 6 June 1894, Seager and Maguire, *Letters and Papers*, 2: 281.

# 3 Planning for War and Empire

Mahan brought the *U.S.S. Chicago* into New York harbor late in March 1895. The vessel was decommissioned 1 May after a board of inspection had found her to be in first-class condition, thereby confirming the wisdom of Roosevelt's recommendation at the time of the imbroglio with Erben. Roosevelt by this time had taken up the job of police commissioner of New York City, and was busy making the dust fly at Mulberry Street. Mahan and his family settled in the New York City area as well, acquiring a winter home at 160 West 86th Street and a summer residence at Quogue on Long Island. Thanks to various special-duty assignments by the navy prior to his retirement from active service in 1896, Mahan was able to resume his writing. He completed his biography of Admiral Nelson in November of that year and, more importantly, had begun to discover the pecuniary benefits of writing articles for some of the leading journals on topics of current interest. The issue of Hawaiian annexation represented a case in point.

Mahan, who took a very dim view of the Democratic party's position on many foreign policy issues, was pleased with William McKinley's victory in the 1896 election. He was delighted to hear of Theodore Roosevelt's appointment to the post of assistant secretary of the navy in the McKinley administration. He congratulated Roosevelt and hoped that the assistant secretary would not mind his writing from time to time on "service matters."[1] He was not interested in matters of the nuts-and-bolts variety that Roosevelt was grappling with at the time. What concerned him far more was the future of the Western powers in Asia. Even though they dominated the globe, the Eastern nations (the Ottoman Empire, China and Japan), having imbibed Western institutions and attitudes, were beginning to bestir themselves. "We stand," Mahan wrote, "at the opening of a period when the question is to be settled decisively, though the issue may be long delayed, whether Eastern or Western civilization is to dominate throughout the earth and to control its future."[2] What Mahan feared was the raw power of a reinvigorated East which rejected the moral and spiritual tutelage of the West. The Sino-Japanese War of 1894–1895 was ample evidence that at least one of the Asian nations was emulating the West all too well.

With these thoughts in mind Mahan wrote Roosevelt to express his concern over the rising naval strength of Japan. He urged that American naval forces in the Pacific be augmented as well. In brief, he expected trouble with Japan over Hawaii, and bemoaned the failure of the Cleveland administration to acquire the islands in 1893. For those who might view annexation as an "insoluble problem," Mahan had a simple piece of advice: take the islands first, then solve the problem of having done so.[3]

Mahan's appreciation of the strategic value of the Hawaiian Islands was long-standing; his interest in their acquisition was of more recent vintage, coinciding with the 1893 revolution and the Hawaiian government's request for American annexation. Mahan certainly was not the first naval officer to show an interest in acquiring the Hawaiian Islands; he was, however, one of the first to sense Japanese interest in them also. In a letter to the editor of the *New York Times*, he had urged the islands' acquisition by "a great, civilized maritime power" rather than risk their domination by the "comparative barbarism" of a nation like China—or Japan.[4] He soon thereafter received a request from the editors of the *Forum* magazine for a piece on the Hawaiian question. As noted in the previous chapter, he was in Washington to coordinate the campaign to remain on shore, and may well have exchanged views with Roosevelt on the Hawaiian matter. In the article, entitled "Hawaii and Our Future Sea Power," Mahan noted the relationship between the islands and the proposed isthmian canal. Hawaii was the key to the commercial and military control of the Pacific, particularly the northern Pacific. "Whether we wish or no, we *must* answer the question, we *must* make the decision. The issue cannot be dodged."[5] Mahan did not attempt to dodge it, although the Cleveland administration did. The immediate result was the administration's determination to send Mahan to sea with the *U.S.S. Chicago*.

Clearly the memory of the episode still rankled. In a subsequent letter to Roosevelt Mahan recalled his *Forum* article on Hawaii. The reluctance of the Cleveland administration to take Hawaii when it was offered on a silver platter only showed the "crass blindness" of the government. Failure to act then had led to "present danger of war" with Japan. Mahan closed his letter with words which were to reappear in an article he was then composing: "The decision not to bring under the authority of one's own government some external position, when just occasion offers, may by future generations be bewailed in tears of blood."[6]

Roosevelt replied to Mahan's 1 May letter that "as regards Hawaii I take your views absolutely, as indeed I do on foreign policy generally. If I had my way we would annex those islands tomorrow. If that is impossible I would establish a protectorate over them...." He added that Secretary of the Navy John Davis Long shared these views. Roosevelt had been providing Long with memoranda to use in a forthcoming cabinet meeting. He assured Mahan that he hoped to prod the administration into action before Japan could further augment her battleship strength. "With Hawaii once in our hands," he concluded, "most of the danger of friction with Japan would disappear."[7] Roosevelt, like Mahan, had been disgusted with the Cleveland administration's handling of the Hawaiian issue and, like Mahan, linked the acquisition of the islands to the construction of an isthmian canal and augmentation of American naval strength.[8]

Early in June 1897 Mahan sent Roosevelt a copy of a letter from the Oriental Association of Tokyo, which stated that the Club of Naval Officers of Japan had translated his *Influence of Sea Power Upon History* into Japanese. Several thousand volumes had been sold in a matter of days. This notice was accompanied by an observation from Mahan that this constituted further evidence of Japan's intention to develop its naval power. Roosevelt promptly showed the "very remarkable" letter to Long, and urged President McKinley to take "immediate action ... as regards Hawaii."[9]

Roosevelt subsequently on at least two occasions enlisted Mahan's help in convincing wavering senators to support Hawaiian annexation. George Frisbie Hoar, senior senator from Massachusetts, was "in doubt" on the annexation issue. Roosevelt asked Mahan to write to Hoar personally (which Mahan did), and said he would try to persuade the senator to read Mahan's *Interest of America in Sea Power*, which had just been published.[10] Early in 1898 Senator James H. Kyle of South Dakota, at Roosevelt's behest, wrote to Mahan asking his opinion of the strategic importance of Hawaii to the United States. Its possession, Mahan replied, would certainly strengthen the United States militarily. A naval detachment based there would threaten an enemy's lines of communication should an attack be mounted against the Pacific Coast from East Asia. Conversely, in hostile or neutral hands, Hawaii would make the prospect of invasion more likely, thus requiring the United States to maintain a larger naval force in the Pacific to defend the West Coast.[11] Both senators voted with the majority when the annexation resolution was approved on 6 July 1898, by a vote of 42 to 21.

If Mahan's concern tended to center on Japan and Hawaii, Roosevelt's did not. In his 3 May letter to Mahan, Roosevelt, while agreeing "absolutely" with Mahan's views on Hawaii, took exception to the latter's belief that trouble was more likely in the Pacific than the Atlantic. He, himself, foresaw "big problems" in the Caribbean so long as strategically important territories were in the possession of weaker powers. The acquisiton of Spain's Caribbean possessions as well as the Danish West Indies "should serve notice that no strong European power, and especially not Germany, should be allowed to gain a foothold."[12] Roosevelt did not fear any of the Great Powers; he was, however, suspicious of their designs.

He had evolved the theory that the basis of American foreign policy should be the gradual elimination of the European powers from the Western Hemisphere and the approaches to it. He proposed to begin with Spain. Conflict with England, France, Russia, and Italy he considered unlikely. Either they had no hemispheric possessions, or they were prepared to accept American preeminence. The powers to be watched were Japan—because of her expansion in Asia and the western Pacific and her interest in Hawaii—and Germany. Germany, Roosevelt thought, wanted to establish additional overseas colonies as a safety valve for her surplus population. The only areas suitable for white settler colonies were eastern and southern Africa (already claimed) and temperate South America (southern Brazil, Argentina, and Chile). America's self-interest lay in preventing a German challenge to the Monroe Doctrine either in the strategically important Caribbean or further south.

Mahan had been slower to appreciate the threat posed by Germany to American interests than was Roosevelt.[13] True, in his 1890 article, "The United States Looking Outward," he spoke of the German "commercial and colonial push" which was bringing that country into conflict with other nations. [14] But his concern appears more contrived than real. Germany and Spain were useful enemies; their navies were approximately the size of the United States Navy, and if conflict arose, the likely theatre of operations would be the Gulf of Mexico and the Caribbean.[15] Yet by late 1897 Mahan's concern was genuine. The German seizure that year of Kiaochow in China, and the subsequent Lüders affair* in Haiti, undoubtedly made a strong impression on him, as they did on other naval officers and government officials. "At the

---

*The murder of a German merchant, Emil Lüders, in Port-au-Prince brought prompt demands from the commander of a German gunboat for an apology and an indemnity . Threatened with bombardment of the city, the Haitian authorities complied.

present time," he wrote a British acquaintance, "Germany represents the probable element of future trouble for us, and perhaps for you."[16] Although Mahan and Roosevelt did not agree completely on matters of foreign policy, both could with little difficulty adjust to each other's views. Neither, however, thought that war with Spain over Cuba was at all imminent. Roosevelt's efforts to improve naval preparedness had been undertaken with no specific crisis in view; Mahan was hurrying to complete a contribution on the American Revolutionary War for William Laird Clowes's multivolume history of the British Royal Navy, before his family's scheduled departure for Europe late in March. The sinking of the *Maine* on 15 February 1898 changed all that.

Before considering the contributions of Mahan and Roosevelt in the sphere of planning for war with Spain, it will be necessary to recount briefly where the navy's plans stood when the McKinley administration took office. As early as 1894, before the outbreak of the second Cuban insurrection, students and staff at the Naval War College had considered the possibility of war with Spain. In one scenario, assuming that Spain was allied with Great Britain and France with the United States, it was recommended that Nassau in the Bahamas be captured, an invasion of Cuba undertaken, and Kingston, Jamaica, attacked before the allies could dispatch their main naval forces from Europe. After "running wild" in the early phases of the conflict, the weaker United States fleet would have to retreat to its East Coast bases.[17] As subsequent Naval War College studies suggested, the above scenario was unrealistic, assuming a far greater degree of naval and military preparedness than could reasonably be expected. Much more suggestive was the solution proposed by Lieutenant Commander Charles J. Train. In his scenario, the United States had to combat only Spain. Train suggested that the United States Navy concentrate its operations against Cuba, assuming in the process that the Cubans themselves would be unable to render much assistance. Train believed that the Spanish fleet would make for Cuba but might first touch at Puerto Rico or some point further south in the Caribbean, in order to refuel and refit before offering battle.[18]

Late the following year (1895), the Naval War College staff again studied the possibility of conflict with Spain. An attack on the Iberian peninsula was rejected because it would involve an "unduly large" expenditure of both lives and funds; the outcome of such a campaign "would be somewhat doubtful." Spain's possessions in Asia might be more vulnerable. While an attack on the Philippines might well succeed, given the lack of enemy naval strength there, such success "would not be of great value to us, as it would not certainly bring the enemy to terms." It also would be more costly than an attack on Spain's West Indian possessions. Thus, by a process of elimination, an attack on

Cuba and Puerto Rico would be mounted. While a successful campaign against both islands might not result in Spain's surrender, it at least would throw the burden of further conflict on Spain. Equally important, the staff report noted—with a bow to Mahan—"the strategic relation of Cuba to the Gulf of Mexico is so close and intimate that the value of that island to the United States in a military and naval way is incalculable." An expedition therefore would be mounted against Havana from Tampa and Charlotte Harbor in Florida, convoyed by the navy. Scouting vessels would be dispatched along the north and south coasts of Cuba to search for Spanish naval forces, and the U.S. battle fleet would rendezvous in the Windward Passage to await the arrival of an enemy squadron from Spain.[19]

A pencilled notation indicates that a copy of this memorandum was sent to the Navy Department in Washington in January or February 1896. Lieutenant Commander Richard Wainwright, named head of the Office of Naval Intelligence (ONI) in April 1896, undoubtedly saw this memorandum. He appointed one of the members of his staff, Lieutenant William W. Kimball, staff intelligence officer at the Naval War College.[20] Kimball devised another variant of the plan, taking issue with the existing Naval War College version. He wanted to liberate Cuba and also collect an indemnity from Spain. The best way of accomplishing the former was to blockade Cuba, bombard the major island ports, and defeat any Spanish naval forces sent across the Atlantic. The Cubans themselves could liberate the island. The way to obtain an indemnity would be for the Asiatic Squadron to capture and hold Manila, thereby controlling the revenues of the Philippines. Other naval vessels would be dispatched to European waters to harass the Spanish coast. These subsidiary operations would presumably make the Spanish amenable to the idea of an indemnity.[21]

Late in 1896 the secretary of the navy created a special board to study the problem, consisting of Lieutenant Commander Wainwright; William T. Sampson, chief of the Bureau of Ordnance; John G. Walker, commander of the North Atlantic Squadron; Francis M. Ramsay, chief of the Bureau of Navigation, and Henry Clay Taylor, president of the Naval War College. Taylor's position embodied that previously staked out by the Naval War College staff. In his handwritten synopsis, Taylor made a brief obeisance to Kimball's planned attack on Manila. "It is premised," he said, "that our forces in Asia and the Pacific will demonstrate against the Philippines." He advocated recalling naval forces from European waters so that they could operate with the Cuban expeditionary force, and ruled out "serious demonstrations" against Spain itself until Cuba was taken. Before Spain could reinforce Cuba, Taylor proposed, the navy should blockade Cuban ports, harass Spanish commerce, and bombard Havana to force its surrender. Failing the latter, an Army expeditionary force of 90,000 men would be convoyed to Cuba to attack Havana, assisted by the navy. Taylor rejected the notion of a passive blockade of Cuba or its attempted reduction by the Navy without Army support, or vice versa, as not being "based upon the principles of warfare as deduced from Naval & Military History." The other approaches suggested—and Taylor almost certainly had Kimball's plan in mind as he wrote this—did have a "certain ingenuity," and appeared "attractive because they seem to offer large returns for small expenditure of life & treasure," but were to be avoided at all costs.[22]

The 1896 Naval War College plan stated that a purely naval blockade of Cuba had its own built-in disadvantages. Spanish relief vessels might be able to dodge American warships, attack the lightly armed auxiliary cruisers on blockade duty, and raise the blockade of one or more ports. If the main American fighting vessels were scattered to enforce the blockade, they risked defeat in detail at the hands of a superior Spanish naval squadron. If the Spanish force could first be defeated, the blockade would be much more effective, but

Long continued work at the War College with the constant end in view of determining the possibilities of thus meeting the Spanish fleet, result in the conviction that the chances of finding them and bringing them to battle are not good if they wish to evade our fighting fleet and strike our blockading detachments.[23]

To Taylor's distress, this prophetic statement and, indeed, the Naval War College's entire proposal were rejected by the ad hoc board. Wainwright, obviously, supported the Kimball plan; Ramsay was an inveterate opponent of the Naval War College and all its works; Walker and Sampson had no vested interest in either version. Though the board accepted Kimball's plan of "a purely naval war of blockades, bombardments, harassments, raids on exposed colonies, and naval actions," the attack on Manila, one of Kimball's pet projects, was thrown out. The Asiatic Squadron instead would be ordered to European waters to join other elements of the American fleet in an attack on the Canary Islands and selected Spanish mainland ports.[24] Thus matters stood when the McKinley administration took office.

Commander Caspar F. Goodrich, who replaced Henry C.Taylor as president of the Naval War College in 1897, sent a letter to the Navy Department requesting that it submit a special problem which the college staff could consider. The letter was referred to the new assistant secretary, who was in the process of familiarizing himself with the navy's existing war plans. Mindful of Japanese interest in the Hawaiian Islands, and their strategic importance to the United States,

Roosevelt suggested that the Naval War College study a possible Japanese—United States conflict in the Pacific over Hawaii ("Japan makes demands . . . this country intervenes".)[25] The staff solution assumed that the vessels of the Asiatic Squadron and the Pacific Squadron together could defend either the Hawaiian Islands or the West Coast of the United States against the Japanese navy, depending upon the point of attack. Existing plans—at least those pushed by the Naval War College—for war against Spain in the Caribbean theatre would not be seriously affected. Nevertheless, the planners were concerned that the growing strength of the Imperial Japanese Navy would require the detachment of ships from the East Coast to the Pacific, thus reducing the margin of safety against the forces Spain could muster. Lieutenant Commander Bowman H. McCalla of the Naval War College staff, author of the report, concluded that the staff members were aware of the "necessity for the immediate building of more battle ships and more torpedo boats."[26]

Giving Roosevelt time to digest this report, Goodrich wrote the assistant secretary to suggest that prior to the outbreak of hostilities with Japan naval units should seize and garrison Honolulu. Roosevelt replied that "the determining factor in any war with Japan would be the control of the sea," not the occupation of Hawaii. Therefore, he urged that "our objective should be the Japanese fleet."[27] Goodrich knew Mahanian doctrine as well as Roosevelt did. He agreed in principle with the assistant secretary (a wise decision in any case), yet tried as diplomatically as possible to point out the difficulties entailed in trying to "smash" the Japanese fleet. Our naval forces in the Pacific were divided; Japan's were united. We could not attack the Japanese fleet in its home waters without seizing a base nearer Japan; Hawaii would certainly help in this respect. The American fleet also was weaker than the Japanese navy in torpedo boats and protected cruisers. All these factors would force us initially onto the defensive. Goodrich hoped that the American seizure of Hawaii, the original bone of contention between the two powers, might end the conflict; if not, the navy could wait for Japan to assume the offensive, knowing that she would need to acquire a base either in the Hawaiian Islands or, perhaps, at Dutch Harbor in the Aleutians in order to attack the West Coast. He concluded: " . . . you have done the College the honor to ask its opinion, and the College is bound to express that opinion frankly, while it regrets that facts seem to forbid a rapid, vigorous, aggressive war."[28] Roosevelt must have asked himself whether there wasn't some way the navy could conduct a "rapid, vigorous, aggressive war" in the Pacific. Anything else was foreign to his nature.

While this exchange between Goodrich and Roosevelt was in progress, the Navy Department reconvened the special board which had

studied the problem of war with Spain six months previously. Lieutenant Commander Wainwright of ONI was the only holdover from
the original group; the other members were Goodrich; Captain Arent
S. Crowninshield, chief of the Bureau of Navigation; Commander
Charles O'Neil, chief of the Bureau of Ordnance; and Rear Admiral
Montgomery Sicard, commander of the North Atlantic Squadron. All
parties agreed that Havana was too tough a nut to crack by *coup de
main*, as Taylor had proposed. Instead, the navy would first seize Matanzas (threatening to cut off Spanish forces in eastern Cuba by sev-
ering the rail line inland), then perform a similar operation against a
harbor west of Havana such as Bahia Honda. It was assumed that the
Spanish command would counter the threat to Havana by concentrat-
ing its forces in the vicinity of the capital; this in turn would make it
necessary for the navy to blockade only the central Cuban coast—both
north and south—to prevent reinforcements from reaching the island.
The main United States fleet would remain in Cuban waters ready to
take on any Spanish squadron that appeared. In order to keep as many
Spanish ships as possible in home waters, the board proposed to detach
a flying squadron of two armored cruisers and two protected cruisers
to demonstrate against the coast of Spain. Thus the previous board's
recommendation of an attack on the Canary Islands was quietly buried.
The Asiatic Squadron, too, would be more profitably employed in Asian
waters by sending it against Manila. Not only would this assist the
Philippine insurgent cause, but it might also give the United States a
"controlling voice" in the ultimate disposition of the islands. Finally,
the board meditated an attack on Puerto Rico once the Cuban situation
was stabilized. By implication, war with Spain would be a naval war—
if the U.S. Army eventually showed up, it could accept the surrender
of Spanish forces in Cuba.[29]

Roosevelt in the main approved of the latest plan; being Roosevelt,
however, he constantly sought for ways to strengthen it. While serving
as acting secretary of the navy, in Long's absence, he had a couple of
chats with President McKinley in September. He wanted the fleet on
the Cuban Coast within forty-eight hours of a declaration of war. He
suggested that the flying squadron be beefed up, consisting of "four
big, fast, heavily armed cruisers." The Asiatic Squadron would, in the
meantime, "blockade, and if possible, take Manila."[30] In a letter to
William W. Kimball, author of the ONI plan, who was serving in a
torpedo boat squadron, he mentioned that the four cruisers he would
select for the flying squadron would be the *Brooklyn*, *New York*, *Columbia*, and *Minneapolis*. Roosevelt also referred to the landing at
Matanzas, the naval blockade of Cuba, an army expeditionary corps
of 30,000–40,000 troops, and, above all, the fact that the navy "would
be the main factor in producing the downfall of the Spaniards."[31] He

also wanted to effect a concentration in American waters of the smaller cruisers and gunboats on foreign stations (principally from the European and South Atlantic squadrons) and to reinforce Admiral George Dewey, the new commander of the Asiatic Squadron. He apparently had been tinkering with the special board's plan of campaign; like the board, he was leery of an attempt against Havana by *coup de main*. He felt it all the more important that "if we do not bombard [Havana], then we must do something else...." The "something else" would be launching the flying squadron against the Spanish coast which, in addition to keeping the Spanish from reinforcing their position in the Caribbean, would "gain the inestimable moral advantage of the aggressive."[32]

Unfortunately, Mahan's letters to Roosevelt in early March of 1898 are missing. It is possible, however, to piece together his contribution to the plan for war against Spain. Roosevelt, either orally or in writing, undoubtedly had conveyed the major features of the June 1897 special board plan to Mahan.[33] Mahan also was in contact with Goodrich, and could have obtained the details from him. In any event, Mahan wrote Roosevelt on 10 or 11 March to raise several objections to the plan—all of them relating to the principle of concentration. He did not like the idea of detaching major units to go raiding the Spanish coast, nor did he want any capital ships held back to defend the East Coast. He had no objection to the capture of Puerto Rico, but he did not want to see any operation mounted against the island until Cuba had fallen.

Roosevelt accepted Mahan's suggestions, saying: "I entirely agree with you." He noted that he favored sending a flying squadron against Spain had war broken out in 1897 but, with only six capital ships against eight Spanish vessels, thought it no longer a wise idea. He promised to show Mahan's letter to both Long and Goodrich. "I have Captain Goodrich at work on a plan of attack," he added, "for we haven't a plan of any kind excepting that prepared last June."[34] Two days later the assistant secretary sent Mahan a copy of the revised plan and requested his comments. The only substantive change from the June 1897 version was, predictably, the dropping of the idea of a flying squadron altogether.[35]

The problems associated with a blockade of the Cuban coast were becoming increasingly apparent. The U.S. Army was woefully unprepared to launch operations in Cuba on short notice. The navy might be required to maintain its blockade for months—during which time local defense forces, principally the much-feared torpedo boat, might damage or destroy major naval units. Mahan's advice would be to have an inshore screen of torpedo-boat destroyers and unarmored or lightly armored auxiliary warships, whose chief role was to prevent Spanish torpedo boats from reaching the battle squadron.[36] As actual events at

Manila Bay and Santiago were to prove, the torpedo boat's potential—at least in Spanish hands—was greatly exaggerated. Mahan and other naval strategists at the time, many of whom as veterans of the Civil War had a healthy respect for what smaller enemy vessels could do, should not be censured for exhibiting excessive concern before the fact.

Roosevelt was effusive in his thanks. "There is no question that you stand head and shoulders above the rest of us!" He said he would show Mahan's letter to Long "and then get some members of the board to go over it." Roosevelt continued: "You probably don't know how much your letter has really helped me clearly to formulate certain things which I had only vaguely in mind. I think I have studied your books to pretty good purpose."[37] The assistant secretary subsequently sent Mahan's letters—four in number—via Captain Robley D. Evans to Rear Admiral William T. Sampson, commander of the fleet then assembling at Key West. Mahan and his family sailed for Europe, certain that the war crisis would subside; Roosevelt, hoping that it would not, planned to resign his post and form a volunteer cavalry regiment. Simply stated, Roosevelt could not bear to stay out of the conflict. He did not feel he possessed the necessary expertise to serve aboard a naval vessel, hence his choice of the cavalry.

One result of the 19 April declaration of war by the United States Congress was the dispatch to Mahan, vacationing in Italy with his family, of orders from the Navy Department to report for duty. On his appearance in Washington 9 May, Secretary Long assigned him to the Naval War Board.[38] Mahan moved into Roosevelt's Washington house; Roosevelt left for San Antonio, Texas, to join the Rough Riders 12 May, his wife and family returning to Sagamore Hill. Other than this four-day overlap, there is no evidence of direct contact between Roosevelt and Mahan during these eventful months. Such news as they had of each other's affairs appears to have been communicated by Henry Cabot Lodge, who was in touch with both of them. Both Lodge and Mahan in Washington were inevitably closer to the decision-making levels of government than was Roosevelt in Texas, Florida and Cuba, who was reduced to writing Lodge concerning possible terms of peace. Roosevelt, in blunt fashion, urged the independence of Cuba and the retention of both Puerto Rico and the Philippines by the United States.[39]

Mahan not only was concerned with wartime naval operations and planning while serving as a member of the Naval War Board,[40] but had some input into the matter of territorial acquisitions as well. On at least three occasions (26 May, 19 June, 13 July) Mahan attended meetings at the White House. On 3 June President William McKinley transmitted peace terms to Ambassador John Hay in London (they were meant to find their way to Madrid). The Spanish were to evacuate Cuba and cede Puerto Rico to the United States. Furthermore, the

United States required an island in the Ladrones (Marianas) possessing a harbor which could be utilized for coaling purposes, and a port in the Philippines.[41] It is probable that these terms were discussed at the 26 May meeting which Mahan attended; their strategic flavor is unmistakable.

Soon after the 19 June White House meeting, Lodge and Mahan had dinner with Secretary of State William A. Day. "Mahan and I talked the Philippines with him for two hours," Lodge told Roosevelt.[42] A month later Lodge informed Roosevelt that President McKinley was "very clear and strong" about both Cuba and Puerto Rico. Even though McKinley was "not giving much consideration" to the Philippines, the fact that he had ordered the occupation of the Ladrones "way back in May" was a hopeful sign.[43] On 26 July the Spanish government asked for terms. McKinley immediately convened the cabinet.[44] Secretary of the Navy Long noted that the Philippines issue was "difficult and complicated"; he hoped that it would be resolved by taking only Guam and a port on Luzon.[45] On the same day (27 July) Mahan, who may well have discussed the proposed terms with Long following the cabinet meeting, wrote a note to Lodge.

In connection with the negotiations for peace, although all I have seen of the President has tended to give me a higher opinion of his decisiveness of character than I had before entertained, I suppose he certainly is a man more disposed to follow public opinion than to lead, or even guide, it. Public opinion I assume will insist that Spain quit America for ever. But feeling as to the Philippines is much more doubtful. I myself, though rather an expansionist, have not fully adjusted myself to the idea of taking them, from our own standpoint of advantage. It does seem to me, however, that the heavy force, army and navy, we have put into Luzon has encouraged the revolutionists to an extent for which we are responsible. Can we ignore the responsibility & give them back to Spain? I think not. Spain cannot observe a pledge to govern justly, because she neither knows what good government is, nor could she practise it if she knew. As to an agreement with other Powers, I hope no entangling alliances for us. But we have done nothing in the other islands of the group. Might it not be a wise compromise to take only the Ladrones & Luzon; yielding to the "honor" & exigencies of Spain the Carolines and the rest of the Philippines. [46]

The terms conveyed to Spain 30 July made no final disposition of the Philippines but in other respects conformed closely to those of early June; clearly, they represented what McKinley wanted. On 12 August the protocol ending hostilities was signed in Washington. Whether Mahan was entirely satisfied is another matter. His sense of what was strategically necessary warred with his concern as to what might happen should the Cubans and Filipinos be left prematurely to their own devices.[47]

The Naval War Board at this time had been requested by the Senate Naval Committee to provide an estimate of the number and location of coaling stations the United States Navy would need outside its own territory. The reply, drafted by Mahan between 15 and 20 July sheds some further light on Mahan's thinking at this time.[48] In the Pacific Ocean, Mahan recommended either Manila Bay or Subic Bay on the island of Luzon, Guam in the Ladrones, Pago Pago in Samoa, and a base in the Chusan archipelago off the mouth of the Yangtze River in China. He also urged that bases be established on either side of the Central American isthmus. Guantanamo Bay in Cuba and a second base in the vicinity of Puerto Rico (Culebra, St. Thomas, or Samana Bay in the Dominican Republic) would serve the latter purpose.

Roosevelt and Mahan worked well together in 1897 and 1898. Mahan's pen served to mobilize public opinion behind the "large policy" in the 1890s in ways that neither Roosevelt nor Henry Cabot Lodge, holding similar views, could hope to match. Roosevelt, for his part, as assistant secretary of the navy helped to transform theory into fact: the navy and the navy's strategic requirements became the cutting edge of American expansionism thanks in no small degree to Roosevelt's dynamism and drive. As the plan of campaign matured in the months preceding the war with Spain, he was able to enlist Mahan's assistance; the latter's suggestions were well-received and duly incorporated. Roosevelt's departure from Washington coincided with Mahan's arrival to serve on the Naval War Board. Even had Roosevelt remained as assistant secretary, it is difficult to imagine operations proceeding in substantially different fashion. Mahan's cautiousness (in, for instance, the issue of concentration of the navy's principal units) would have nicely counterbalanced Roosevelt's impetuosity. As for the issue of territorial acquisitions, Mahan had serious misgivings about the desirability of acquiring the Philippines—let alone Spain's other Pacific island possessions. Roosevelt and Lodge, on the other hand, saw the acquisition of Spain's empire as both desirable and inevitable— symbolic of the American public's acceptance of the country's great power status. Events of the next decade were to prove Mahan's concern justified. Yet in the first flush of triumph, it was as well that neither he nor Roosevelt could foresee some of the personal and professional strains which were to develop in their partnership.

## NOTES

1. Mahan to Theodore Roosevelt, 1 May 1897, Seager and Maguire, *Letters and Papers*, 2: 505–6.

2. Alfred Thayer Mahan, "A Twentieth Century Outlook," *The Interest of*

*America in Sea Power, Present and Future* (Port Washington, N.Y.: Kennikat Press, 1970; o.d. 1897). p. 243.

3. Mahan to Roosevelt, 1 May 1897, Seager and Maguire, *Letters and Papers*, 2: 505–6.

4. Alfred Thayer Mahan to the editor of the *New York Times*, 30 January 1893, Seager and Maguire, *Letters and Papers*, 2: 92.

5. Alfred Thayer Mahan, "Hawaii and Our Future Sea Power," *Interest of America in Sea Power*, p. 33.

6. Mahan to Roosevelt, 6 May 1897, Seager and Maguire, *Letters and Papers*, 2: 507; see also Mahan, "A Twentieth Century Outlook," *Interest of America in Sea Power*, pp. 261–62.

7. Roosevelt to Mahan, 3 May 1897, Pennsylvania State University Libraries Microfilms Collection, Theodore Roosevelt Papers (hereafter cited as PSU - TR Papers), Series 2, Reel 313.

8. See, for example, Theodore Roosevelt to Anna Roosevelt, 20 May 1894, Morison, *Letters of Theodore Roosevelt*, 1: 379.

9. Roosevelt to Mahan, 9 June 1897, PSU - TR Papers, Series 2, Reel 313.

10. Roosevelt to Mahan, 9 and 11 December 1897, PSU - TR Papers, Series 2, Reel 315.

11. Mahan to James H. Kyle, 4 February 1898, Seager and Maguire, *Letters and Papers*, 2: 538–39.

12. Roosevelt to Mahan, 3 May 1897, PSU - TR Papers, Series 2, Reel 313.

13. Mahan to Samuel Ashe, 26 July 1884 and 11 March 1885, Seager and Maguire, *Letters and Papers*, 1: 573–74, 593.

14. Alfred Thayer Mahan, "The United States Looking Outward," *Interest of America in Sea Power*. pp. 7–8.

15. Mahan to Charles H. Davis, 23 December 1890, Seager and Maguire, *Letters and Papers*, 2: 37.

16. Mahan to James R. Thursfield, 1 December 1897 and 25 January 1898, Seager and Maguire, *Letters and Papers*, 2: 529, 536–37.

17. Intelligence and Technological Archives, Naval War College (hereafter cited as NWC), Newport, R.I., Record Group (RG) 8, Container #21. The authors were Lieutenant Commander John B. van Bleeker and Lieutenant W. E. Reynolds.

18. Lieutenant Commander Charles J. Train, "Strategy Upon a War with Spain," NWC, RG 8, Container #21.

19. Naval War College Staff, "Situation in the Case of War with Spain," #260, 1895, NWC, RG 8, Container #21.

20. Jeffery M. Dorwart, *The Office of Naval Intelligence: The Birth of America's First Intelligence Agency, 1865–1918* (Annapolis, Md.: U.S. Naval Institute Press, 1979), pp. 55–57.

21. Ronald Spector, *Admiral of the New Empire: The Life and Career of George Dewey* (Baton Rouge: Louisiana State University Press, 1974), pp. 32–33.

22. Henry Clay Taylor, "Synopsis of War College Plan for Cuban Campaign in a War with Spain," NWC, RG 8, Container #21.

23. "Situation in the Case of War with Spain," December 1896, NWC, RG 8, Container #21, p. 4b.

24. Spector, *Admiral of the New Empire*, p. 35.

25. Roosevelt to Caspar F. Goodrich, 28 May 1897, Morison, *Letters of Theodore Roosevelt*, 1: 617–18.

26. Board on Defenses, "War with Spain and Japan," 1897, #253, NWC, RG 8, Container #21, p. 11.

27. Roosevelt to Goodrich, 16 June 1897; Morison, *Letters of Theodore Roosevelt*, 1: 626.

28. Goodrich to Roosevelt, 23 June 1897, NWC, RG 8, Container #47, #265.

29. "Rough Draft of Official Plan in Event of Operations Against Spain in Cuba, with Suggestions by Captain C. F. Goodrich," 1897, #262, NWC, RG 8, Container #21.

30. See Roosevelt to Henry Cabot Lodge, 21 September 1897, Morison, *Letters of Theodore Roosevelt*, 1: 685–86.

31. Roosevelt to William Wirt Kimball, 19 November 1897, Morison, *Letters of Theodore Roosevelt*, 1: 716–17.

32. Roosevelt to John D. Long, 14 January 1898, Morison, *Letters of Theodore Roosevelt*, 1: 761.

33. See Roosevelt to Mahan, 30 August 1897 and 8 January 1898, PSU - TR Papers, Series 2, Reels 314, 315.

34. Roosevelt to Mahan, 14 March 1898, PSU - TR Papers, Series 2, Reel 315.

35. See Roosevelt to Robley D. Evans, 20 April 1898, and to Benjamin F. Tracy, 18 April 1898 and 21 April 1898, Morison, *Letters of Theodore Roosevelt*, 2: 818–19. There is no evidence, as Karsten suggests, that Roosevelt was "testing" Mahan's strategic sense. Mahan's comments and suggestions concerned the 1897 special board plan, not Goodrich's plans for operations in the Pacific which Roosevelt had objected to on grounds of their being too defensive in nature. See Karsten, "The Nature of 'Influence,'" *American Quarterly* 23 (October 1971): 592–93.

36. Seager, *Alfred Thayer Mahan*, pp. 362–63. Seager places the date of Mahan's letter as 12, 13 or 14 March; in all probability it was between the 18th and 20th.

37. Roosevelt to Mahan, 21 March 1898, Harvard collection, Roosevelt Papers. See also David F. Trask, *The War with Spain in 1898* (New York: MacMillan, 1981) pp. 84–85.

38. John D. Long's diary entry of 9 May read as follows: "Captain Mahan, on the retired list, returns under orders from abroad for duty on the War Board. He has achieved great distinction as a writer of naval history, and has made a very thorough study of naval strategy. No naval officer stands higher to-day. Yet I doubt very much whether he will be of much value practically. He may be, or he may not. That remains to be seen.

"Attended Cabinet meeting at the White House, in which we consider some questions of the term of peace, in case it shall become practicable." Lawrence Shaw Mayo, ed., *America of Yesterday, as Reflected in the Journal of John Davis Long* (Boston: Atlantic Monthly Press, 1923), p. 191.

39. Roosevelt to Lodge, 19 May and 12 June 1898, Morison, *Letters of Theodore Roosevelt*, 2: 831, 842.

40. Mahan as a member of the Naval War Board (from 9 May through

August of 1898) tended to approve of operations that conformed to his understanding of the Navy Department's prewar plan of campaign: the attack on the Philippines, the blockade of Cuba, fleet concentration, and the subsequent move against Puerto Rico. Similarly, Mahan disapproved of ventures which departed from the departmental plan or the strategic principles by which he was guided, such as Sampson's early move against San Juan, the temporary retention of Schley's flying squadron at Hampton Roads, and the proposed dispatch of certain naval vessels to bombard Spanish ports after the victory over Admiral Cervera's squadron at Santiago. See chapter 14 in Seager, *Alfred Thayer Mahan*, pp. 354–96.

41. Trask, *The War with Spain*, p. 425.

42. Lodge to Roosevelt, 24 June 1898; Henry Cabot Lodge, ed., *Selections from the Correspondence of Theodore Roosevelt and Henry Cabot Lodge*, 2 vols. (New York: Charles Scribner's Sons, 1925), 1:313.

43. Lodge to Roosevelt, 23 July 1898, ibid., 1: 330.

44. Trask, *The War with Spain*, p. 428.

45. Mayo, *Journal of John Davis Long*, p. 210.

46. Mahan to Lodge, 27 July 1898, Seager and Maguire, *Letters and Papers*, 2: 569. Mahan was willing to acquire additional territory in the Caribbean. St. Thomas, he thought, "would form a compact strategic entity" with Puerto Rico and its dependencies. Lodge, on the other hand, was not averse to acquiring the Ladrones and Carolines as well as the Philippines. See Mahan to Lodge, 4 August 1898, Seager and Maguire, *Letters and Papers*, 2: 572; also Stephen B. Luce to Lodge, 10 May 1898 and Lodge to Luce, 12 May 1898, Gleaves, *Life and Letters of Stephen B. Luce*, pp. 279–80.

47. To an English correspondent Mahan wrote: "I think, however, the islands will be forced upon us by the refractoriness of the insurgents themselves. As in Cuba, so in Luzon, long before the Commissioners at Paris can act, our nation will be forced to feel that we cannot abandon to any other the task of maintaining order in the land in which we have been led to interpose." Mahan to George Syndenham Clarke, 17 August 1898, Seager and Maguire, *Letters and Papers*, 2: 579–80.

48. The text of the document is reproduced in Seager and Maguire, *Letters and Papers*, 2: 581–91.

# 4 Geopolitics and Anglo-American Relations

One wintry day in mid-January, 1900, New York Governor Theodore Roosevelt penned a brief invitation to Alfred Thayer Mahan to join him for lunch the following Saturday at his sister Corinne's New York City residence. "Did you see my article in *The Independent* on Expansion and Peace?" Roosevelt inquired. "I think you would like it."[1] Mahan accepted the invitation and promised to look up the article in question.[2]

The conversation at luncheons involving Theodore Roosevelt invariably tended to be both lively and wide-ranging. Certainly there was no shortage of topics to discuss at this particular one. The 21 December issue of the *Independent*, in which Roosevelt's piece appeared, carried a number of items of interest to the reader in its "Survey of the World." William McKinley's renomination on the first ballot of the forthcoming Republican national convention was seen as a "foregone conclusion"; Secretary of War Elihu Root was being mentioned for the vice-presidency. The Democratic party continued to oppose the administration's Philippine policy. Emilio Aguinaldo, leader of the Philippine independence movement, was in hiding; Leonard Wood, the former colonel of the Rough Riders, had been appointed military governor of Cuba. Cipriano Castro continued to consolidate his hold on Venezuela; though no one knew it at the time, his rule would embroil the United States with both England and Germany within two years. The British army in South Africa had suffered three stunning defeats at the hands of the Boers: Stormberg Mountain, the Modder River, and Tugela. General Kitchener and Field Marshal Lord Roberts were ordered to the theatre of operations. Rumors of Russian designs on the Afghanistan

city of Herat were rife, as were accounts of a Russian advance southward toward the Persian Gulf, the latter move bringing her into conflict
with both Great Britain and Germany in western Asia.[3]

Nor would these topics exhaust the conversation between Roosevelt
and Mahan. Roosevelt's struggle to oust Louis F. Payn, New York
State's superintendent of insurance, was reaching a climax, bringing
the governor once again into conflict with Boss Thomas C. Platt and
the Republican machine. It was suggested in some circles that Platt
was prepared to dump the governor, wanting someone more amenable
in Albany. Senator Henry Cabot Lodge was working strenuously to
boost Roosevelt for the vice-presidential nomination. Roosevelt himself
was torn between a number of possibilities: a second term as governor,
the vice-presidency, secretary of war, governor general of the Philippines. If he and Mahan touched on matters of interest to the navy, the
smouldering Sampson-Schley controversy must have been discussed.
Both men were partisans of William T. Sampson.[4] Both also were aware
that negotiations were nearing a conclusion between Secretary of State
John Hay and British Minister Lord Julian Pauncefote concerning the
revision of the Clayton-Bulwer Treaty. Mahan's "The Problem of Asia"
was to be serialized by *Harper's Monthly* beginning in March, and the
lunch table would be a perfect place to test some of his views on the
subject on Roosevelt.

Mahan surely thanked the governor for his flattering reference in
the latter's "Expansion and Peace" essay. Roosevelt had approvingly
quoted Mahan's denunciation of those who indiscriminately advocated
"peace at any price." The colonel called Mahan "a Christian gentleman"
who was "incapable of advocating wrongdoing of any kind, national or
individual."[5] Roosevelt's essay was a thinly disguised polemic supporting the McKinley administration's position in the Philippines. To
leave the islands, he said, would mean turning them over to "rapine
and bloodshed" until some stronger civilizing nation stepped in. "Fun-
damentally, the cause of [American] expansion is the cause of peace."
Wars between the civilized nations, Roosevelt suggested, were becoming less frequent. "With England our relations are better than ever
before, and so they ought to be and will be with Germany." All the
civilized powers—the United States, England, Germany, France, Austria, and Russia—had the right and the duty to expand to bring peace
to the barbarian peoples of the world. "In other words every expansion
of a great civilized Power means a victory for law, order and righteousness."[6] With all of this Mahan concurred, having by this time
overcome his initial doubts concerning American retention of the
Philippines.

Roosevelt earlier that day had met with Thomas Collier Platt. Roosevelt was determined to get rid of Louis F. Payn, a spoilsman par

excellence. Payn's term in office expired that month, but with the support of the Republican machine and the insurance companies, he seemed determined to defy the governor's express wishes and remain in office. Roosevelt that morning had insisted to Platt that Payn had to go; Platt, equally obdurate, had said that Payn would stay. The governor then gave Platt an ultimatum: either accept a new individual from the list of names Roosevelt had tendered, or Roosevelt would send in his own nominee when the legislature reconvened Wednesday. Mahan supported Roosevelt's stand. In his note accepting the luncheon invitation he had expressed his confidence "that if you decide it [the Payn affair] in utter disregard of the effect on your own future—which I am sure you will—you will be guided aright."[7]

As for Roosevelt's political future, Platt had said to him that morning "that he believed I ought to take the Vice Presidency both for National and State reasons."[8] Platt clearly had the power to deny Roosevelt the renomination as governor of New York, but Roosevelt also saw the pitfalls involved in accepting the vice-presidency. Both men knew that Roosevelt had his eye on the White House. It all boiled down to how best to remain in the public eye for the next four years. Roosevelt earlier had toyed with the idea of becoming secretary of war, but his fellow New Yorker Elihu Root had accepted the post and done superlatively well. "As you know," Roosevelt wrote Henry Cabot Lodge two days after his luncheon with Mahan,

the one thing I should really like to do would be to be the first civil Governor General in the Philippines. I believe I could do that job, and it is a job emphatically worth doing. I feel that being Vice President would cut me off definitely from all chance of doing it; whereas in my second term as Governor, were I offered the Philippines, I could resign and accept it.[9]

The adventurous aspects of the position would have appealed to Roosevelt; whether he was seriously interested, or was merely trying to dampen Lodge's enthusiasm for Roosevelt as the number two man on the Republican ticket is a matter of conjecture. Mahan could sympathize with the governor's problem; but what was the right thing to do?

Although Roosevelt and Mahan agreed on the foregoing issues, they did not see eye to eye on the Boer War. For Mahan it was a conflict the British could not afford to lose. He recently had written a British correspondent of his "deep sorrow and anxiety" at the recent defeats. He wondered if British efforts in Africa shouldn't be concentrated largely on Egypt, rather than the Cape. "From Bryce's book I draw one conclusion: that Africa has little promise of permanent intrinsic value."[10] To his way of thinking the Boer War represented merely a sideshow in the more basic geopolitical conflict between land power

(Russia and her ally France) and sea power (Britain, the United States, Germany, and Japan). This conflict was being waged across the "debatable ground" of Asia: China, Afghanistan, Persia, and Asiatic Turkey. Russia was seeking access to the sea. Mahan felt that she must at all costs be barred from control of the Dardanelles and the Persian Gulf. Russian control of those two key locations would threaten Britain's maritime lifeline to India via Suez. In China, the maritime powers must hold the Yangtze valley, although Russia could be expected to control those portions of China contiguous to her own territory—i.e., Mongolia and Manchuria. The United States had to take a more active role in East Asia to support the British position there—commercially, culturally, religiously, and militarily. Though a formal Anglo-American alliance in Asia was neither necessary nor politically possible, both Britain and the United States should if necessary retrench elsewhere: the British in southern Africa, the United States in South America below the Amazon.[11]

Roosevelt did not agree. He shared Mahan's regret that the Boer War was being waged, but for somewhat different reasons. He compared the conflict to the War of 1812, in the sense that each party was in the right from its own standpoint.[12] As the conflict dragged on, Roosevelt grew more and more troubled. Writing to a British friend, he commented: "The two races are so near together; they both fight with such valor; they both have such splendid qualities. It seems dreadful, when there is so much evil to combat in the world, that the powers that ought to tell for good should be employed in mutual destruction."[13] Roosevelt agreed with Mahan that the downfall of the British Empire would be "a calamity to the race," but intuitively sensed, as Mahan did not, that the Boer War represented a degree of "deterioration in the English-speaking peoples."[14] He spelled out one of the consequences of British defeat: a future conflict between Germany and the United States.

Many of my friends need to understand that if the British Empire suffers a serious disaster, I believe in five years it will mean a war between us and some one of the great continental European military nations, unless we are content to abandon the Monroe Doctrine for South America.[15]

Roosevelt thus could not share Mahan's enthusiasm for an increased Anglo-American commitment to East Asia. If Britain had to make a choice between Asia and Africa, Roosevelt's preference was for the latter. If worst came to worst, and Britain was forced out of Asia, "I cannot help thinking that the blow instead of cowing the English-speaking race would serve thoroughly to arouse and anger all their communities."[16] In any case, he did not see how British domination of "southern and South East Asia" could last "through the ages." Furthermore, "Russia's march over barbarous Asia does represent a real and great advance for civilization."[17]

Later that year Mahan, writing to Lodge, "rejoiced" that he and Lodge saw eye to eye concerning "the community of interest between ourselves & Great Britain." He did not, however, think that Britain's performance in the Boer War was a sign of "her practical decadence."[18] To Roosevelt himself, in the spring of 1901, Mahan commended *The Problem of Asia*. He saw no way to deny Russia control of northern China but thought that Great Britain and the United States should continue to control the Yangtze valley,"the heart of China in every sense of the word," with naval power.[19]

Roosevelt said that he had indeed read Mahan's book "with the greatest interest, and in the main, with entire agreement." He was concerned, though, that American public opinion would not support a more forward position in East Asia. Americans (and, one suspects, Roosevelt himself) were far more concerned "about the Nicaragua Canal and the Alaskan boundary." Almost sarcastically, Roosevelt wrote:

But I do not have to tell you, with your wide and profound historical research, that while something can be done by public means in leading the people, they cannot lead them much further than public opinion has prepared the way. They can lead them *somewhat* further, but not very much. Now, as yet our public opinion is dull on the question of China, and moreover, we are all somewhat in the dark as to the true facts.[20]

The impending construction of an isthmian canal also led to disagreement. Both Roosevelt and Mahan for some years had supported the idea of an exclusively American-controlled canal; both wanted to see the Clayton-Bulwer Treaty of 1850, which specified a jointly-owned Anglo-American canal through Nicaragua, annulled. Both undoubtedly approved of the Hepburn bill which, introduced in the Senate 15 January 1900, had precisely that end in mind. Secretary of State John Hay, his hand forced by the Senate, felt it necessary to reach some formal agreement with Great Britain, so he proceeded to institute discussions with the British ambassador, Sir Julian Pauncefote. Agreement was quickly reached, and the Hay-Pauncefote Treaty was signed 5 February and submitted to the Senate for ratification the next day. Up to this point, Mahan and Roosevelt undoubtedly had seen eye to eye on the course of events. Their reactions to the Hay-Pauncefote Treaty, once its terms were known, differed considerably.

Roosevelt issued a terse statement to the press on 12 February urging that the pending treaty not be ratified unless amended to provide for a wholly American-controlled canal. "This seems to me vital," he argued, "from the standpoint of our sea power, no less than from the standpoint of the Monroe Doctrine."[21] Hay was outraged by what he saw as Roosevelt's gratuitous interference. Admitting that the Clayton-Bulwer Treaty had outlived its usefulness, Hay felt it would be dishonorable to unilaterally abrogate it. "As to 'Sea Power' and the Monroe Doctrine," he declared, "we did not act without consulting the best living authorities on those subjects."[22] Roosevelt responded in measured words to Hay's outburst. He maintained that a canal open to ships of all nations in time of war, and unfortified, would become "an added burden, an additional strategic point to be guarded by our fleet." The navy, he maintained, should be free "for offensive purposes," not fettered by having to guard the approaches to the canal. His other objection was that by inviting other powers to adhere to the Hay-Pauncefote Treaty, we were inviting "similar joint action" by the European nations elsewhere in the hemisphere. "To my mind," Roosevelt concluded, "we should consistently refuse to all European powers the right to control, in any shape, any territory in the western Hemisphere which they do not already hold."[23]

There is a strong presumption that Hay, or someone in the State Department acting on his behalf, consulted Mahan prior to the signing of the first Hay-Pauncefote Treaty, if Hay's statement in his 12 February letter to Roosevelt can be taken at face value. Mahan set out his thinking about the treaty in a letter to Seth Low, president of Columbia University. Mahan felt the press was making too much of the idea of a joint "guarantee." The "invitation to the other Powers to adhere" was asking them only not to "violate the neutrality of the canal." Mahan thus saw the treaty as essentially bilateral (which it was), not multilateral, as Roosevelt implied. He readily admitted that a hostile warship or squadron could utilize the canal, but did not see that they would gain anything strategically by doing so. If, for instance, a German squadron passed through from the Caribbean into the Pacific, what damage could they do to San Francisco or Seattle, unless those locales were "miserably undefended"? *Why* they should want to attack them, leaving "unnoticed the far more important Atlantic centres" was even more to the point. Mahan, in short, favored the Hay-Pauncefote Treaty, provided the United States government adopted the policy of keeping American naval strength "equal at least to that of Germany."[24] Mahan's letter to Low was written two days after one to Roosevelt, suggesting that he (Mahan) used similar arguments attempting to defuse the governor's concern regarding the treaty. If so, Roosevelt remained dubious:

As you know, I am heartily friendly to England, but I cannot help feeling that the State Department has made a great error in the canal treaty. We really make not only England but all the great continental powers our partners in the transaction, and I do not see why we should dig the canal if we are not to fortify it so as to insure its being used for ourselves and against our foes in time of war.[25]

One senses that the basic disagreement between Roosevelt and Mahan at this time was in the realm of Anglo-American relations. Mahan urged support for Britain's position in East Asia and acceptance of the Hay-Pauncefote Treaty. Roosevelt felt that the British were overextended in Asia and that the Hay-Pauncefote Treaty, unamended, was contrary to America's national interest. As events turned out, Roosevelt had a surer sense of public opinion than did Mahan. The treaty, amended by the Senate, was rejected by Great Britain. The second Hay-Pauncefote Treaty was far closer to Roosevelt's position than the first had been. By disagreeing with the terms of the first Hay-Pauncefote Treaty, he clearly went further than Mahan wished. In similar fashion, his Caribbean policy during his first term in office, which began in September 1901 following McKinley's death, exceeded those measures that Mahan felt were necessary and wise.

## NOTES

1. Roosevelt to Mahan, 16/17 January 1900, PSU - TR Papers, Series 2, Reel 322.

2. Mahan to Roosevelt, 18 January 1900, Seager and Maguire, *Letters and Papers*, 2: 676.

3. *Independent* 51 (21 December 1899): 3393–98.

4. For an account of this affair, and particularly Mahan's views, see Seager, *Alfred Thayer Mahan*, pp. 400–405.

5. Theodore Roosevelt, "Expansion and Peace," *Independent* 51 (21 December 1899): 3401.

6. Ibid., 3403–4.

7. Mahan to Roosevelt, 18 January 1900, Seager and Maguire, *Letters and Papers*, 2: 676.

8. Roosevelt to Lodge, 22 January 1900, Lodge, *Correspondence of Roosevelt and Lodge*, 1: 437.

9. Ibid.

10. *Mahan to James R. Thursfield, 15 December 1899, Seager and Maguire, Letters and Papers*, 2: 673.

11. Alfred Thayer Mahan, *The Problem of Asia and Its Effect upon International Policies* (Boston: Little, Brown, 1905), pp. 201–2.

12. Roosevelt to John St. Loe Strachey, 27 January 1900, Morison, *Letters of Theodore Roosevelt*, 2: 1144.

13. Roosevelt to Frederick Courteney Selous, 7 February 1900, ibid., 2: 1177.

14. Theodore Roosevelt to Anna Roosevelt Cowles, 17 December 1899, ibid., 2: 1112–13.

15. Roosevelt to Arthur Hamilton Lee, 30 January 1900, ibid., 2: 1152; see also Roosevelt to Elihu Root, 29 January 1900, ibid., 2: 1151.

16. Roosevelt to Cecil Spring-Rice, 11 August 1899, ibid., 2: 1052.

17. Ibid., 2: 1051. See also Roosevelt to Spring-Rice, 2 January 1900, ibid., 2: 1128; Roosevelt to Frederick Rene Couder, 3 July 1901, ibid., 3: 107.

18. Mahan to Lodge, 8 December 1900, Seager and Maguire, *Letters and Papers*, 2: 698.

19. Mahan to Roosevelt, 21 March 1901, ibid., 2: 706, 708.

20. Roosevelt to Mahan, 18 March 1901, PSU - TR Papers, Series 2, Reel 325. Both Lodge and Roosevelt were concerned that an expanded American presence in East Asia would be matched by a contraction of the area covered by the Monroe Doctrine in South America. See Roosevelt to Lodge, 27 March 1901, and Lodge to Roosevelt, 30 March 1901, Lodge, *Correspondence of Roosevelt and Lodge*, 1: 484–88.

21. See Roosevelt to Albert Shaw, 15 February 1900, Morison, *Letters of Theodore Roosevelt*, 2: 1186–1187.

22. John Hay to Roosevelt, 12 February 1900, William Roscoe Thayer, *The Life and Letters of John Hay*, 2 vols., (New York: Houghton, Mifflin, 1908), 2: 225. Thayer disguised the fact that the letter had been written to Roosevelt.

23. Roosevelt to Hay, 18 February 1900, Morison, *Letters of Theodore Roosevelt*, 2: 1192.

24. Mahan to Seth Low, 15 February 1900, Seager and Maguire, *Letters and Papers*, 2: 682–84. Mahan evidently believed that the McKinley administration had erred initially by failing to obtain the opinion of any leading military or naval figures. "It is not only a mistake in itself," he had written to Low, "but a grave political blunder in tactics; for the statement that [General Nelson A.] Miles and [Admiral George E.] Dewey approved would have immense weight with the public."

25. Roosevelt to Mahan, 14 February 1900, PSU - TR Papers, Series 2, Reel 323: see also Roosevelt to William Sheffield Cowles, 2 March 1900, and to Cecil Arthur Spring-Rice, 2 March 1900, Morison, *Letters of Theodore Roosevelt*, 2: 1208–9.

# 5 Muted Differences over Caribbean Issues

Speaking of the American role in the Panama revolution of November 1903, Mahan observed:"The question then was not one of law, but of morals; and, except in cases of absolute right and wrong, morals in the case of nations . . . [are] often a matter of expedience."[1] This statement by itself was not remarkable; other defenders of Roosevelt's policies had said as much. What was remarkable about it was that it appeared not immediately after the United States recognized the independence of Panama, but in 1912—nine years later. Mahan would normally have been expected to comment at length on such foreign policy concerns as the second Venezuelan crisis, the Panama imbroglio, and events leading up to the Dominican customs receivership of 1905. Yet a close scrutiny of Mahan's correspondence during these years (1902–1905) yields no reference to the country's Caribbean policy.

A partial explanation is that Mahan's gaze was still riveted on eastern Asia. Letters to English correspondents (Bouverie Clark, Leopold J. Maxse, William Henderson) during this period contain little mention of affairs in the Western Hemisphere. It is clear that Mahan hoped, despite existing tensions between Germany and Great Britain, that the two countries would undertake to cooperate in Asia—and perhaps elsewhere. Russia and France, he felt, would always be Britain's "inevitable enemies."[2] Mahan nevertheless deplored Britain's close association with Germany during the second Venezuelan crisis, not because of a new-found distrust of the efficacy of gunboat diplomacy, but because American public opinion, aroused against Germany by the episode, might lash out against Britain as well.[3] Even after the outbreak of the Russo-Japanese War, Mahan hoped that Russia could retain Port Arthur and "remain engaged in Manchuria & a Pacific seaport. She cannot tackle both that [East Asia] and the Persian Gulf."[4]

Mahan clearly found the Monroe Doctrine useful as a spur for "the creation of a powerful navy by the United States."[5] In similar fashion, the bogey of European interference in this hemisphere also had its uses. Yet at the time, Mahan was not convinced that a serious European threat to the Monroe Doctrine existed. Writing to Captain Henry Clay Taylor, chief of the Bureau of Navigation, shortly after the independence of Panama, he declared: "In considering possible wars with the great nations of the world, it seems to me inconceivable that any one of them should expect seriously to modify, or weaken, our position in this hemisphere."[6] In an article on the Monroe Doctrine written in the fall of 1902, Mahan mused that what the doctrine really stood for was the responsibility of the United States to preserve the independence of the nations in the hemisphere. This did not imply that Latin American states could flout their obligations either to the United States or other nations, but any action to compel the observance of such obligations should never be undertaken lightly. Should the United States compel the Latin American states "to observe their international obligations to others . . . which has been by some argued a necessary corollary of the Monroe Doctrine, [this] would encroach on the very independence which that political dogma defends; for to assume the responsibility which derives from independence, and can only be transferred by its surrender, would be to assert a *quasi* suzerainty." Although the United States was clearly "the preponderant American Power," she did not aspire to be "paramount. She does not find the true complement of the Monroe Doctrine in an undefined control over American States, exercised by her and denied to Europe."[7] Just as the United States enjoyed "a priority of interest and influence" in the Western Hemisphere, so the European powers were preeminent in Africa, the Levant, and India. China, Japan, and the Pacific would be open to influence from both the United States and Europe.

It would soon become clear that the Roosevelt administration did not share Mahan's views, particularly with respect to any threat to the Western Hemisphere from Europe and, consequently, the need for American intervention in the affairs of the several Caribbean states.

The second Venezuelan crisis of 1902–1903 arose from the default of the Venezuelan government on payments of debts owed to foreign nationals. The governments of Great Britain and Germany, after mutual consultation, decided to institute a blockade of the principal Venezuelan ports to compel payment to their own citizens at least. They did not take this action without first clearing it with the Roosevelt administration. Both Roosevelt and Secretary of State John Hay acquiesced, adding only that no permanent occupation of Venezuelan territory would be countenanced. As the blockade progressed, the American public became seriously alarmed over reports of Venezuelan vessels being sunk, and ports and customs houses shelled, by German gunboats. Roosevelt requested the powers (subsequently joined by Italy) to agree to a peaceful settlement of the dispute. As a means of enforcing his demands, he publicized American naval maneuvers then taking place in the vicinity of Puerto Rico. The settlement reached with the Venezuelan government for resumption of payments, and the lifting of the blockade, eased the crisis so far as the American public was concerned. The blockading powers, however, submitted a claim on behalf of their nationals for priority in the distribution of money paid by Venezuela in settlement of claims. The Hague world court decision reached in February 1904 supported this contention and created fresh problems for the Roosevelt administration in the Dominican Republic—a nation where revolution and instability seemed chronic.

Dominican insurgents had formed the habit of swooping down from the hills and helping themselves to funds from the nearest customs house, then using these funds to procure weapons and supplies from local merchants before marching on the capital. Customs house revenues represented almost the only source of foreign exchange in the Dominican Republic, and its government, like that of Venezuela, found itself with an empty treasury and importunate foreign creditors. The Hague decision, in a manner of speaking, forced the Roosevelt administration, much against its will, to act. The Italian government sent a cruiser to the Dominican Republic to enforce its demands on behalf of its nationals. It seemed other nations, buttressed by the court decision, might not be far behind. Roosevelt did not want foreign powers meddling in strategically sensitive Dominican waters any more than in Venezuelan territory.

To forestall such action, he had initially sent down a fact-finding team led by Admiral Dewey and Assistant Secretary of State Francis B. Loomis, which reported that the situation was every bit as bad as rumor had it. Next he engineered a Dominican government "request" for the establishment of an American-controlled customs receivership, backing up his action with American naval patrols in Dominican waters. He then promulgated the famous (or infamous) Roosevelt corollary to the Monroe Doctrine, through which the United States, "in cases of chronic wrongdoing," undertook to discipline recalcitrant Latin American nations so that the European powers need not interfere. When the Senate balked and refused to ratify the accord, the president put it into effect by executive agreement.[8]

Given Mahan's views noted previously, it is not surprising that he was not in full accord with the administration's actions in Venezuela and the Dominican Republic. He supported the right of intervention by Germany, Great Britain, and Italy in Venezuela, and agreed with the decision of the Hague Tribunal concerning priority of payment. "It can scarcely be alleged," Mahan noted, "that anything like an international consensus now obtains as to the ethical propriety of forcing a nation to pay its creditors . . . but, as international law till now has tolerated the forcible collection of such debts, I own to thinking that the peoples who by resort to authorized methods obtained redress for all parties were entitled for their trouble and expense to have the first lien upon the security pledge."[9] In a 1907 postscript to his Monroe Doctrine essay written five years earlier, Mahan clearly expressed doubts about the propriety of the administration's actions in the Dominican Republic: "An end, however beneficent, does not necessarily justify the means."[10] He finally rationalized the episode to himself on the grounds that public opinion clearly favored Roosevelt's stand, and (which was not in fact true) that the Dominican government had requested us to take action. Yet even if Mahan in time reconciled himself to the Dominican intervention, he had much more difficulty justifying the Roosevelt administration's actions in Panama.

The need for an isthmian canal having been demonstrated afresh during the Spanish-American War, both public and governmental interest quickened in the project. The second Hay-Pauncefote Treaty permitted the United States government to build and fortify a canal under its exclusive control. An isthmian canal commission appointed in 1899 by the McKinley administration reported favorably on the Nicaragua route. Supporters of the Panama alternative then launched a frantic lobbying effort to convince Congress to change its mind. The subsequent Spooner Amendment favored the Panama route provided no more than $25 million was spent to acquire the rights of the New Panama Canal Company.

At this stage, the Roosevelt administration negotiated the Hay-Herrán Treaty with the Colombian government, acquired the rights of the New Panama Canal Company for $25 million, as stipulated, and was ready to begin construction. The Colombian government, however, balked. It was unhappy with the Hay-Herrán Treaty, and with the amount of money it was realizing from the arrangements. Roosevelt and Hay, neither knowing nor caring anything about Colombian politics or the issue of Colombian sovereignty over the proposed canal, became increasingly impatient and began to cast about for alternatives during the summer of 1903. Clearly they could opt for the Nicaragua route, but this course of action did not appeal to Roosevelt, whose blood was up. Hearing from a variety of sources that a revolution against Bogotá was brewing on the isthmus, Roosevelt resolved to put it to good use. He ordered a number of American warships dispatched toward the isthmus late in October. In his mind, they had the dual purpose of preventing Colombia from squelching the uprising (troop reinforcements would have to come by sea) and deterring outside (i.e., European) interference.

The revolution occurred almost on schedule; American naval intervention, although initially tentative, ultimately proved decisive. The new republic of Panama was recognized, and an even more favorable canal treaty was quickly negotiated. Domestic critics of the administration's actions had a field day. Mahan, however, kept quiet about the whole affair.

Mahan was never reluctant to advocate the acquisition of strategically valuable territory, particularly if it was contiguous to the Western Hemisphere. He had long urged the acquisition of Hawaii and, while a member of the Naval War Board, believed the Danish West Indies should be purchased. Cuba, too, belonged in the United States' orbit. "I myself thought," Mahan wrote some years later, "if we went to war [with Spain] we had better take Cuba, the military importance of which to our position had been evident ever since we became a nation."[11] He should have been in the forefront, then, of those who supported the "taking of Panama" and defended the Roosevelt administration's actions on grounds of strategic necessity.

One reason for his reticence might have been his indifference to the "battle of the routes" which had been of such consuming interest to Roosevelt. "As regards the canals I have always been a Nicaragua man, though without any personal knowledge of the merits of the case," he confessed in 1902.[12] That being the case, why not let the Colombians stew in their own juice and opt for the Nicaragua route?

His initial reaction to the events of November 1903 almost certainly was negative. From a legal point of view, he suspected that the United States had broken the 1846 Bidlack-Mallarino Treaty with Colombia. Its terms stated that American travellers and goods transiting the isthmus were guaranteed equality of treatment with Colombian nationals and goods vis-a-vis the cost and mode of transportation. In return the United States guaranteed the positive neutrality and freedom of transit of the isthmus: a provision aimed at preserving Colombian sovereignty over the isthmus in cases of either internal rebellion or external assault. On numerous occasions during the next half century or so the United States had in fact intervened—sometimes with ships and, on occasion, sending forces ashore as well—but always at the invitation of the Colombian government.[13] "I certainly do not hold that any advantage to the United States or to Panama could be advanced to justify the action of 1903, if certainly in contravention of the treaty," Mahan later wrote.[14] A man of conservative temperament, Mahan also was distressed at the way the episode was handled and at the president's subsequent fit of self-righteousness: " ... the strenuousness of Mr. Roosevelt's character communicates itself to his speech and writings; the vigor of which, when exerted in necessary self-justification, tends rather to confirm the first impression of indefensibleness."[15]

When Mahan broke his long-standing silence on the issue in 1911, it is all too evident that he was trying to convince himself, with only partial success, that the administration had acted honorably. In a letter to John Bassett Moore, the noted international jurist who had been an assistant secretary of state at the time of the Panama affair, Mahan acknowledged that the government's actions in 1903 did not violate international law, but nevertheless might have violated the Treaty of 1846. He reasoned, however, that the ensuring of freedom of transit of the isthmus was a principle which overrode the assurance of Colombian sovereignty over the isthmus—except "against *foreign* conquest or invasion. If all this be so, we fulfilled our obligations." Mahan went on to say:

The endeavor to state the case to you has gone far to clarify my own mind, and to convince me of the integrity of our action. That men as keen sighted as Roosevelt and Hay should have perceived at once an opportunity and should have purposed to embrace it, is nothing to the point of law or equity. We have to do only with the act, and that is the discharging of our guaranteed assurance of quiet. It may be that the Colombian force was so overwhelming as to insure submission without disturbance; but as to that our Government was at liberty to form its own conclusions. It was not called upon to permit a landing that might be followed by fighting, nor to sustain Colombia against domestic outbreak.[16]

One further factor in Mahan's belated conversion may have been his desire to recruit the support of Roosevelt in his own efforts to vitiate the Taft administration's attempt to make a series of arbitration treaties with the major powers. He also began to show concern that the United States was falling behind Germany in naval construction, permitting Germany, if she wished, to mount a challenge to the Monroe Doctrine.[17]

Roosevelt, for his part, made no acknowledgement of Mahan's breaking silence on the Panama episode. The ex-president no doubt noted Mahan's continued ambivalence, and although the two men cooperated to help defeat the arbitration treaties, they exchanged no views on the Caribbean policy, past or present. By contrast, Roosevelt had been quick to praise Mahan's June 1911 piece in *Century Magazine*, "The Panama Canal and Sea Power in the Pacific," which despite its title had little to do with the Panama Canal; it was a rehash of Mahan's long-standing objections to Japanese immigration in the "white settler" portions of the Pacific littoral.[18]

Mahan's reluctance to mobilize public support for the Roosevelt administration's actions in the Venezuela, Dominican Republic, and Panama episodes may have weakened what little inclination the president had to consult the apostle of sea power on diplomatic issues during the 1901–1908 period. Perhaps Mahan would have been isolated from policy-making circles during Roosevelt's presidency in any event, given the president's determination to be both his own secretary of state and his own secretary of the navy. A careful reading of Mahan, combined with his silence on Caribbean issues, must have convinced Roosevelt that such advice as he might elicit would be unwelcome. Whether the very real differences between the two were ever the subject of discussion is a moot point. The Russo-Japanese war, and the all-big-gun controversy which it triggered, only deepened Mahan's exclusion.

## NOTES

1. Alfred Thayer Mahan, "Was Panama a Chapter of National Dishonor?" *Armaments and Arbitration, or The Place of Force in the International Relations of States* (New York: Harper & Brothers, 1912), p. 243.

2. Mahan to Leopold J. Maxse, 21 February 1902, Seager and Maguire, *Letters and Papers*, 3: 12.

3. Mahan to Maxse, 22 December 1902, ibid., 3: 50.

4. Mahan to Maxse, 17 June 1904 and 22 November 1904, ibid., 3: 98–99, 109.

5. Alfred Thayer Mahan, "Conditions Determining the Naval Expansion of the United States," *Retrospect and Prospect: Studies in International Relations Naval and Political* (Boston: Little, Brown, 1903), p. 52.

6. Mahan to Henry Clay Taylor, 7 December 1903, Seager and Maguire, *Letters and Papers*, 3: 80.

7. Alfred Thayer Mahan. "The Monroe Doctrine," *Naval Administration and Warfare: Some General Principles* (Boston: Little, Brown, 1908), pp. 395–96.

8. For a discussion of both the second Venezuelan crisis and the Dominican customs receivership in a broader strategic context, see Richard W. Turk, "Defending the New Empire, 1900–1914," in *In Peace and War: Interpretations of American Naval History, 1775–1978*, ed. Kenneth J. Hagan (Westport, Conn.: Greenwood Press, 1978), pp. 189–90, 191–93.

9. Alfred Thayer Mahan, "The Practical Aspect of War," *Some Neglected Aspects of War* (Boston: Little, Brown, 1907), p. 61.

10. Mahan, "The Monroe Doctrine," *Naval Administration and Warfare*, pp. 405–6.

11. Mahan, "The Practical Aspect of War," *Neglected Aspects of War*, pp. 74–75.

12. Mahan to Bouverie Clark, 8 February 1902, Seager and Maguire, *Letters and Papers*, 3: 9.

13. See Richard W. Turk, "The United States Navy and the 'Taking' of Panama, 1901–1903," *Military Affairs* 38 (October 1974): 92–96.

14. Mahan, "Was Panama a Chapter of National Dishonor?" *Armaments and Arbitration*, p. 243.

15. Ibid., p. 220.

16. Mahan to John Bassett Moore, 1 June 1912, Seager and Maguire, *Letters and Papers*, 3: 462–63.

17. Mahan to Moore, 26 February 1912; ibid., 3:445.

18. Roosevelt to Mahan, 8 June 1911, PSU - TR Papers, Series 2, Reel 367.

# 6 Roosevelt Unlimbers His Big Guns

The Russo-Japanese war accomplished a number of things. To Russia, and the West in general, it was a sharp rebuke to those European nations who aspired to dominate the "lesser breeds." Russian aspirations in the Far East were set back for half a century; Japan, conversely, was universally recognized as an Asian power, if indeed her victory in the Sino-Japanese War had not already accomplished that. Theodore Roosevelt had an opportunity to exercise his talents as a peacemaker. Alfred Thayer Mahan had an opportunity to muse upon, and write about, the lessons of the conflict, both strategic and tactical. Last, but not least, the battle of Tsushima engendered a controversy on battleship construction that involved Mahan, Roosevelt, and a brash young inspector of target practice, Lieutenant Commander William S. Sims.

United States naval officers on the Asiatic station did not normally correspond directly with the president of the United States. Certainly Lieutenant Commander Sims was aware that he was taking a calculated risk when he penned a letter to Roosevelt late in 1901. It was, briefly, a plea that the president could hardly ignore: Sims argued that naval gunnery was not nearly as effective as it should be, and asked the president's intercession with the upper echelons of the bureaus concerned.[1] The letter may not have been as risky an act as it seemed. Roosevelt already knew of Sims, having been impressed with the latter's naval attaché reports from Paris while the president was serving as assistant secretary of the navy in 1897–1898. One of Sims's closest associates on the Asiatic station was Albert Lenoir Key, then serving as naval attaché at Tokyo. Key had worked as secretary of the Personnel Board under Roosevelt's direction in 1897, and his sister-in-law had married Leonard Wood, a close friend of the president's.

Sims's audacity was rewarded by his nomination to the position of inspector of target practice in the fall of 1902, although the appointment was opposed by Roosevelt's brother-in-law, William S. Cowles, who was serving at the time as the president's naval aide. Roosevelt thereafter kept an eye on Sims, helped him to obtain new gunsights for naval vessels, and solicited his opinion on a variety of issues. It was understandable that Roosevelt would turn to Sims for assistance when in due course the all-big-gun controversy came to a head.

Mahan, unlike Sims and many other young naval officers, was uncomfortable with the technological complexities of modern warships. He sought balanced fleets composed of destroyers, cruisers and battleships—analogous to the sloops, frigates, and ships-of-the-line of the age of sail. Each class of vessel would have standardized tonnage and armament. The battleships would have mixed batteries of both long-range guns to oppose other battleships and quick-firing five- and eight-inch guns to combat the enemy's smaller vessels. Standardization, Mahan believed, would slow down the arms race and go far toward solving the problem of rapid obsolescence.

Late in 1902 Mahan urged the president to consider a standardized battleship for the American fleet.[2] Undeterred by the president's noncommittal reply, Mahan returned to the issue in the fall of 1903. Referring to the pending Naval General Staff Bill, Mahan noted that it was "of utmost importance" that "the designing of ships—their classes, numbers, and qualities—should be brought into direct relation with the naval policy and strategy of the country."[3] There is no evidence that Roosevelt responded to this letter, preoccupied as he was with Colombia's intransigence on the Hay-Herrán treaty. Mahan tried once more, shortly after Roosevelt's reelection. "It has occurred to me, as an agreement tending to lessen the expense of armaments," Mahan suggested, "that nations might agree on a limitation of the tonnage of single ships."[4] Again, Roosevelt was evasive. "I shall have to think over the matter before I could answer you at all definitely on this last proposition," he replied.[5]

In fact, however, Roosevelt was already leaning in the other direction. On 5 October 1904, he wrote to Sims asking for his opinion on the all-big-gun ship. Sims, in reply, said that it was the only "logical battery" for a battleship. The larger the vessel, the steadier the gun platform; target practice results had shown that big guns were more accurate than smaller ones.[6] Roosevelt subsequently suggested to the Board of Construction that the *New Hampshire*'s battery consist only of eleven- or twelve-inch guns, but he was overruled by the Bureau of Construction and Repair. This exchange took place nearly a year before the keel of *H.M.S. Dreadnought*, the first all-big-gun warship, was laid down.

What both proponents and opponents of the all-big-gun ship needed was evidence from actual combat. This gradually emerged from eyewitness accounts of the battle of Tsushima in 1905. Mahan, writing both for the general public and for professional naval opinion, maintained that the six and eight inch guns of the Japanese had wrought the greatest damage to the Russian ships and crews. Mixed-battery vessels, in his opinion, had a tactical firepower advantage over all-big-gun ships. The speed of the vessels was not decisive at Tsushima. There was inherent in Mahan's argument a concern that, should proponents of the all-big-gun vessel triumph, a new arms race between the naval powers would ensue. His earlier proposal to standardize naval vessels had addressed a related issue.

There was a great deal at stake. Should Mahan's arguments carry the day, the president's shipbuilding program might be irretrievably damaged by Congress. The United States could not permit other powers to forge ahead and still retain its claim to world power status. Roosevelt called on Sims to answer Mahan, which he did in convincing fashion. He demonstrated, based on the number of hits registered by both fleets at Tsushima, that an all-big-gun fleet would deliver "a greater volume of hitting—a greater number of hits, twice the weight of metal hitting, and twice the weight in bursting charges" than would a mixed-battery fleet of the same strength.[7] Speed, he held, was decisive; had the Russian fleet been faster than the Japanese, there would have been no battle. As it was, Admiral Togo had been able to choose his range, with decisive results. Mahan, given the opportunity to rebut Sims's paper, attempted to do so in two letters to Roosevelt (30 September and 22 October 1906) with a noticeable lack of success.[8]

Mahan was on firmer ground in discussing the strategic lessons of the Russo-Japanese war. In a May 1907 article which appeared in the *National Review*, he explained to his readers the "terrible danger" of dividing a battle fleet. Russia had dispersed her naval strength between her Pacific Fleet (based on Port Arthur and Vladivostok), her Black Sea Fleet, and her Baltic Fleet. The loss of Port Arthur and the destruction of her naval power in the western Pacific led inevitably, so Mahan thought, to the defeat of Rozhdestvenski's Baltic squadron at Tsushima. In case anyone missed the point, Mahan then added: "To an instructed, thoughtful, naval mind in the United States [Mahan, obviously], there is no contingency . . . so menacing as the fear of popular clamor influencing an irresolute, or militarily ignorant, administration to divide the battle-ship force into two divisions, the Atlantic and the Pacific."[9]

Mahan almost certainly did not intend to imply that Roosevelt was "irresolute, or militarily ignorant," since he noted in the same paragraph that a "determined President, instructed in military matters" would not yield to the outcry. Yet it is possible that Roosevelt, reading this piece may have felt himself to be the target. Had he not told Mahan some years before that he had read his books "to pretty good advantage?" It would have taken a far less keen mind than Roosevelt's little time to absorb the immutable principle of concentration of force from Mahan's early works, not to mention the captain's proclivity in this direction while serving as a member of the Naval War Board in 1898.

Early the following year Mahan was incautious enough to return to these issues in a manner almost guaranteed to stir Roosevelt's wrath:

I fear I may trespass on your indulgence, but the statement in a morning paper that four of our best battleships are to be sent to the Pacific has filled me with dismay.

In case of war with Japan what can four battleships do against their navy? In case of a war with a European power, what would not the four battleships add to our fleet here?

I apprehend, should war with Japan come before the Panama Canal is finished, the Philippines and Hawaii might fall before we could get there; but, had we our whole fleet in hand, all could be retrieved. Between us and Japan any hostilities must depend on sea power. Invasion in force is possible to neither.

I had inferred from our recent sustained withdrawals of our battleships from Eastern waters, that this was the policy of our Government; and it may be I should at once apologize for writing upon a mere newspaper statement.

Have you chanced to see in the *Athenaeum*, December 22 (p. 799) some comments attributed to Sir George Clarke, Secretary of the British Defense Committee, sustaining the opinion advanced by me concerning the 8 in. and 6 in. guns at Tsushima?[10]

Despite Mahan's disclaimers, the tone of the letter is that of a teacher patiently lecturing a rather backward pupil. Whatever Roosevelt's thoughts when he received this remarkable missive, his reply to Mahan suggests that he was having some difficulty controlling his temper.

don't you know me well enough to believe that I am quite incapable of such an act of utter folly as dividing our fighting fleet? I have no more thought of sending four battleships to the Pacific while there is the least possible friction with Japan than I have of going thither in a rowboat myself.[11]

On some matters Mahan was irrepressible. He did not cease advising Roosevelt not to divide the fleet. As the president was about to leave office in March 1909, Mahan asked him to give his successor, William Howard Taft, a "last earnest recommendation" not to divide the battleship force. Roosevelt, good-naturedly this time, told Mahan that he had already warned Taft on the subject, but said that he would "send him in writing one final protest."[12] The president could afford to be magnanimous. He had won both the battle and the war. The United States Navy henceforth would build only all-big-gun battleships.

## NOTES

1. Elting E. Morison, *Admiral Sims and the Modern American Navy* (Boston: Houghton Mifflin, 1942), pp. 102–5.

2. Mahan to Roosevelt, 16 October 1902, Seager and Maguire, *Letters and Papers*, 3: 38–40; Roosevelt to Mahan, 25 October 1902, PSU - TR Papers, Series 2, Reel 329.

3. Mahan to Roosevelt, 7 September 1903, Seager and Maguire, *Letters and Papers*, 3: 73–74.

4. Mahan to Roosevelt, 27 December 1904, ibid., 3: 112–14.

5. Roosevelt to Mahan, 29 December 1904, PSU - TR Papers, Series 2, Reel 336.

6. Morison, *Admiral Sims*, p. 161.

7. Seager, *Alfred Thayer Mahan*, p. 526.

8. Seager's biography of Mahan contains an excellent account of the entire episode. The upshot was that Mahan lost considerable standing among naval officers, even though his reputation with the public was undimmed. The battle of Jutland in 1916, which Mahan did not live to see, proved Sims right. Yet from another perspective the naval arms limitation agreements of the 1920s represented at least a partial vindication of Mahan's point of view concerning tonnage limitation. See pp. 523–35.

9. Alfred Thayer Mahan, "Retrospect upon the War between Japan and Russia," *Naval Administration and Warfare* (Boston: Little, Brown, 1908), pp. 168–69; see also pp. 172–73.

10. Mahan to Roosevelt, 10 January 1907, Seager and Maguire, *Letters and Papers*, 3: 202.

11. Roosevelt to Mahan, 12 January 1907, PSU - TR Papers, Series 2, Reel 344.

12. Mahan to Roosevelt, 2 March 1909, Seager and Maguire, *Letters and Papers*, 3: 290; Roosevelt to Mahan, 3 March 1909, PSU - TR Papers, Series 2, Reel 354.

# 7 Refighting the War of 1812—in 1905

The War of 1812 spawned a series of conflicts. Potentially one of the more serious, though heretofore neglected, was that which developed between Mahan and Roosevelt. Though less spectacular than some— neither man wanted to publicize their disagreement—its effect was to contribute to Mahan's limited effectiveness in his dealings with Roosevelt during much of the latter's presidency. How each interpreted the War of 1812 also reveals much of each man's view of both past and current naval policy.

Roosevelt's *Naval War of 1812* was the first of his literary offspring and reflected his lifelong interest in ships and seafaring. What spurred Roosevelt to undertake the work were misstatements in British author William James's "Chief Naval Occurrences of the Late War".[1] Roosevelt, wanting to set the record straight, composed the first two chapters during his senior year at Harvard. He returned to the book in earnest in 1881. Aided substantially by his uncle, James Dunwody Bulloch, with whom he spent hours "talking over naval history," the work was completed and delivered to the publisher in December 1882.

For a 22-year-old's first book, it was quite an achievement. The work can be read on a number of levels. Roosevelt managed, by scrupulous research, to show at the tactical level why the American navy had emerged victorious in most of the single-ship engagements at sea: its ships were, on the whole, superior to the British vessels; its officers and crews were better trained. Admittedly, these victories did not seriously affect British naval power, "but morally the result was of inestimable benefit to the United States."[2]

As an amateur strategist, he correctly noted the importance of Perry's victory on Lake Erie and Thomas Macdonough's on Lake Champlain. Perry's success gave the navy command of the upper Great Lakes, ensured the conquest of upper Canada, and "increased our prestige with the foe and our confidence in ourselves." Macdonough's victory at the battle of Plattsburgh cleared the northern frontier for the remainder of the war and "had a very great effect on the negotiations for peace."[3] Roosevelt also recognized the significance of the British blockade of major East Coast ports. On the other hand, though he tabulated the number of prizes taken by American warships, he failed to deal substantively with commerce raiding by privateers and the extent to which this succeeded in injuring the enemy. Finally, his contempt for Jefferson's policy of building gunboats for coastal defense blinded him to the fact that these same gunboats, used in combination with land fortifications and batteries, could be extremely useful in protecting ports and shallow estuaries.

The author's own character and combativeness suffuse the work. The emphasis was on ship-to-ship engagements. Roosevelt was at his best recounting the murderous impact of the 36-pounder carronades on men and equipment in battle after battle, detailing the carnage aboard Perry's flagship *Lawrence* or the obstinate defense of the *U.S.S. Essex* off the coast of Chile in 1814 against a superior British force. Commanders were judged not only by how well they maneuvered, but by how well they fought. Perry's victory was tempered in Roosevelt's eyes because Perry *ought* to have won. His highest praise was reserved for Macdonough, who defeated a British squadron superior in firepower to his own. His distress over Stephen Decatur's surrender of the *U.S.S. President* near the close of the war after a token resistance was scarcely concealed. Both Jefferson and Madison were indicted by Roosevelt because of their willingness to turn the other cheek in the face of British and French depredations before the war, and their reluctance to prepare for probable conflict. Roosevelt had little patience with those who meekly accepted adversity.

Finally, Roosevelt's work at the dawn of an era of naval regeneration and modernization represented a plea to the American public. A respectable force of ships-of-the-line might have averted war entirely. Failing that, American victories showed how vital it was to have a few vessels "unsurpassed" by any foreign ship of the same class. "It is too much to hope that our political short-sightedness will ever enable us to have a navy that is first-class in point of size; but there certainly seems no reason why what ships we have should not be of the very best quality...."[4] A war in 1882 against a major European naval power would be "folly," the young naval historian implied.

The essay on the War of 1812 which Theodore Roosevelt wrote for William Laird Clowes's multivolume history of the Royal Navy is arguably less balanced in its judgments than its predecessor. Begun in April of 1896 when the author was a police commissioner in New York City, and completed in August 1897 while Roosevelt served as assistant secretary of the navy, its tone may have reflected Roosevelt's growing frustration in his police job, or perhaps represented a deliberate attempt to awaken his Anglo-American readership to the perils of naval unpreparedness. It reads, in places, like a polemic. In a brief nod towards impartiality, Roosevelt observed that both Britain and the United States considered themselves in the right in the dispute which was to lead to war in 1812. Britain, "engaged in a life and death grapple with a powerful foe," was in no position to overly concern itself with neutral rights. Nor could it be expected that the United States, "when wronged," would "refrain from retaliation."[5] Roosevelt asserted that by the standards of his day Britain's position under international law was unjustifiable; he recognized, however, that a different standard had prevailed at the beginning of the nineteenth century "and, moreover, Great Britain was fighting for her life, and nice customs curtesy to great crises as well as to great kings."[6] The author was to make this same argument initially in 1914 after Germany invaded Belgium in violation of her treaty obligations.

American naval weakness in the years preceding the War of 1812 invited British and French depredations. "There was but one possible way by which to gain and keep the respect of either France or Britain," Roosevelt declared, "and that was by the possession of power, and the readiness to use it if necessary; and power in this case meant a formidable fighting navy."[7] He castigated both the American public and the national Republican party. A fleet of twenty ships-of-the-line would have averted war, yet the Jeffersonians "lacked the wisdom" to see this. The people "showed criminal negligence" by refusing to countenance a naval buildup. The conduct of Jefferson, Madison, and their followers was "humiliating to the national honor; it was a crime, and it left a stain on the national character and reputation."[8]

Roosevelt acknowledged that the British blockade "was exceedingly effective." It was so effective, he mused, that historians "have paid little heed to the ceaseless strain on American resources caused by the blockade."[9] The assistant secretary of the navy had scarcely noted the existence of privateers in his earlier study, but he now observed that "the American privateers rendered invaluable service to their country." Yet, as a devotee of sea power and with Mahan's works clearly in mind, Roosevelt maintained that "commerce destroyers were in no sense satisfactory substitutes for great fighting ships of the line, fitted to wrest victory from the enemy by destroying his powers, both of offence and defence, and able to keep the war away from the home coasts."[10]

Again and again the assistant secretary of the navy returned to the issue of preparedness. It is clear that Roosevelt had in mind the efforts then being made to make the United States Navy an effective fighting force. Once war broke out in 1812, the American government and people had been "powerless . . . to make good the shortcomings of which they had been guilty." There was no substitute for adequate preparation and training *before* a conflict. What was true in the age of sail was infinitely more valid in his own day, Roosevelt asserted, "because the fighting machinery for use on the sea is so delicate and complicated."[11] If Mahan ever read this, given his experiences as captain of the *Chicago*, he must have nodded in rueful agreement.

Both America and Britain were ill-prepared for the War of 1812. The Americans were unable to contest British command of the sea because of the lack of ships-of-the-line; the British, smug in their "dream of invincibility," were defeated by the better-trained, better-led Americans in many of the individual ship battles. Yet American impotence in the face of the British naval blockade illustrated that to conduct war solely on the defensive was ruinous. War must be waged aggressively: "the foe must himself be struck, and struck heavily."[12] Roosevelt confidently asserted that victory in wars of the future would rest with the side which was best prepared. The results of the naval phase of the Spanish-American War showed that he was correct.

Mahan up to this point (1897) had said little about the War of 1812. In an article published in 1895 he noted that the conflict had demonstrated the "usefulness" of a navy by the very absence of a force "at all proportionate to the country's needs and exposure." The single-ship victories may have been admirable, but they were "utterly unavailing" in the face of British sea power.

Never was there a more lustrous example of what Jomini calls "the sterile glory of fighting battles merely to win them" . . . never was blood spilled more uselessly than in the frigate and sloop actions of that day. . . . They were simply scattered efforts, without relation either to one another or to any main body whatsoever, capable of affecting seriously the issues of the war, or indeed, to any plan of operations worthy of the name.[13]

What Roosevelt thought of these views of Mahan's is not known. It is clear, however, that he was concerned that Mahan's proposed War of 1812 study might be published at an awkward time for him (Roosevelt). He was finishing his contribution for Clowes's multivolume history and asked, somewhat anxiously, when Mahan intended to bring out his own work. He admitted that he hoped the two wouldn't "come out at the same time" and added that what Mahan wrote would "be the final word on the subject, and will be rightfully so accepted."[14]

Roosevelt need not have worried; Mahan did not even begin to write the third and final volume of his trilogy of sea power until 1902, and it was not published until 1905.

Certainly Mahan was active in a number of areas in the decade between volumes 2 and 3 of the trilogy, but there is also much to be said for the idea that Mahan didn't particularly want to write the book. The War of 1812 clearly illustrated the awesome nature of sea power. The Royal Navy, with almost contemptuous ease, could and did drive American commerce from the seas and seal up its principal seaports. Sea power, "a positive and commanding element in the history of the world," operated as a "negative quantity" upon the United States in the conflict. Wars between maritime powers, Mahan believed, were decided "not by rambling operations, or naval duels... but by force massed, and handled in skillful combination."[15] The United States, with no ships-of-the-line at all, scarcely even deserved the appellation of maritime power. Of what lasting value would be the recounting of successful ship-to-ship duels in the face of such overwhelming maritime superiority as the British exercised? Little wonder that Mahan, holding such views, was reluctant to write the book for an American audience. It might prove gratifying to the British reading public; it could scarcely endear its author to his American readership.[16]

While researching the subject, Mahan relied on primary sources as much as possible, utilizing archival materials in Washington, Ottawa and London. Inevitably both he and Roosevelt used some of the same source materials, but Mahan, taking a broader approach to the subject, dealt in greater detail with the prewar years than had Roosevelt. Although Mahan unquestionably had read Roosevelt's own work on the War of 1812, there is no evidence that he worked with it extensively— or, indeed, at all. Writing to Admiral Luce, he noted: "As regards the surrender of the *President*, I know Roosevelt's general ground, but have purposely refrained from studying his reasons till I shall have formed my independent conclusions."[17] He also asked the chief of the Bureau of Ordnance to supply him with information on the range of the carronades and long guns utilized by both sides in the conflict—again, his intent was to form his own opinions rather than rely upon Roosevelt's research. Given Roosevelt's antipathy towards the British historian James's account of the conflict, it is interesting to note that Mahan, in his account of the *Chesapeake-Shannon* engagement, stated that he "preferred to follow James in the main, because, dying as he did in 1827, his authorities are necessarily partly contemporaneous, and he is known to have been painstaking."[18]

The first third of Mahan's study was devoted to an account of the maritime origins of the war—best summarized by the American cry of "Free trade and sailors' rights." Running throughout this section are several interrelated themes. Great Britain, locked in mortal combat with revolutionary and Napoleonic France, could not as a matter of national security afford to be tolerant of neutral flag cargoes destined for its opponent. Nor, in the matter of manning its warships, could it admit that British nationals could change their citizenship; many had become naturalized Americans. Only force, or the threat of force, could bring about a change in British attitudes—and Jefferson and Madison were as unwilling to build ships-of-the-line as they were to acquiesce in British maritime practices. Mahan, to his credit, did not attempt to sugarcoat the pill. The record of the United States during the war was "one of gloom, disaster, and governmental incompetence.... This was so even upon the water."[19] The real lessons of the war, therefore, lay in appreciating the impact of British naval power in conjunction with American unpreparedness. The blockade of America's ports and the strangling of her seaborne and coastal commerce, largely invisible, had been forgotten. In its place, the public had "a prevalent impression of distinguished success, because of a few brilliant naval actions and the closing battle of New Orleans."[20] Fortunately for Mahan—and his American readers—there were victories on Lakes Erie and Champlain to celebrate.

The lake campaigns of 1813 and 1814 thus emphasized the teaching of history as to the influence of control of the water upon the course of events; and they illustrate also the too often forgotten truth, that it is not by brilliant individual feats of gallantry or skill, by ships or men, but by the massing of superior forces, that military issues are decided. For, although on a small scale, the lakes were oceans, and the forces which met on them were fleets; and as, on a wider field and in more tremendous issues, the fleets of Great Britain saved their country and determined the fortunes of Europe, so Perry and Macdonough averted from the United States, without further fighting, a rectification of frontier.[21]

Given the different approaches to—and emphases placed upon—the origins and events of the War of 1812, Roosevelt and Mahan were in agreement in certain respects. Both castigated the government and public for blindness to the navy's needs; both recognized the value of advanced preparation and training: both felt the victories at sea had had a beneficial effect on public morale; both recognized the significance of Perry's and Macdonough's victories; both (Roosevelt a bit grudgingly) noted the effectiveness of the British blockade and the resulting damage to America's commerce; both appreciated the fact that commerce raiding by American warships and privateers, though annoying to British interests, could not be decisive. The two men were far apart, however, on the ultimate utility of ship-to-ship engagements, the causes of the conflict (and, indeed, the necessity and desirability of it), who "won" the war, and (which ultimately was to lead to much acrimony) whether private property should be exempt from capture on the high seas. The president, after reading the book, confessed to one correspondent: "Incidentally I may add that I was as disappointed as you with Mahan's *War of 1812*. He is a curious fellow, for he cannot write in effective shape of the navy or of the fighting of his own country."[22]

The differences of opinion were serious and go beyond the confines of scholarly debate. There is a vast gulf between Roosevelt's assertion that "the foe must be struck, and struck heavily," and Mahan's disgust over "the useless effusion of blood." Each felt his own view of the war was correct and had difficulty in accepting contrary opinions. Coming to a head when it did, the dispute added to the growing estrangement between Roosevelt and Mahan—and undoubtedly affected Mahan's ability to sway the president on such issues as the balanced fleet and the all-big-gun ship discussed in chapter six, as well as the question of immunity of private property from seizure. This issue would carry the dispute over the War of 1812 into yet another dimension.

## NOTES

1. Carleton Putnam, *Theodore Roosevelt: The Formative Years, 1858–1886* (New York: Charles Scribner's Sons, 1958), p. 220.

2. Theodore Roosevelt, *The Naval War of 1812: The History of the United States Navy During the Last War with Great Britain to Which is Appended an Account of the Battle of New Orleans*, Hermann Hagedorn, ed., *The Works of Theodore Roosevelt*, 20 vols. (New York: Charles Scribner's Sons, 1926), 6: 363.

3. Ibid., 223, 328.

4. Ibid., 114.

5. Theodore Roosevelt, "The War with the United States, 1812–15," in *The Royal Navy: A History from the Earliest Times to the Present*, ed. William Laird Clowes, 7 vols. (London: Sampson Low, Marston and Company, 1901), 6: 2.

6. Ibid., 8.

7. Ibid., 6.

8. Ibid., 24–25.

9. Ibid.. 68.

10. Ibid.,73–74. See also Roosevelt's reference to Mahan's writings in his footnote on p. 58.

11. Ibid., 66.

12. Ibid,, 177.

13. Alfred Thayer Mahan, "The Future in Relation to American Naval Power," *The Interest of America in Sea Power, Present and Future* (Port Washington, N.Y.: Kennikat Press, 1970, o.d. 1897). pp. 149–50.

14. Roosevelt to Mahan, 17 May 1897, PSU - TR Papers, Series 2, Reel 313. See also Roosevelt to William Laird Clowes, 4 March 1898, Morison, *Letters of Theodore Roosevelt*, 1: 789.

15. Alfred Thayer Mahan, *Sea Power in Its Relation to the War of 1812*, 2 vols. (Boston: Little, Brown, 1905), 1: v.

16. The book did not sell well in the United States. See Seager, *Alfred Thayer Mahan*, p. 570.

17. Mahan to Stephen B. Luce, 17 June 1903, Seager and Maguire, *Letters and Papers*, 3: 64. Both Mahan and Roosevelt concluded that Captain Stephen Decatur struck his flag prematurely. See Roosevelt, *The Naval War of 1812*, pp. 333–35, and Mahan, *Sea Power in Its Relation to the War of 1812*, 2: 402–3.

18. Mahan to Charles W. Stewart, 14 October 1804, Seager and Maguire, *Letters and Papers*, 3: 103. For a scathing account of James's objectivity, see David F. Long, *Sailor-Diplomat: A Biography of Commodore James Biddle, 1783–1848* (Boston: Northeastern University Press, 1983). pp. 54–55.

19. Mahan, *Sea Power in Its Relation to the War of 1812*, 1: 290.

20. Ibid., 2: 208.

21. Ibid., 2: 101.

22. Roosevelt to James Jeffrey Roche, 7 March 1906, Morison, *Letters of Theodore Roosevelt*, 5: 173.

# 8 Private Property and Arbitration

Mahan had the misfortune to become involved in yet another controversy with President Roosevelt. Growing in part out of Mahan's study of the War of 1812 and its origins, it represented an attempt by Mahan to reverse the long-standing American position on the immunity of private property from capture at sea. It came on top of the foreign policy disagreements between the two men, occurring about the time of the publication of Mahan's *Sea Power in Its Relation to the War of 1812* and while the all-big-gun controversy was brewing. This unfortunate conjunction may have contributed to Roosevelt's reluctance to examine the issue on its merits.

The United States government had raised the issue of immunity of private property while publicly calling for a second Hague conference.[1] Mahan wrote to President Roosevelt 27 December 1904 to express his concern, enclosing several pages excerpted from his forthcoming work on the War of 1812.[2] He pointed out that the government of the United States in 1800 had in an ill-considered fashion put forth the suggestion that naval blockades of enemy ports would be recognized as such under international law *only* if accompanied by a simultaneous blockade by land. Clearly, it was designed to make it more difficult for a maritime power such as Great Britain to disrupt American commerce in future conflicts. Had this self-serving measure become accepted practice, Mahan noted, the government would not have been able to institute its blockade of the Confederate coastline in 1861 with any prospect of international recognition. If the proposed Hague conference were to endorse the resolution on immunity of property now sponsored by the government, it would seriously restrict the ability of the maritime powers to control the seas. Mahan warned the president that the United States in all probability would be forced by international conditions into a position of cooperating with Great Britain at least until mid-century. "It may very well be that under such conditions the power to control commerce...may be of immense, of decisive, importance."[3]

Roosevelt misunderstood—perhaps deliberately—the point Mahan was trying to make. In simplest terms, Mahan wanted Roosevelt to make a distinction between personal property (e.g., clothing, jewelry, money, household furnishings), and corporate property. It was the old argument about contraband restated in modern guise. Virtually any product shipped could be utilized directly or indirectly for military purposes. Mahan wanted the broadest possible definition of contraband; Roosevelt did not. "There is a strong tendency," the president noted, "to protect private property and private life on sea and land. Of course the earlier races killed or enslaved every private citizen of the hostile nation whom they could get at and destroyed or took his property as a matter of course."[4] Roosevelt promised to take the subject up with Secretary of State John Hay. If he did so, it must have been in perfunctory fashion. Hay was in poor health at the time and was well aware that Roosevelt wanted to control the pace in foreign affairs. If Roosevelt didn't wish to pursue the issue, neither did Hay. Mahan may well have heard nothing further from the president, and suspected that Roosevelt was attempting to bury the issue.[5]

Yet Mahan was unwilling to drop the matter. He returned to the fray by reopening the subject in a letter to Hay's successor, Elihu Root, requesting Root, if he found merit in Mahan's position, to intercede with the president. Mahan enclosed several pages entitled "Comments on the Seizure of Private Property at Sea" for the secretary of state's edification. These paragraphs had originally been included in Mahan's May 1906 article, "Retrospect upon the War Between Japan and Russia," but Mahan, "upon reflection, seeing that they traversed a declared policy of the Administration," deleted them.[6]

Roosevelt's earlier dismissal of the subject still rankled, and Mahan tried to respond obliquely to the president's concern in his memorandum to Root.

The practice has been given a bad name of late, partly by the emphasis laid on the phrase "private property," partly doubtless because it is in direct descent from the old freebooting system prevalent when there were no standing navies, when war at sea was carried on by private venture wholly, or at best by private vessels impressed for the occasion.[7]

Root did forward Mahan's letter and accompanying memorandum to the navy's General Board for comment. The board supported Mahan's position.[8] Even so, Root warned Mahan (perhaps after receiving Roosevelt's reaction) that although he personally "had already entertained and in private expressed serious doubts" about the blanket immunity of private property, "the subject is no longer an open one for us. The United States has advocated the immunity of private property at sea so long and so positively that I cannot see how it is possible to make a *volte face* at the Hague."[9]

Mahan, having meanwhile been commissioned by the Navy Department to write a history of the Naval War Board, travelled to Oyster Bay 31 July to obtain President Roosevelt's recollections of the board's origins, Roosevelt having been assistant secretary of the navy at the time. This gave Mahan the opportunity for direct discussion with the president of the private property issue—and to air as well his advocacy of a mixed battery on battleships. As subsequent events indicated, neither man succeeded in changing the other's views.

Mahan tried once more. He asked the president's permission to "write for publication concerning matters that might come before the approaching Hague Conference; notably the question of exemption of private property, so called, from maritime capture." He went on to reiterate his arguments at length, in compelling fashion. He foresaw the possibility of Great Britain and the United States having to face Germany in the future. Exempt Germany's carrying trade from capture, he warned, "and you remove the strongest hook in the jaws of Germany that the English speaking peoples have; a principal gage for peace." Mahan did not begrudge Germany an overseas empire, "but her ambitions threaten us as well as Great Britain," and it would be the better part of wisdom to take no action at all on the private property question.[10] Roosevelt granted Mahan the desired permission. "You have a deserved reputation as a publicist which makes this proper from the public standpoint," he noted. "Indeed I think it important for you to write just what you think of the matter."[11] Roosevelt may have been implying that if Mahan could swing public opinion to his side on the issue, then Roosevelt would modify his own position.

A series of letters to the editor of the British magazine *National Review*, in which Mahan's articles on the subject were to appear, shows that Mahan did indeed hope to sway opinion in both British and American governmental circles. He asked the editor, Leopold J. Maxse, to be sure that copies of both articles went to Roosevelt, Root, Dewey, and former U.S. Ambassador to Great Britain Joseph H. Choate.[12] In late April, Mahan commented disparagingly about peace rallies being held in Britain in advance of the Hague session, adding: "Luckily, Roosevelt, Root, and Choate have heads as clear and hard as ice. Their hearts too are all right, especially the President's; but they don't prevent their brains from seeing both sides." Significantly, Mahan noted:

"I am not without hopes that I may carry conviction in influential quarters which have hitherto accepted tradition without query."[13] It wasn't hard to guess which "influential quarter" Mahan had in mind.

Shortly after, Roosevelt wrote Mahan to wish him a speedy recovery from prostate surgery, and he promised to read Mahan's private property articles "with interest."[14] All Mahan could do, convalescing as he was, was hope for the best. He was unable to play a more active role while the Hague conference was in session. Nothing in fact came of this issue at the conference; nor did the conferees agree, as Mahan had hoped they might, to restrict battleship tonnage.[15]

The issue of the immunity of private property from seizure had not arisen formally at the first Hague conference in 1899. Of more immediate concern to Mahan at that time was the issue of compulsory arbitration of disputes. Largely at his instigation, the American delegation succeeded in inserting in the arbitration convention a reservation exempting any disputes which could be traced to differing interpretations of the Monroe Doctrine. The United States, in short, was not prepared to let other powers intervene in hemispheric concerns. What had drawn the subject to Mahan's attention was an editorial in the *Manchester Guardian* of 21 July 1899, pointing out that if the arbitration convention (specifically, Article 27) had been in effect in 1898, the European powers might have intervened to prevent war between the United States and Spain.[16] Mahan upon reading this raised the issue with other members of the American delegation.

In a letter to his long-time friend Samuel Ashe, Mahan confessed that the conference had been "interesting in a way; but ten weeks of it was rather too much." He thought Russia had called the conference because of its alarm at the prospect of the United States and Great Britain drawing more closely together to oppose Russia's advance in East Asia. Being unprepared for war with those powers, Mahan thought, Russia wished for "peace—by pledge." He called Ashe's attention to his forthcoming essay. Conceding that arbitration should always be a country's "first thought," Mahan believed that a nation "should never pledge itself . . . to arbitrate before it knows what the subject of dispute is."[17]

The first Hague conference, and Mahan's role therein, seems to have had little impact at the time on New York governor Theodore Roosevelt—and virtually none on the Mahan-Roosevelt relationship. If Roosevelt then was concerned about either the immunity of private property or compulsory arbitration, he showed little evidence of it in his comments on the conference and its doings.[18] He may have taken note of the dispute which erupted a bit later between Mahan and a fellow Hague conference delegate, George Friedrich Wilhelm Holls, over who was entitled to the credit for the Monroe Doctrine reservation at the conference. Holls, in a book which he authored, claimed credit for the reservation, engendering a long and acrimonious dispute with Mahan which ended only with Holls's death in July 1903. Roosevelt knew Holls, a respected and influential member of New York City's German-American community and "a particular friend of mine."[19] Holls was an international lawyer of some note and used his European connections to work for better relations between Germany, England, and the United States. By the time the dispute with Mahan erupted, though, Roosevelt was no longer intimately involved with New York politics. Having less need to court Holls and the German-American vote than would have been the case had he remained governor of the state, he appears to have stayed out of the Mahan-Holls imbroglio.

The compulsory arbitration issue lay dormant for some years until it was revived by the Taft administration. Both Roosevelt and Mahan opposed the pending arbitration treaty with Great Britain, and in consequence drew together while separately combatting the treaty. Thus, briefly, the triumvirate of Mahan, Roosevelt and Henry Cabot Lodge, which had worked so successfully in the 1890s, was revived in 1911.

In a letter to the editor of the *New York Times*, Mahan spoke highly of Roosevelt and castigated the press for insinuating that the president had sent the U.S. fleet to the Pacific in 1908 because he wanted war with Japan.[20] Some months later, in another letter to the editor, he took exception to an editorial which was critical of the ex-president. Roosevelt, in a Decoration Day address, had said:

There are certain questions which we Americans would never think of arbitrating. One is the Monroe Doctrine, and another is the allowing of vast quantities of Asiatics to come here. We have got to stand out against agreeing to do these dangerous things, no matter what the short-sighted, false-peace advocates say.[21]

The editorial writer claimed that Roosevelt had in effect called President William Howard Taft a "short-sighted, false-peace advocate," because Taft was supporting the proposed arbitration treaty with Great Britain. Mahan pointed out that while Taft, in a 17 December 1910 speech did suggest that "an agreement with some great nation to abide the adjudication of an international arbitral court in every issue which cannot be settled by negotiation" would be a "long step forward" toward world peace, much of the same speech was devoted to the subject of military preparedness, particularly fortification of the Panama Canal. This, and President Taft's consistent advocacy of a strong United States Navy, scarcely permitted him to be classified as a "short-sighted, false-peace advocate."[22]

Mahan's defense of Roosevelt elicited a warm note from the former president. He admitted that "with Great Britain ... no difficulty can rise which we cannot solve by arbitration." The problem lay in extending the principle of general arbitration treaties to nations with whom real difficulties existed—such as Germany or Japan. Such issues as the fortification of the Panama Canal, exclusion of unwanted immigrants, and the Monroe Doctrine surely were not arbitrable.[23] Roosevelt thought so highly of Mahan's second letter to the editor that he reprinted it in the *Outlook*.

Mahan in turn thanked Roosevelt for his letter. He foresaw the immigration question in particular as fraught with difficulty regarding Japan. Since, in his opinion, Japanese emigrants to Korea and Manchuria were unable to compete economically for wages vis-à-vis Korean and Chinese laborers, they would in consequence tend to emigrate to Australia, Canada, and the United States, where they could continue to compete successfully in the labor market.[24]

In a subsequent letter to Roosevelt, Mahan was disturbed lest the Senate, by agreeing to the proposed Anglo-American arbitration treaty, might part "forever with its power of advice and consent as to the determination whether a particular question is 'justiciable.' " Could we refuse to another country what we had been willing to grant Great Britain? Sir Edward Grey, the British foreign secretary, had endorsed the idea of exclusion of the Monroe Doctrine from justiciable issues, but this exclusion was not formally part of the treaty. The Monroe Doctrine, "without a shred of legal right," was to Mahan even more vulnerable than the question of Asiatic immigration.[25] Roosevelt replied: "I absolutely agree with you. I think that these arbitration treaties are hopelessly wrong, and I am extremely sorry."[26]

The more he thought about it, the more convinced Mahan became that the Monroe Doctrine was justiciable, whatever Sir Edward Grey maintained. "This alone, if correct, condemns the treaty as it stands." He went on to note that Asiatic immigration was alien to the spirit of the Monroe Doctrine, because the Asiatics "don't assimilate, they colonize, and virtually annex."[27] Again Roosevelt concurred with Mahan's reasoning, and said so editorially in The *Outlook*.[28]

Mahan expanded upon his concern about the Monroe Doctrine's justiciability in two letters to Henry Cabot Lodge and one to John Bassett Moore. Transfer of territory from one power to another was recognized by international law. How then, Mahan asked, could the Monroe Doctrine, forbidding transfer of territory in the hemisphere from one European power to another, be applicable if the *principle* of transfer was indeed justiciable (or, to use the words of the 1911 arbitration treaty, "capable of settlement by principles of international law")? Mahan's solution was to declare the Monroe Doctrine in its entirety non-justiciable—to raise the doctrine to the level of "national policy" which "thereby ceases to be justiciable by law, however long the applicable law may have existed."[29] Germany's colonization efforts, he noted in his second letter to Lodge, had been directed eastward and southward. The justiciability of the Monroe Doctrine would give Germany an opening to seek territory in the Western Hemisphere, and could "cause serious trouble" between her and the United States.[30]

In his letter to John Bassett Moore, Mahan noted that Germany could insist that acquisition or transfer of territory "is legal not only generally, but always and everywhere." An arbitration treaty with Germany surely would follow the pending treaties in the Senate. "If under the treaty she raises the point that buying the Danish Islands is determinable by law, therefore justiciable, & we refuse, we shall be much nearer war than if the understanding is clear from the first. Germany will soon have a decisive navy."[31]

The growing outcry against the arbitration treaties was merged imperceptibly with the struggle between the two wings of the Republican party. In the preelection turmoil the arbitration treaty was amended to death. Critics have claimed that Roosevelt's and Mahan's opposition was narrowly opportunistic. Seeing an opportunity to strike another blow at the faltering Taft administration, they lost an opportunity to advance detente in East Asia by defusing the possibility that Japan could invoke her alliance with Great Britain in the event of trouble with the United States. Mahan, however, did not see the Anglo-Japanese treaty leading to a "collision" between Great Britain and the United States in the absence of the arbitration treaties unless the latter sought "to deprive Japan of territory—a most impossible contingency."[32]

Both issues, being related, suggest once again the limits of Mahan's influence with the president. Mahan's instincts were correct in wishing to scrap the long-standing American attachment to immunity of private property from capture. Roosevelt's reluctance to go along may have stemmed less from lack of sympathy with Mahan's arguments than from a realization that to take such action unilaterally would appear to be truckling to Great Britain's interests. It was better to temporize, as Roosevelt did, awaiting either a shift in public opinion or changing international conditions. On the issue of compulsory arbitration Roosevelt, now out of office, could more freely afford to range himself alongside Mahan. In a stand reminiscent of the one he had taken on the first Hay-Pauncefote Treaty, Roosevelt's objection to the Taft administration's position was that it did not sufficiently safeguard the country's crucial needs. In similar fashion, Roosevelt had in the waning days of his second administration coopted Mahan to attempt to push through a major reorganization within the Navy Department—one designed to better meet the navy's need to coordinate strategy, ship construction, and technological change.

## NOTES

1. Mahan had attended the first Hague conference in 1899 as a member of the American delegation. Secretary of State John Hay had instructed the delegates to press for an exemption of private property from capture; the issue, however, did not come up for substantive consideration. See Calvin DeArmond Davis, *The United States and the First Hague Conference* (Ithaca, N.Y.: Cornell University Press, 1962), pp. 80, 133–35.

2. The relevant pages are in Mahan, *Sea Power in Its Relation to the War of 1812*, 1: 146–48.

3. Mahan to Roosevelt, 27 December 1904, Seager and Maguire, *Letters and Papers*, 3: 112–14.

4. Roosevelt to Mahan, 29 December 1904, PSU - TR Papers, Series 2, Reel 336.

5. Mahan to Elihu Root, 20 April 1906, Seager and Maguire, *Letters and Papers*, 3: 157–59.

6. Ibid. Some of the excised material reappeared in an article by Mahan entitled "The Hague Conference: The Question of Immunity for Belligerent Shipping," which appeared in the June 1907 issue of the British publication *National Review*.

7. Alfred Thayer Mahan, "Comments on the Seizure of Private Property at Sea," Seager and Maguire, *Letters and Papers*, 3: 625.

8. Ibid., 3: 158.

9. Elihu Root to Mahan, 21 May 1906, cited in William E. Livezey, *Mahan on Sea Power* (Norman, University of Oklahoma Press, 1947), pp. 250–51.

10. Mahan to Roosevelt, n.d. (ca. 20 July 1906), Seager and Maguire, *Letters and Papers*, 3: 164–65.

11. Roosevelt to Mahan, 16 August 1906, PSU - TR Papers, Series 2, Reel 342. Retired officers were forbidden to comment publicly on matters of state or on military concerns. Both McKinley and Roosevelt permitted Mahan to do so. Woodrow Wilson, following the outbreak of World War I, did not.

12. Mahan to Leopold J. Maxse, 5 March and 15 April 1907, Seager and Maguire, *Letters and Papers*, 3: 207, 209.

13. Mahan to Maxse, 30 April 1907, ibid., 210.

14. Roosevelt to Mahan, 24 May 1907, PSU - TR Papers, Series 2, Reel 345.

15. Seager, *Alfred Thayer Mahan*, pp. 507–10.

16. Some years later Mahan ran across the same clipping in his files and sent it to President Roosevelt with the warning that the issue of compulsory arbitration might well be raised again at the proposed second Hague conference. Mahan to Roosevelt, 9 September 1905, Seager and Maguire, *Letters and Papers*, 3: 139; Roosevelt to Mahan, 12 September 1905, PSU – TR Papers, Series 2, Reel 339.

17. Mahan to Samuel A. Ashe, 23 September 1899, and to James R. Thurs-

field, 28 October 1899, Seager and Maguire, *Letters and Papers*, 2: 658, 664–65; see also Alfred Thayer Mahan, "The Peace Conference and the Moral Aspect of War," *Some Neglected Aspects of War* (Boston: Little, Brown, 1907), pp. 23–53.

18. Roosevelt to Maria Longworth Storer, 28 October 1899, and to Cecil Arthur Spring-Rice, 19 November 1900, Morison, *Letters of Theodore Roosevelt*. 2: 1089, 1422–23.

19. Roosevelt to Spring-Rice, 11 August 1899, and to Albert Shaw, 15 February 1900, ibid., 1051, 1186.

20. Alfred Thayer Mahan to the editor of the *New York Times*, 25 October 1910, Seager and Maguire, *Letters and Papers*, 3: 363–65.

21. Mahan to the editor of the *New York Times*. 2 June 1911, ibid., 408.

22. Ibid., 409.

23. Roosevelt to Mahan, 8 June 1911, PSU - TR Papers, Series 2, Reel 367.

24. Mahan to Roosevelt, 19 June 1911, Seager and Maguire, *Letters and Papers*, 3: 411–12.

25. Mahan to Roosevelt, 11 August 1911, ibid., 420–21.

26. Roosevelt to Mahan, 15 August 1911, PSU - TR Papers, Series 2, Reel 368.

27. Mahan to Roosevelt, 2 December 1911, Seager and Maguire. *Letters and Papers*, 3: 435–36.

28. Roosevelt to Mahan, 5 December 1911, PSU - TR Papers, Series 2, Reel 370; see also Roosevelt to Millard J. Bloomer, 5 December 1911, Morison, *Letters of Theodore Roosevelt*, 7: 499; Roosevelt to Mahan, 21 December 1911, PSU - TR Papers, Series 2, Reel 371.

29. Mahan to Lodge, 6 January 1912, Seager and Maguire, *Letters and Papers*, 3: 442

30. Mahan to Lodge, 8 January 1912, ibid., 443–44.

31. Mahan to John Bassett Moore, 26 February 1912, ibid.; see also Mahan to Carter Fitzhugh, 9 March 1912, ibid., 446.

32. Alfred Thayer Mahan, "The Hague Conference and the Practical Aspect of War," *Some Neglected Aspects of War*, pp. 80–81.

# 9 Reorganizing the Navy

That Alfred Thayer Mahan would be appointed to the President's Commission on Naval Reorganization late in January 1909 was by no means certain. He had to an extent alienated himself from both Roosevelt and the so-called "insurgents," or progressive younger officers, by his stance on the all-big-gun controversy. Yet the fact that he, like the insurgents, had been critical of the power exercised by the eight bureau chiefs within the Navy Department, plus the value of his pronouncements with the public, ultimately were decisive in obtaining his appointment to the commission.

Not only was Mahan in favor of lessening the power of the bureau chiefs; he also urged the formation of a naval General Staff. His experience as a member of the Naval War Board in 1898 had made him aware of the desirability of an agency which could "coordinate the work of the Department and the Fleet, and . . . keep a general surveillance over . . . larger strategical and technical questions."[1] The formation of the General Board in 1900 constituted a step in the right direction, in Mahan's opinion, but it suffered from lack of authority over the bureaus and its purely advisory status with the secretary of the navy. It was not Mahan, but rather Rear Admiral Henry Clay Taylor, a member of the General Board, who spearheaded an effort for the creation of a true General Staff—as he had done while president of the Naval War College from 1893 to 1897.[2]

Taylor proposed in 1901 that the Bureau of Navigation, already responsible for personnel, could serve as the nucleus of a General Staff by absorbing the duties and functions of the General Board, the Office of Naval Intelligence, and the Naval War College. The chief of the

Bureau of Navigation, relieved of routine administration, could head the bureau as chief of staff. Mahan knew of and approved of Taylor's proposal.[3] President Roosevelt, who also supported the idea, had it presented by Secretary of the Navy William H. Moody to Congress in the spring of 1904. Despite favorable testimony before the House Naval Affairs Committee, the bill never reached the floor of the House. Taylor died unexpectedly in July 1904, and the movement for departmental reorganization passed into the hands of the insurgents.[4] The insurgents opposed the diffusion of power inherent in the bureau system as it pertained to operational planning.

Given Mahan's diminished influence with the navy and the Roosevelt administration, when the issue of reorganization was activated once more in 1908 there was little likelihood of Mahan's playing any role at all. What caused the issue to resurface was an insurgent defeat in 1908 at the hands of the Bureau of Construction and Repair over the issue of alleged defects in battleship design. Failing to curb bureau power in one way, the insurgents attempted it through administrative change. The effort to trim the bureaus down to size while Roosevelt still was in the White House was spearheaded initially by Roosevelt's naval aide William S. Sims and retired Rear Admiral Stephen B. Luce.

Luce, like Mahan, had long held that the existing administrative system was "archaic."[5] It took little urging from Sims to obtain his support. In a lengthy letter to the president, Sims suggested that a mixed commission of both civilians and naval officers would be advantageous, "the civilians to be gentlemen of such high character, national reputation and large experience in public affairs, and the naval officers to be of such high rank and knowledge of Department methods that their report and recommendations would command the attention and respect of the congress and of the people." Mahan's name was conspicuous by its absence from the list of individuals Sims suggested. Sims argued that the commission might consider both the consolidation of certain bureaus and a reduction of their authority, as well as the existing divided responsibility and "lack of co-ordination in the preparation for war and in the conduct of war" and the need to provide the secretary of the navy with "military advisors." Sims added that Admiral Luce fully concurred with the above, and thought it much more likely to produce "immediate results" than a report by the members of the Newport battleship conference who "clearly were at loggerheads."[6]

Roosevelt replied favorably to Sims's proposal, but nothing occurred for several months, much to the distress of those pressing for the commission. At some point Mahan's name was introduced as a potential member, probably by Luce, possibly by the president. Even if Sims had not wanted Mahan on the commission, as the initial absence of his

name from the list of candidates suggests, he knew that Mahan's im-
primatur would go far to provide a favorable impression on the public
mind as well as a favorable mood in Congress toward the committee's
recommendations.

With the appointment on 1 December 1908 of Truman H. Newberry
as secretary of the navy (the sixth in seven years under Roosevelt)
action of a sort was taken. Newberry had his own ideas on reorganization: he would enlarge the General Board to include representatives
from all the bureaus; the Board of Construction would have a few line
officers added to its membership (thus meeting one of the insurgents'
objections). Finally, the Bureau of Construction and Repair would in-
corporate the Bureau of Steam Engineering. This seemed too cosmetic
to suit those pushing for fundamental administrative changes.[7] Sims,
in a memorandum to President Roosevelt early in December, pointed
out that the Newberry proposals violated the principle that the secretary's policy advisory group have no administrative responsibilities.
He even cited Mahan's 1903 essay on "The Principles of Naval Administration," which had just been reprinted, in support of his contention.
Sims warned the president that if Congress approved Newberry's proposal, it would diminish the effectiveness of the General Board.[8] Roosevelt early in January sent Mahan a copy of this memorandum, asking
him for his views, and formally appointing him a member of a commission on reorganization.

Mahan, accepting the appointment, went right to the heart of the
matter. He was not disturbed with the bureaus *per se*; but, run along
business and professional lines, they required a secretary equipped
with similar expertise to control them. Both the president and the
secretary of the navy should be master of "diplomatic, military and
naval considerations" which might at any given time affect the nation's
foreign policy. Since neither individual in the ordinary course of events
had the necessary military-naval expertise (although Roosevelt came
close), "the only means by which such consecutive knowledge can be
maintained is by a corporate body, continuous in existence and gradual
in change. That we call a General Staff." Mahan continued:

For best results, the Chief of Staff should so possess the confidence of the
Administration, as to be aware of the relations existing between our own
Government and the various states interested in a possible theatre of war; and
also of the attitude these states bear to one another, and hence their possible
action in case of hostilities. . . .

Have you read Corbett's *Seven Years War*? It is a good book. He brings out
clearly that Pitt, besides eminent ability, had control of all three threads,—
diplomatic, military, and naval,—and that in this, concentrated in one efficient
man, consisted his great advantage. Jomini taught me from the first to scorn

the sharp distinction so often asserted between diplomatic and military considerations. Corbett simply gives the help of putting the same idea into other words. *Diplomatic conditions affect military action, the military considerations diplomatic measures.* [italics added] They are inseparable parts of a whole; and as such those responsible for military measures should understand the diplomatic factors, and vice versa. No man is fit for Chief of Staff who cannot be intrusted with knowledge of a diplomatic situation. The naval man also should understand the military conditions, and the military the naval.

Corbett makes another excellent point: that for a military establishment the distinction between a state of war and a state of peace is one of words, not of fact. Nothing so readily as a general staff will insure this.[9]

Roosevelt passed Mahan's letter along to Sims, who termed it "in all respects an admirable presentation." Sims, a belated convert to Mahan's inclusion, thought it "fortunate" that the "highest authority on this subject" would be available to serve on the commission.[10] Roosevelt, emulating the grand old duke of York, marched his commissioners up to Washington (16 January 1909), then marched them home again, after having them rubber-stamp the Newberry proposals. The reason for this turn of events lay in the president's reluctance to jeopardize his naval construction program in Congress by presenting too radical proposals for reform, particularly since many members of Congress had little sympathy for the General Staff idea.

With naval appropriations successfully dealt with, the president on 27 January formed another commission to consider Navy Department organization. The commissioners—who included former Secretaries of the Navy William H. Moody and Paul Morton; Judge Alston Dayton, a former member of the House Naval Affairs Committee; and Admirals Alfred T. Mahan, Stephen B. Luce, William M. Folger, William S. Cowles (Roosevelt's brother-in-law), and Robley D. Evans—were to address themselves to the issues raised by Sims with the president the previous August. Roosevelt wanted "specific recommendations" concerning changes in the present organization of the department which would "insure an efficient preparation for war in time of peace."[11]

The preliminary report, "General Principles Governing Naval Organization," was submitted on 20 February to the President. Drafted by Mahan, and little altered by the other members of the committee, it began by making obeisance to the idea of civilian supremacy, then proceeded to develop the rationale for a General Staff. Although power ultimately should rest with the secretary, "owing to the shortness of tenure in office" and the "inevitable unfamiliarity with naval conditions," secretaries lacked the ability to make their authority effective. "What the Secretary needs, specifically and above all, is a clear understanding and firm grasp of leading military considerations." This could be provided by an advisory body of line officers, who would be expected to have frequent intervals of sea duty to familiarize themselves with fleet tactical and administrative matters.

In conclusion, it should be distinctly laid down as a cardinal principle that no scheme of naval organization can possibly be effective which does not recognize that the requirement of war is the true standard of efficiency in an administrative military system; that success in war and victory in battle can be assured only by that constant preparedness and that superior fighting efficiency which logically result from placing the control and responsibility in time of peace upon the same individuals and the same agencies that must control in time of war. There should be no shock or change of method in expanding from a state of peace to a state of war. This is not militarism; it is a simple business principle based upon the fact that success in war is the only return the people and the nation can get from the investment of many millions in the building and maintenance of a great navy.[12]

President Roosevelt, in his own letter of transmittal to Congress, asked that "all other considerations . . . be subordinated to keeping the navy in the highest condition of military efficiency." Although much good had come from the creation of the General Board, the Joint Army-Navy Board, and the war colleges, more could be done. The army's general staff system, he argued, deserved a naval counterpart. All the great naval powers had systems that observed the principles of administration laid down in Mahan's memorandum. The United States should do no less.[13]

Following the principles of reorganization set forth by Mahan, the commission proposed five major subdivisions within the Navy Department, the head of each reporting directly to the secretary. The assistant secretary would be in charge of the first division, having under his aegis the bureaus of Yards and Docks, Supplies, and Medicine and Surgery, along with general accounting, legal, and personnel branches. The second area, Naval Operations, would be headed by an officer of flag rank, the "principal military advisor to the Secretary." This individual, the chief of naval operations, would be *ex officio* head of the General Board and the Board of Construction, and would be responsible for coordinating the work of the Office of Naval Intelligence and the Naval War College, devising war plans, and formulating naval policy. The third area, Personnel, would include the Bureau of Navigation, the Marine Corps, the Office of the Judge-Advocate-General, and all service educational institutions except the Naval War College. The fourth area, Inspection, would be responsible for ships' trials, inspection of vessels and naval yards, and selection of sites for naval stations. The fifth division, Matériel, would supervise the bureaus of Construction and Repair, Ordnance, Engineering and Equipment.

The chiefs of the five divisions would comprise the secretary's General Council. The chiefs of the divisions of Operations, Personnel, and Inspection would comprise the secretary's Military Council, "but of these the chief of Naval Operations is the sole responsible advisor. No chief of bureau, while acting as such, [is] to act as chief of a division."[14] Roosevelt, in his letter of transmittal, stated, as well he might: "I have expressed to Justice Moody and his associates my profound sense of obligation for the admirable work they have done."[15]

All parties concerned knew there was not the slightest chance that Congress would act on the commission's recommendations in the waning days of the Roosevelt administration. The deliberations had been intended all along as guidelines for the incoming Taft administration and Secretary of the Navy George von Lengerke Meyer. Meyer had served the Roosevelt administration as ambassador first to Italy and then to Russia, and was recalled to become postmaster general during Roosevelt's second term. Roosevelt had recommended him for the navy post. Meyer had been briefed by Moody about the commission's deliberations. At Meyer's request, Mahan met with him in New York City the evening of 26 February for additional discussion.[16] Upon assuming office, Meyer convened another commission, which approved the work of the Moody-Mahan group, then proceeded to institute substantially what had been recommended. The system was maintained through the remaining years of his tenure as secretary, and one segment of it, the Office of Naval Operations, was formally approved by Congress in 1915.

Mahan must have felt a sense of vindication as he saw his proposals bearing fruit at last. Once again he was playing a significant role in naval affairs: his recommendations endorsed by the president, the secretary of the navy, and service professionals. It was illustrative of what the Mahan-Roosevelt relationship might have been. Just as Roosevelt utilized Mahan's prestige in the matter of administrative reorganization, he was to similarly utilize Mahan's pen in publicizing certain aspect of the navy's around-the world cruise.

## NOTES

1. Seager and Maguire, *Letters and Papers*, 3: 628; see also Alfred Thayer Mahan, *Naval Administration and Warfare: Some General Principles* (Boston: Little. Brown, 1908), pp. 64–65.

2. See Spector, *Professors of War*, chaps. 5 and 6; and also Ronald Spector, *Admiral of the New Empire: The Life and Career of George Dewey* (Baton Rouge: Louisiana State University Press, 1974), p. 125.

3. Mahan to Roosevelt, 7 September 1903, Seager and Maguire, *Letters and Papers*, 3: 73–74.

4. Spector, *Admiral of the New Empire*, pp. 154–55.

5. Stephen B. Luce to Roosevelt, 14 July 1908, Luce Papers, LCMD, Container #12.

6. William S. Sims to Roosevelt, 10 August 1908, Sims Papers, LCMD, Container #97.

7. Paolo Coletta, K. Jack Bauer and Robert G. Albion, *American Secretaries of the Navy*, 2 vols. (Annapolis, Md.: Naval Institute Press, 1980), 1: 490–91.

8. William S. Sims to Roosevelt, 3 December 1908, Sims Papers, LCMD, Container #97.

9. Mahan to Roosevelt, 13 January 1909, Seager and Maguire, *Letters and Papers*, 3: 275–77.

10. Sims to Roosevelt, 14 January 1909, Sims Papers, LCMD, Container #97.

11. Roosevelt to Mahan, 27 January 1909, PSU - TR Papers, Series 2, Reel 353.

12. Certain Needs of the Navy. Message from the President of the United States, transmitting two preliminary reports of the Commission appointed to consider certain needs of the Navy, Sen. Doc. No. 740; 60th Cong., 2nd sess., Mahan Papers, LCMD, Container #6. See also Mahan to John S. Billings, 30 January 1909, Mahan to William H. Moody, 1 February 1909, and Mahan to Moody, 3 February 1909, Seager and Maguire, *Letters and Papers*, 3: 279, 280–81, 283.

13. Certain Needs of the Navy, Mahan Papers, LCMD, Container #6.

14. Final Report of the Commission on Naval Reorganization, Sen. Doc. No. 743. 60th Congress, 2nd sess.

15. Theodore Roosevelt letter of transmittal, 27 February 1909, ibid.

16. See Mahan to Spencer Gordon, n.d., Seager and Maguire, *Letters and Papers*, 3: 289.

# 10 Cruise around the World

The outcome of the Russo-Japanese war had convinced Mahan that his geopolitical and strategic views had received vindication. It was this sense of vindication that was in part responsible for his involvement in the all-big-gun imbroglio and his incautious letter to Roosevelt warning him not to divide the fleet. The Russian statesmen had failed to heed the principle of concentration prior to the war, and so the Russian navy suffered defeat in detail. Japan's victory, however, created a new set of problems for the United States in East Asia with which both Mahan and Roosevelt, each in his own fashion, attempted to grapple.

Mahan initially had welcomed, or at least tolerated, the Anglo-Japanese alliance of 1902 because it served as a check upon Russian ambitions. He began to realize, however, that Japan's success might merely have whetted her appetite for more territory—that a rapacious Russia might have been replaced by a rapacious Japan. Nor was it at all certain that Great Britain could continue to restrain Japanese ambitions. "I think I have before told you," Mahan wrote to an English friend, "that I thought you had made a mistake in helping drive Russia out of Manchuria."[1] Although Japan had temporarily exhausted her economic and military power for fresh adventures, her eyes might well be focused on American possessions in the Pacific, particularly the Philippines. Militarily, Japan seemed to Mahan to represent an Asian version of Imperial Germany.[2]

The chief difficulty to Mahan, however, was not Japanese territorial ambitions in Asia, but rather the immigration question. U.S.-Japanese relations had deteriorated sharply in 1907 under the dual impact of the San Francisco school board decision to segregate Asian children in the schools, and the clamor from the western states to shut off Japanese immigration altogether. To another British correspondent, he wrote: "After my concern as to permitting yellow immigration, my great anxiety is as to the effect upon our relations with you. It does seem an awful pity that your treaty may force you into a position of apparent antagonism."[3] A Japanese-American clash on the issue of Asiatic exclusion threatened the laboriously constructed Anglo-American entente. Mahan feared that the United States would be driven to seek closer ties with Germany, "which would contradict the whole of my life policy."[4] If he was concerned privately about the danger of conflict with Great Britain because of the Anglo-Japanese treaty, publicly he attempted to minimize the problem. The Anglo-Japanese alliance would come into effect with respect to the United States only if the latter sought territorial gains at Japan's expense. Furthermore, American public opinion would not support the idea of war with Great Britain.[5]

Roosevelt also became deeply involved with East Asian issues. His efforts to bring about a satisfactory resolution of the Russo-Japanese war were based in large part on his desire to preserve the balance of power in East Asia and, by extension, in Europe. Should one power become militarily dominant, it would threaten American interests in both China and the Philippines. The Japanese victory gave Japan the dominance that Roosevelt feared. Realistically, he knew that Congress and public opinion would not countenance a massive increase in American military and naval strength in the Philippines, so he sought alternatively to protect them by reaching a *modus vivendi* with Japan. The Taft-Katsura agreement (1905) and the subsequent Root-Takahira convention (1908) gave Japan a free hand in Korea and southern Manchuria in return for a Japanese pledge of noninterference in the Philippines. The eruption in 1907 of the San Francisco school board crisis forced Roosevelt to consider the possibility of war with Japan—something neither power wished, but both recognized might come. It was in this context that Roosevelt seized upon a suggestion originating with Captain Nathan Sargent, a member of the General Board, to send some battleships to the Pacific Coast, and decided to send the entire fleet on what became an around-the-world cruise.

As regards the fleet going to the Pacific, there has been no change, save that the naval board decided sooner than I had expected. I could not entertain any proposition to divide the fleet and send some vessels there, which has been the fool proposition of our own jingoes; but this winter we shall have reached the period when it is advisable to send the whole fleet on a practice cruise around the world. It became evident to me, from talking with the naval authorities, that in the event of war they would have a good deal to find out in the way of sending the fleet to the Pacific.

Now, the one thing that I won't run the risk of is to experiment for the first time in a matter of vital importance in time of war. Accordingly I concluded that it was imperative that we should send the fleet on what would practically be a practice voyage. I do not intend to keep it in the Pacific for any length of time; but I want all failures, blunders, and shortcomings to be made apparent in time of peace and not in time of war. Moreover, I think that before matters become more strained we had better make it evident that when it comes to visiting our own coasts on the Pacific or Atlantic and assembling the fleet in our own waters, we cannot submit to any outside protests or interference. Curiously enough, the Japs have seen this more quickly than our own people.[6]

Both Mahan and Roosevelt, approaching the problem of Japan from different perspectives, remembered the fate of Rozhdestvenski's squadron. It had prompted Mahan's incautious letter to the president in January 1907. Roosevelt's testiness was evidence that the chief executive knew full well what could happen to a divided fleet. Both men, despite their disagreement on other issues, saw merit in the idea of an extended cruise by the fleet. Mahan, recovering from prostate surgery, was moved to write about the forthcoming cruise because of criticism of the move made from his old opponent William S. Sims.

Sims had commented about the slowness with which preparations for the voyage had gone and about the logistic difficulties so lengthy a cruise would engender.[7] Apparently, too, the inspector of target practice believed the fleet could do a better job of gunnery exercising in home waters. As Mahan commented to Luce, Sims's remarks "greatly excited and enraged" him, and he lost no time taking advantage of a request by *Scientific American* for an article on the forthcoming cruise.

Mahan began the article by defending Roosevelt against attacks in the press to the effect that the cruise was not intended for practice purposes at all. Rather, one writer hinted strongly, Roosevelt was sending the fleet to the Pacific for the express purpose of stirring up trouble with the Japanese. Anyone who believed the contrary was, in the journalist's opinion, "a miracle of innocent credulity."[8] Mahan freely confessed that he numbered himself among the ranks of the credulous. In bittersweet fashion, he noted: "I am not in the councils of either the government or the Navy Department. I have neither talked with nor heard from any person who from official position could communicate to me any knowledge of the facts. My own information has been confined throughout to the newspapers."[9] The balance of his essay in *Scientific American* was a reasoned exposition on the benefits of the cruise to the fleet. Mahan clearly wished to downplay the danger of war with Japan, for with the exception of his dig at the journalist, he made no mention of the issue at all. There the matter rested for some months until Mahan, meditating a follow-up piece, wrote Roosevelt to request the president's permission for an inquiry directed to Admiral Robley D. Evans, commander of the fleet, on the value to the navy of the cruise.

With his article he enclosed a piece by Edward Dicey which had appeared in the January 1908 edition of the *Empire Review*, a British publication. Dicey had harsh words for the U.S. Navy's discipline, and called the entire cruise a crude attempt to bluff the Japanese into backing down on the immigration imbroglio—an attempt, moreover, which the Japanese could puncture whenever they chose. Roosevelt replied warmly to Mahan's request, and told him to get whatever information he needed from Evans. As for that "ridiculous creature" Dicey, the president asserted, he "knows no more about the alleged 'brutal discipline' in the navy than he does about our motive in sending the fleet abroad."[10]

Thus encouraged, Mahan early in July mailed Roosevelt portions of his forthcoming "Retrospect" article, asking if the president would object to their publication. Far from objecting, Roosevelt was in complete accord, noting: "In especial I think what you say about the misconduct of the press in that very delicate matter may be of real interest."[11] The "delicate matter" referred to was the Japanese-American negotiations on the issue of Japanese immigration. In his article, published in the 28 August issue of *Collier's Weekly*, Mahan took the press to task for assuming that the fleet was sent to the Pacific to overawe Japan into making a settlement favorable to the United States. This commentary was "particularly inconsiderate and ill-timed, not to say unpatriotic," because it rendered agreement less likely, not more so.[12] Mahan apparently feared an upsurge of anti-American feeling in Japan comparable to that which had followed the Treaty of Portsmouth.[13] This would be particularly unfortunate if it should coincide with the fleet's visit to Japan, and Mahan freely admitted he would be much "more at ease when the fleet gets safely away from Japan without shore rows and the typhoon season."[14]

The fleet got safely away, but Mahan did not. His Naval War College ally from earlier days, Caspar F. Goodrich, had become a recent convert to the all-big-gun school. As such, he apparently was looking for an opportunity to further erode Mahan's credibility with the officer corps. Since Sims had been dubious about the efficacy of the around-the-world cruise, Goodrich took up the same cudgel in objecting to Mahan's rose-colored reporting. "Had you known the real history of the trip from Trinidad to Magdalena Bay of the Atlantic Fleet, you would have framed your *Collier's* article very differently," Goodrich wrote. "We all look up to you as the model of accuracy. Greatness has its own responsibilities you see."[15] Mahan's essay was about to be reprinted for inclusion in his book, *Naval Administration and Warfare*, so he asked Goodrich if he could offer corrections to "specific misstatements" which Mahan might inadvertently have made.[16] Goodrich, spurning this olive branch, declined to do so, merely reiterating that Mahan should be sure of his facts.[17]

At this point, Mahan, "after much consideration," requested Roosevelt's opinion as to whether the article should be submitted "to some person sufficiently cognizant of the facts" before its republication.[18] Roosevelt recognized a tempest in a teapot when he saw one. Mahan's favorable publicizing of the around-the-world voyage had been useful to the president, who probably felt that he owed Mahan a favor in return. Having encouraged the captain to write the piece, and having read portions of it prior to its publication, he had no wish to have its accuracy questioned at this point. His reply therefore stated that Mahan had been justified in relying upon statements made by Rear Admiral Charles S. Sperry, who assumed command of the fleet in San Francisco. "Incidentally I may add that the reports from Sperry and the reports from the officers under Sperry, as to what Sperry has done on the voyage to Australia, show a constant and steady improvement in the fleet and warrant us in taking as accurate Sperry's original statements," Roosevelt noted.[19]

Perhaps the entire episode was blown out of proportion. Yet there is ample evidence that both Roosevelt and Mahan believed that war with Japan was a distinct possibility some day. The immigration issue, if combined with lack of American military preparedness, could lead to war and a Japanese decision to attack the Philippines, Hawaii, or even the West Coast. The Mahan-Sims dispute over the all-big-gun ship had for a time obscured the more fundamental areas of agreement which Mahan and Roosevelt shared concerning U.S.-Japanese relations. As the dispute receded into the background, the convergence of views emerged. Indeed, this convergence extended to each man's perception of the international scene, and was to serve as a legacy for Assistant Secretary of the Navy Franklin Delano Roosevelt.

## NOTES

1. Mahan to Leopold J. Maxse, 30 May 1907, Seager and Maguire, *Letters and Papers*, 3: 213–14.

2. Mahan to Maxse, 19 June 1908, ibid., 251.

3. Mahan to Bouverie F. Clark, 6 September 1907, ibid., 225–26.

4. Mahan to Maxse, 28 June 1907, ibid., 215–16.

5. Alfred Thayer Mahan, "The Practical Aspect of War," *Some Neglected Aspects of War* (Boston: Little, Brown, 1907), pp. 80–81.

6. Roosevelt to Lodge, 10 July 1907, Morison, *Letters of Theodore Roosevelt*, 5: 709–10. See also Roosevelt to Elihu Root, 13 July 1907, ibid., 717; Roosevelt

to Speck von Sternberg, 16 July 1907, ibid., 270; Roosevelt to Truman H. Newberry, 24 July 1907, ibid., 724; Roosevelt to Willard H. Brownson, 26 July 1907, ibid., 730.

7. Seager, *Alfred Thayer Mahan*, p. 480.

8. Alfred Thayer Mahan, *Naval Administration and Warfare: Some General Principles* (Boston: Little, Brown, 1908), p. 314.

9. Ibid.

10. Roosevelt to Mahan, 8 June 1908, PSU - TR Papers, Series 2, Reel 349. See also Roosevelt to Whitelaw Reid, 13 June 1908, Morison, *Letters of Theodore Roosevelt*, 6: 1073.

11. Roosevelt to Mahan, 10 July 1908, PSU - TR Papers, Series 2, Reel 350.

12. Mahan, *Naval Administration and Warfare*, p. 345.

13. Ibid., p. 346.

14. Mahan to Bouverie F. Clark, 11 September 1908, Seager and Maguire, *Letters and Papers*, 3: 262-3.

15. Goodrich to Mahan, 12 September 1908, ibid., 263.

16. Mahan to Caspar F. Goodrich, 14 September 1908, ibid., 264.

17. Goodrich to Mahan, 15 September 1908, ibid., 264.

18. Mahan to William Loeb, 30 September 1908, ibid., 265.

19. Roosevelt to Mahan, 1 October 1908, PSU - TR Papers, Series 2, Reel 351.

# 11 Darkening Horizons

Perhaps Mahan's realization that he could no longer decisively influence technological developments in the navy led him to concentrate increasingly on the international scene. Perhaps it was the mixture of force and diplomacy which the voyage of the Great White Fleet symbolized. Or perhaps it was a desire to awaken the American public to the darkening clouds over Europe, and Britain's increasing peril.[1] Whatever it was, Mahan produced four essays in the winter of 1909–1910 which were published the following fall.

He stressed the growing military preponderance of Germany in Europe, and of Japan in East Asia. Only the British navy stood between Germany and control of Europe. Germany's growing naval strength, and the concentration of the British and German battle fleets in North Sea waters, meant that neither of the powers could or would pose an amphibious challenge to American interests in the Western Hemisphere, for fear the other might be tempted to attack. Should war break out in Europe, and Germany succeed in winning it, the United States would then face a more serious threat to her hemispheric preeminence than ever before. Noninterference with European matters, Mahan maintained, "does not imply absence of concern in them, nor should it involve heedlessness of the fact that the shifting of the balance in Europe may affect our interests and power throughout the world."[2]

In East Asia the situation for the United States was far more troublesome. The government could not rely on any other power to support its Open Door policy. Worse yet, Japan and Russia, recent enemies, had come together to delineate spheres of influence in Manchuria. Britain, needing Russian support to counterbalance Germany's military power in Europe, and relying upon the Anglo-Japanese treaty to buttress its position along the western Pacific littoral, would do nothing to antagonize either power in East Asia. Thus Mahan reasoned that the American navy perhaps should be shifted to the Pacific Ocean from the Atlantic, to serve as a deterrent to Japanese ambitions.[3]

Roosevelt, meanwhile, had embarked on a safari to British East Africa. From comments made both before and during his African and European trip, it is evident that he saw world conditions much as Mahan did. He told incoming Secretary of State Philander C. Knox just prior to his departure that he did not think Germany had any designs currently on the Western Hemisphere. Nor did he expect war with Japan. It would, however, be idle to deny that tensions existed between the United States and Japan on a number of issues. There was always a chance that war would come, and while the president felt that the United States ultimately would win, he thought "there is at least a chance of disaster." He noted the lack of defenses on the West Coast, the absence of an army which could either hold or reconquer the Philippines and Hawaii, and the relative lack of auxiliary naval forces (cruisers and destroyers)—all of which must tempt the Japanese to attack American possessions.[4]

He was, however, troubled by the growth of Germany's navy and the threat that that posed to British maritime predominance. He believed Germany's naval power would make her more intransigent, rather than less, in future European diplomatic crises. "If she had a Navy as strong as that of England," he mused, "I do not believe that she would *intend* to use it for the destruction of England; but I do believe that incidents would be very likely to occur which might make her so use it."[5]

Precisely when Roosevelt read Mahan's *The Interest of America in International Conditions* is not certain. It probably was late in 1910, upon his return to Oyster Bay after his strenuous campaign swing earlier in the fall. Mahan, as was his wont, had seen to it that Roosevelt was sent a complimentary copy by the publisher.[6] Roosevelt, meanwhile, had agreed to write for the *Outlook*. In answer to a question concerning his influence on the magazine's content, Roosevelt explained that the decision as to which books would be reviewed in the pages of the *Outlook* was not his, but the editors'. He felt that Mahan's book warranted a review, because it was "of capital importance" and "would have appealed to the general reader," but the editors apparently felt otherwise.[7] Elsewhere, he observed to his brother-in-law, William S. Cowles, that he had to be careful not to abuse his position on the *Outlook*—not, in short, to use it "in any way for my personal friends or to meet my personal ideas."[8] In yet another letter to Cowles, Roosevelt noted:

If Japan goes on growing, and we go on growing, no human being can be certain that there never will be war between us. If Germany should ever overthrow England and establish the supremacy in Europe she aims at, she will be almost certain to want to try her hand in America; and if ever we became involved with either Germany or Japan and had not fortified the canal, our people might have cause to rue it for generations.[9]

Following the outbreak of World War I, Roosevelt initially believed that Germany, if defeated by the Allies, would be stripped of her colonial empire and fleet, "reduced to international impotence." Should Germany, improbably, win the war, he felt she would not have been able to reduce Russia, and would face the "active hostility" of the United States as well. "Our people have never forgotten the attitude taken by Germany in the Spanish War, and since then threatened by Germany in South America."[10] Yet he clearly had doubts about whether a defeated Britain would be in a position to block German expansion into the Western Hemisphere. To a German sympathizer, he wrote:

Now, not for publication, but frankly between outselves, do you not believe that if Germany won in this war, smashed the English Fleet and destroyed the British Empire, within a year or two she would insist upon taking the dominant position in South and Central America and upon treating the United States precisely as she treated Japan when she joined with Russia and France against Japan twenty years ago and took Kiaochow as her share? I believe so. Indeed I know so.[11]

Roosevelt thus shared some of Mahan's concerns and clearly was impressed by Mahan's earlier analysis of international conditions, not least because they so nearly coincided with his own. Mahan's belated conversion to the necessity of "taking Panama" and their mutual distress at the Taft administration's arbitration treaties clearly served to reinforce the two men's convergence of views at this time. This was fortunate in another respect, because with the election of Woodrow Wilson to the presidency in 1912, another Roosevelt was offered the post of assistant secretary of the navy. Among Franklin Delano Roosevelt's idols, Mahan stood very near to cousin Ted, and it would have been unfortunate had the two mentors not seen eye to eye in the advice which they proferred the fledging assistant secretary.

Theodore Roosevelt wrote FDR in the spring of 1913 that although he did not anticipate trouble with Japan, "it may come, and if it does it will come suddenly." He went on to warn that the fleet should never be separated. "Russia's fate ought to be a warning for all time as to the criminal folly of dividing the fleet if there is even the remotest chance of war."[12] The subsequent war scare with Japan led to a growing uneasiness along the West Coast as to their defenselessness. The imminent opening of the Panama Canal made it appear possible to divide the fleet with little danger, and Franklin Roosevelt enlisted the help of both Theodore Roosevelt and Mahan to head off the agitation. Writing Mahan that his voice would "carry more conviction than that of anybody else," FDR asked him to write an article or two. Mahan obliged, and his article, "The Panama Canal and the Distribution of the Fleet," appeared in the September issue of the *North American Review*. Mahan also suggested that FDR enlist the aid of his cousin, the ex-president; Roosevelt replied that he had already done so.[13]

The assistant secretary informed Mahan that he was playing with the idea of establishing an armored cruiser squadron which would be based on the Pacific coast, and which would switch places periodically with the Atlantic Fleet when the latter was in the Pacific. This idea struck Mahan "very favorably." It would ensure concentration of the main fleet and give much-needed practice in transiting the canal, since the squadrons were to be rotated biennially. "Personally," he added, "I feel that our danger in the Pacific much exceeds that in the Atlantic."[14] But in this view Mahan was wrong, as events in Europe were soon to prove.

As the European scene darkened, Mahan continued to be concerned over possible complications between the United States and Japan. He urged Franklin Roosevelt to do all he could to see that the fleet was "brought into immediate readiness and so disposed as to permit of very rapid concentration ready to proceed when desired." He hoped that though the canal was not quite ready, "a sufficient number of battleships could even now be passed through on occasion."[15] The very next day, 4 August 1914, he wrote FDR again to suggest that the United States should inform the belligerent nations in its forthcoming proclamation of neutrality that no coal would be permitted any vessels entering United States ports. The usual formula, which permitted a neutral to provide coal enough for a belligerent vessel to reach the "nearest national port," would in the case of German ships permit them to cross the Atlantic or, alternatively, to prey on British and French vessels carrying American goods. He also called the assistant secretary's attention to an article in the *New York Evening Post* (3 August 1914) in which he sketched out the situation of the belligerents at sea.[16]

Finally, Mahan was disturbed by the Japanese ultimatum to Germany, which he thought both "sudden and ill-conceived." He feared that the effect of Japan's action would be to transfer "popular sympathy" in the conflict from Great Britain, Japan's ally, to Germany, "because the latter, in a moment of extreme embarrassment and danger, has been wantonly and needlessly assailed, on trumpery pretext."

Mahan doubted that Japan had entered into prior consultation with Great Britain before delivering the ultimatum, but foresaw in any case a strain in Anglo-American relations should the Japanese proceed beyond the seizure of Kiaochow to take Germany's islands in the Pacific.

Japan, going to war with Germany, will be at liberty to take the German Islands, Pelew, Marianne, Caroline, and Samoa. The first three flank our Mercator course to the Philippines; and it is one thing to have them in the hands of a Power whose main strength is in Europe, and quite another that they should pass into the hands of one so near as Japan.[17]

This turned out to be Mahan's last letter to either Roosevelt. He and Franklin Roosevelt never met, though Mahan did appear one day at the Navy Department when FDR was out.[18] For a brief time, though, Mahan enjoyed a relationship of advisor to the assistant secretary that must have made up in part for the disappointments of his relationship with Theodore Roosevelt during the latter's presidency.

## NOTES

1. Mahan to Bouverie Clark, 23 July 1909, Seager and Maguire, *Letters and Papers*, 3: 307–8.

2. Alfred Thayer Mahan, *The Interest of America in International Conditions* (Boston: Little, Brown, 1910), p. 178.

3. Ibid., 142–43, 198–99.

4. Roosevelt to Philander C. Knox, 8 February 1909, Morison, *Letters of Theodore Roosevelt*, 6: 1510–14.

5. Roosevelt to George Otto Trevelyan, 1 October 1911, ibid., 7: 395–96.

6. Mahan to Little, Brown, 14 October 1910, Seager and Maguire, *Letters and Papers*, 3: 361.

7. Roosevelt to Archibald Gracie, 23 December 1911, Morison, *Letters of Theodore Roosevelt*, 7: 464.

8. Roosevelt to William S. Cowles, 10 February 1911, ibid., 231.

9. Roosevelt to Cowles, 27 October 1911, ibid., 423. Roosevelt noted that the country would be forced to rely on the fleet for protection for the foreseeable future. Press reports that Secretary of the Navy Josephus Daniels contemplated dividing the fleet between the Atlantic and Pacific, in view of the disaster to Russia a decade previously, "would be literally a crime against the nation." Theodore Roosevelt, *America and the World War* (New York: Charles Scribner's Sons, 1915), p. 162.

10. Roosevelt to Arthur Hamilton Lee, 22 August 1914, Morison, *Letters of Theodore Roosevelt*, 7: 810–11.

11. Roosevelt to Hugo Munsterberg, 3 October 1914, ibid., 8: 823. See also Roosevelt to Bernhard Dernburg, 4 December 1914, ibid., 860.

12. Roosevelt to Franklin Delano Roosevelt, 10 May 1913, ibid., 7: 729.

13. Franklin D. Roosevelt to Mahan, 28 May 1914; Mahan to FDR, 2 June and 16 June 1914; Roosevelt Papers, FDR Library, Hyde Park, N.Y.

14. Mahan to FDR, 26 June 1914, ibid.

15. Mahan to FDR, 3 August 1914, ibid.

16. Mahan to FDR, 4 August 1914, ibid. See also Seager, *Alfred Thayer Mahan*, p. 598.

17. Mahan to FDR, 18 August 1914, Roosevelt Papers, FDR Library.

18. Ellen Lyle Mahan to FDR, 9 January 1915, ibid.

# 12 The Ambiguous Relationship

The Mahan-Roosevelt relationship, which began in 1888 and lasted until Mahan's death in 1914, was "not clearly defined," and was "open to more than one interpretation."[1] On some issues, and at some times, there was close cooperation and harmony of views; on other issues, and at other times, these two strong-willed individuals disagreed. Broadly speaking, three distinct phases emerged. From 1888 to 1898, Roosevelt and Mahan were perhaps as close as they ever became, personally and professionally. From 1899 through 1907, the relationship was characterized by disagreement, sometimes muted but no less real. Beginning in 1908 and continuing through 1914, there was a degree of rapprochement—though without the warmth of the earlier period.

Roosevelt's reviews of Mahan's first two sea-power books illustrate the ambiguity in the relationship even at this early date. Roosevelt agreed with Mahan that it was "folly" to rely on a policy of commerce-destroying in the face of a "resolute and powerful enemy," yet he also criticized Mahan for failure to give credit to the effect produced by American privateers in the Revolutionary War. Roosevelt was generous enough to consider Mahan's work superior to those (including his own *Naval War of 1812*) which limited themselves to describing the "actual battles and forces" on each side. Mahan's treatment of strategy and grand strategy elevated the books, in Roosevelt's view, to the status of "naval classics." The books did indeed become naval classics, and Mahan, praise pouring in from all sides, may well have assumed the existence of a greater degree of deference than Roosevelt ever intended. Mahan elicited Roosevelt's assistance in his efforts to avoid being posted to the *U.S.S. Chicago* because sea duty not only would force him to postpone several major writing projects, but would silence his ability to comment upon "questions of naval policy" in leading journals. This latter argument must have proved conclusive to Roosevelt, no mean publicist himself.

Roosevelt and Mahan also favored the annexation of Hawaii, and worked together to bring this about. Roosevelt wrote Mahan that he shared his views regarding Hawaii "absolutely." This was not altogether true. Mahan had a deeply rooted fear of Japanese expansion and immigration, heralding the opening of a struggle for domination between East and West. Roosevelt was much less concerned *then* about Japan, and indeed admired the advances the government and people had made. Hawaiian annexation, strategically desirable for the United States, would also in Roosevelt's view remove the likelihood of a clash with Japan. It became apparent that Roosevelt feared German expansion more than Japanese, and wished to acquire Spain's Caribbean possessions and the Danish West Indies to forestall possible German designs. Mahan's view was towards the Pacific and Asia, Roosevelt's towards the Caribbean. This divergence would widen.

Meanwhile, Roosevelt enlisted Mahan's assistance in the preparation of plans for war with Spain. One facet of the plan at the time Mahan came into the picture was the dispatch of a "flying squadron," consisting of fast armored cruisers, to operate against the coast of Spain. Mahan felt this violated the principle of concentration., nor did he desire any movement against Puerto Rico until Cuba had been captured. Roosevelt concurred, and was effusive in his thanks for Mahan's subsequent advice regarding the disposition of the blockading fleet off Havana. He may have regretted, though, that much of the counsel he was receiving—Mahan's included—seemed to preclude the prosecution of a "rapid, vigorous, aggressive war." Both men also approved of the attack on the Philippines, but they subsequently had divergent opinions on what should be done with the islands. Roosevelt wanted the government to retain the entire archipelago; Mahan, less certain of the desirability of this course, suggested the retention of Luzon and the return of the rest of the islands to Spain. Nor was he convinced, as Roosevelt was, that independence for Cuba was the best course to follow. Ironically, President Roosevelt intervened in Cuba in 1906 to restore order following a disputed election. Before too many years had passed, he also was to refer to the Philippines as "our heel of Achilles."

The American presence in the Philippines represented, in Roosevelt's words, a victory "for law, order and righteousness." All civilized nations—the United States, England, Germany, France, Austria, and Russia—had both the right and the duty to expand to bring peace to the world. With all this Mahan concurred, but he was to go further with the notion of American expansion in Asia than Roosevelt believed wise. The Boer War, Mahan believed, was for Britain the wrong war, at the wrong time, and in the wrong place. The real struggle was between land power (Russia and France) and sea power (Britain, the United States, Germany, and Japan), waged across the "debatable ground" of Asia: China, Afghanistan, Persia, and Asiatic Turkey. He wanted the United States to support Britain in central China in every way possible. Britain should if necessary retrench in southern Africa, and concentrate on denying Russia access to the Dardanelles and the Persian Gulf. Roosevelt, by contrast, regretted that two civilized peoples, Boers and Britons, should be at each other's throats. The war seemed to him to represent a "deterioration" of the English-speaking peoples. He did not believe America public opinion would support the kind of Asian commitment Mahan sought, nor did he believe Britain could maintain itself indefinitely in southern and southeastern Asia. A "serious disaster" to the British Empire, he mused, would heighten the prospect of German-American conflict in the Western Hemisphere unless (as Mahan at one point advocated) we were prepared to abandon the Monroe Doctrine in South America.

This may in part explain Roosevelt's opposition to the first Hay-Pauncefote Treaty. If British power and resolution indeed was waning, could the United States afford to agree to the neutralization and non-fortification of an isthmian canal? The American fleet, he believed, should be free to conduct offensive operations, not chained to the defense of the canal. Mahan disagreed. The essential element—which the treaty permitted—was an American-controlled canal. Granted that a German squadron could steam through the canal to attack points on the West Coast, Mahan felt it highly unlikely that it would wish to overextend its own communications and forego an attack on the East Coast. It appears also that Mahan was in no hurry to unduly weaken Britain's position in the Western Hemisphere while she was beleaguered elsewhere. Given these differences of opinion, it is not surprising that Mahan failed to support Roosevelt's Caribbean policy from 1902 to 1905 nor that Roosevelt, in turn, failed to call upon Mahan for advice.

Mahan, though circumspect in his comments concerning the Caribbean, believed it "inconceivable" that any of the great powers would seriously threaten the United States's position in the hemisphere. He disliked the Anglo-German blockade of Venezuela in the winter of 1902–1903, partly because it could—and did—exacerbate public fear of a European threat, and partly because it could lead to an upsurge of anti-British feeling. Mahan was ambivalent over the "taking" of Panama, despite his desire for an American-controlled canal, and not until 1911 did he belatedly and publicly support the administration's actions in 1903. The imposition of the Dominican customs receivership left him wondering whether the end justified the means. Mahan's silence and circumspection surely did not escape Roosevelt's attention.

Differences of opinion in the realm of foreign policy were mirrored in naval policy as well. Mahan, increasingly concerned by the international naval arms race, attempted in 1902 to interest Roosevelt in a standardized battleship, limited as to tonnage, and possessing a mixed battery of both long-range and quick-firing guns. He hoped for the president's backing in obtaining international agreement for such a vessel, which could "lessen the expense" of armaments. Mahan believed, correctly, that the classes, numbers, and characteristics of naval vessels should bear a "direct relation" to the country's naval policy and strategy. Roosevelt gave these proposals short shrift. The inconclusiveness of the first Hague conference (to which Mahan was a delegate) may have led him to conclude that the likelihood of substantive international agreement was almost nil. Perhaps he felt such an initiative could jeopardize existing naval construction. He himself was becoming a convert to the all-big-gun ship, and may well have sensed the likelihood of a new arms race—which, in fact, the commissioning of *H.M.S. Dreadnought* was to inspire.

The subsequent all-big-gun controversy pitted Mahan against Roosevelt and Sims. Never was Mahan's lack of understanding of modern technology more pitilessly exposed. Yet by committing the nation to the modern battleship, the Roosevelt administration also was emphasizing the capital ship at the expense of other types of vessels: cruisers, destroyers, torpedo boats, and submarines. Mahan himself was a proponent of the capital ship (perhaps one should say the ship-of-the-line) and the strategy of *grand guerre*: close blockade, decisive fleet-to-fleet engagements, and keeping one's lines of communication open. Somewhere, though, his notion of correlating vessel types with naval policy and strategy got lost in the shuffle.

It might have been better for Mahan if Roosevelt had never written about the War of 1812—had not, in short, established his own credentials as a naval historian. Failing that, surely Mahan could have quoted from Roosevelt's work or at least have acknowledged its contributions to the field. He seems, rather, to have gone out of his way to disagree with the president and to minimize areas of agreement. Where Roosevelt focused upon the single-ship engagements and battles upon lakes Erie and Champlain, Mahan considered the American victories at sea "useless effusions of blood," "utterly unavailing" in the face of British sea power. Roosevelt believed British seizures of American ships and cargoes prior to the war "unjustifiable" by present-day standards; Mahan declared that Britain could not tolerate neutral flag cargoes reaching France. Whereas Roosevelt undertook his study in the first place to refute some of British historian William James's interpretations, Mahan more than once relied upon James's accounts because "he is known to have been painstaking." Perhaps hardest of all for Roosevelt to swallow was Mahan's assertion that the United States's record was one of "gloom, disaster, and governmental incompetence" even upon the water. Small wonder, then, that Roosevelt, upon reading Mahan's work, referred to him as a "curious fellow" who could not write effectively about the navy or the fighting of his own nation.

Had the question of immunity of private property from capture not been so closely tied in with the origins of the War of 1812, it is entirely possible that Mahan's struggle to get the Roosevelt administration to reverse its position might have succeeded. With all the persuasiveness he could command, he pleaded that if the nations were to endorse the American position at the second Hague conference it would seriously restrict the ability of the maritime powers to control the seas. In the event of war with Germany, if her carrying trade were to be exempt from capture, "you remove the strongest hook in the jaws of Germany that the English speaking people have." Though Roosevelt did not attempt to prevent Mahan from speaking out on the issue, he was unwilling to alter the traditional American posture.

Both men also remained concerned about Japan. On Mahan's part, he feared that sometime, somewhere, a chief executive might decide to station a portion of the American battle fleet in the Pacific, inviting an attack by Japan and subsequent defeat in detail, as had happened to the Russians in their recent conflict with Japan. It was this concern that led him to anxiously question Roosevelt whether press rumors of such a move had any truth in them. Another aspect of his concern was the Anglo-Japanese alliance. Should there be trouble with Japan, almost certainly Anglo-American relations also would be affected. Finally, he continued to worry about Japanese immigration, both on racist grounds and because he saw it as a continued source of difficulty. Roosevelt may have shared some of these concerns, but he attempted to deal with them through a combination of force (the around-the-world cruise) and diplomacy (the Taft-Katsura and Root-Takahira agreements, as well as a resolution of the immigration issue). Upon leaving office in 1909, he advised William Howard Taft not to antagonize Japan and not to divide the fleet.

A rapprochement of sorts took root as Roosevelt's second term neared its end. Roosevelt had, after all, quoted from Mahan's *War of 1812* (on preparedness) in his 1906 state-of-the-union message, and had urged him to publicize his viewpoint on the immunity of private property. He saw, also, the value of having Mahan's name associated with the proposed reorganization of the navy department, even if some of the insurgents did not. He welcomed Mahan's assistance a bit later in his campaign against the Taft administration's arbitration treaties. Most importantly, he thought well of Mahan's book, *The Interest of America in International Conditions*.

Mahan stressed the importance of the British fleet to American security. It stood between Germany and her mastery of Europe. Should Britain—and the British navy—be defeated, the United States would face a serious threat to her own hemispheric preeminence. At the same time, Japanese power was increasing in Asia, unchecked by either Russia (with whom a spheres-of-influence agreement had been reached) or Britain (who had to concentrate her strength in European waters). It might therefore be well to consider stationing the American fleet in the Pacific as a check to Japanese ambitions. With much of this analysis Roosevelt concurred.

Clearly Mahan did not, as some have suggested, enter the White House in the person of Theodore Roosevelt. Part of the reason lies in their differing personalities. Both men possessed extraordinarily diverse sets of interests, unusual even in a cosmopolitan age. Roosevelt was a doer as well as a thinker, as Mahan recognized. Writing to Roosevelt at a time when their relationship was as close as it ever became, Mahan noted:

You will believe that when I write to you it is only to suggest thoughts, or give information, not with any wish otherwise to influence action, or to ask information. I have known myself too long not to know that I am the man of thought, not the man of action. Such an one may beneficially throw out ideas, the practical effect of which can rest only, and be duly shaped only, by practical men.[2]

Mahan hoped to assume just such a role with Roosevelt, with some degree of reciprocity, and for a time in the 1890s it appeared these expectations would be realized. But it was not to be. Mahan was, in his daughter's words, "The Cat That Walked By Himself." She noted: "I never heard him speak of Admiral [Robley D.] Evans, nor any of his friends except Mr. [Samuel B.] Ashe and Sir Bouverie Clark."[3] Significantly, Roosevelt's name was not mentioned.

Personality differences notwithstanding, both Roosevelt and Mahan were advocates of sea power, the strategy of *grand guerre*, and reliance upon the battleship as the backbone of the fleet, although each had reached this position via a different route. Both were Anglophiles— Mahan much more so than Roosevelt. Both, in varying degrees and at varying times, feared (in Mahan's case) or respected (in Roosevelt's case) the rising power of Germany and Japan. Both subscribed to Social Darwinist tenets. Yet there were disagreements even within these broad areas of convergence, as well as the open clashes over the all-big-gun ship and the immunity of private property from seizure.

It would be erroneous to suggest, on the other hand, that Mahan lacked any influence with Roosevelt. His international reputation as a publicist and propagandist for sea power, as well as his keen interest in international relations, assured him an extensive audience. Roosevelt, aware of the power of Mahan's pen, sought wherever possible to avoid openly disagreeing with him. Yet as president—and even before—he determined both the nature and extent of the relationship between them. He had, being Roosevelt, little difficulty convincing himself of the correctness of his own viewpoint at all times.

It is the ambiguity of the relationship that is significant. If Mahan's voice had prevailed, Roosevelt might have maintained a lower profile in the Caribbean but become more actively involved in the Pacific and East Asia. The degree of cooperation between Britain and the United States would have been even closer than was the case. The United States also might have clung a bit longer to the mixed-battery battleship. Neither man, however, sensed that the advent of the airplane signaled the end of the battleship's preeminence in the world's navies.

There is, however, no gainsaying the importance of the relationship, nor the prominence of both men at the time of the United States's emergence as a great power. The tensions between them, the shifts and nuances of their relationship help to highlight the development of both naval and foreign policy. If on the one hand it might have been a famous friendship, on the other the Mahan-Roosevelt relationship bore within itself the seeds of serious discord. Neither extreme triumphed, and thus the ambiguity remains.

## NOTES

1. *The Oxford Universal Dictionary on Historical Principles,* rev. and ed. by C. T. Onions (Oxford: Clarendon Press, 1955), p. 53.

2. Mahan to Roosevelt, 6 May 1897, *Seager and Maguire,* Letters and Papers, 2: 507.

3. Recollections of Ellen Kuhn Mahan, ibid., 3: 721.

# Roosevelt-Mahan Correspondence

LC - Mahan MSS
Washington, May 12, 1890

My dear Captain Mahan,

During the last two days I have spent half my time, busy as I am, in reading your book; and that I found it interesting is shown by the fact that having taken it up I have gone straight through and finished it.

I can say with perfect sincerity that I think it very much the clearest and most instructive general work of the kind with which I am acquainted. It is a *very* good book—admirable; and I am greatly in error  if it does not become a naval classic. It shows the faculty of grasping the meaning of events and their relations to one another and of taking in the whole situation. I wish the portions dealing with commerce destroying could be put in the hands of some of the friends of a navy, and that the whole book could be placed where it could be read by the navy's foes, especially in congress. You must read the two volumes of Henry Adams' history dealing with the war of 1812 when they come out. He is a man of infinite research, and his ideas are usually (with some very marked exceptions) excellent.

With sincere congratulations I am

*Letters & Papers*, 2:96–97
March 1, 1893

To Theodore Roosevelt

My Dear Sir:

I present to you herewith the written statement of my wishes, and the arguments pro and con, which you asked me to make.

I have for the past seven years been engaged in the study of matters connected with the Conduct of Naval Warfare, a question entirely distinct from that of the Development of Naval Material.
Upon the latter, it is safe to say, professional attention has been exclusively concentrated; very few, save myself scarcely any, have attempted the systematic investigation of Naval Warfare and Naval Policy.

You are acquainted with some of the results of my work. I have now in contemplation, 1. For the Naval War College, a Systematic Treatise of Naval Strategy, formulating its theories and illustrating its practice, by the historical examples collected in my previous studies. 2. An historical study of the War of 1812, upon the same general lines as my other historical works. I have on my table a request from a leading publishing firm of New York to write a Naval History of the Civil War.

The continuance of my work depends upon my not going to sea. The absorbing administrative work of a modern large ship of war would impose an interruption, which, at my age—53—and for two years, would probably prove final. I propose, therefore, to retire, as allowed by law, after forty years of service, in 1896; if, in view of that intention, I am not meanwhile ordered to sea duty.

The argument *in favor* of this indulgence to me rests upon the character of the work I propose to do, for which that already done by me must be the guarantee. Interrupted now, it is probably interrupted finally; nor, as far as I know, is there any one else likely to take it up.

The argument *against* thus excusing me will probably be that every man must take his turn, that I throw upon others sea service which I should do, and which is essential to my own professional education. The reply is that I will get out of the way as soon as the law allows; and that the experience is not necessary to me, if, as I engage, I retire from active service.

The main argument, however, must be the utility of the work, past and future; the fact of my fitness for it; and the improbability of any one else undertaking it. In support of this I forward to you letters and criticisms, both American and English, which will adequately show the estimation in which the work is held abroad and at home.

In view of these indorsements (all of them unsought) it might also, I think, be safely urged that editors of leading magazines are now seeking from me articles on questions of naval policy, and civil societies asking me to address them on kindred subjects. It is therefore not improbable, seeing the favorable opinion held of me, that I shall by these means be able to contribute to the intelligent comprehension of naval necessities by the country at large.

The question then is: May I not, for the reasons given, be even more useful to the navy by the proposed course than by commanding a ship? And should the simple, and perfectly just, tradition, that each man must go to sea when his turn comes, prevail to prevent me from what is practically a change of profession, probably beneficial to the navy, but which my means will not permit me at my age to risk, except in the way indicated?

It will be important to note that my term of forty years expires in 1896, that is, within the term of the coming administration, upon whose decision my plea rests.

*Letters & Papers*, 2: 98–99
March 18, 1893

My dear Mr. Roosevelt:

I have delayed until to day making my application, on account of Mr. Herbert's absence; and would have waited still longer, until I knew he was back, but that to day I have heard "on good authority," that there was thought of ordering me to temporary command of the *Baltimore*, whose captain, I believe, is ill. Independently of the fact that temporary orders have a tendency to become permanent, the application would come with less grace when under orders. I accordingly sent it by the last mail—three hours ago—and I enclose you a copy, as finally mailed.

I also enclose a clipping from the well known service paper, *Broad Arrow*, chiefly because of the last sentence. Concerning our rise in naval power, Mr. Herbert, I fancy, inclines to think "quorum pars magna fui"; and the connection may touch his convictions. I will ask you to return it to me carefully, as it is one of several sent me by the London publishers with a request to return.

I have thought of only one possible thing to add. It may be objected that other captains might have to go to sea a second time, if I don't. To this I believe an adequate reply can be made that, owing to the retirements of this year, and especially of 1894, there will be a sufficient supply of captains who have never been to sea as such.

I thank you most sincerely for the kind interest you have taken in this matter. It is to me vital—the question, probably, of a career made or a career lost, and I trust that any proper appeal to Mr. Herbert's mind may be made. Other you would certainly not make, and I, I trust, would not ask.

*Letters & Papers*, 2: 100–101
March 26, 1893

Mr. Dear Mr. Roosevelt:

I thank you most gratefully for your letter and for the effort you have made on my behalf. I understand exactly the state of the case, as it now stands i.e. no promise on the Secretary's part, but apparently a disposition to take a view favorable to my wishes. I consider it a particular piece of good fortune to have had my case advocated by you, prohibited as you are by your reputation from seeking to further it on any other ground than the merits of the case, as you see it. It gives you a unique weight when you see reason for speaking.

I shall wait the issue quietly, thought not without grave concern; but sure that in you I have all the support that I ought to desire, and a really interested friend.

I sent you a letter from Laughton, addressed 1215 Nineteenth St. for which I depended upon my memory. I mention it only because you have not. Don't trouble to acknowledge, for unless I hear to the contrary I shall be sure you receive it.

LC - Mahan MSS
Washington, May 1, 1893

My dear Captain Mahan,

Last evening Lodge, Harry Davis, Admiral Luce and I held a solemn council of war, with your last letter to me as a text; and as a result, taking advantage of Herbert's absence, I went up to see McAdoo, who is much more civilized, today. He is on our side; but he can do very little. I fear all hope for the War College (which is nothing without you) has gone; our prize idiots here have thrown away the chance to give us an absolutely unique position in Naval affairs; but I made a very strong bid to at least give you the *Miantonomah*. The obstacle is of course Ramsay, who is bitterly opposing it, or anything else that may help you; he is a blind, narrow, mean, jealous pedant; if I can ever do him a bad turn I most certainly will—and I'll see that Lodge does. Lodge will see Herbert about the *Miantonomah* business.

Oh, what idiots we have had to deal with! And those "Century" geese! Well-meaning, good people, the *Century* folks; but their writing that there were not three men in the navy who could do your work was as if some one had said there were not ten men in the Navy who could do Farragut's.

Your article on Saumerez—May 1893 *Atlantic Monthly* was admirable; of course you will gather all these short essays into a volume some day. By the way, was the action you alluded to as ranking with Rodney's, that of Hawke?

LC - Mahan MSS
Oyster Bay, June 13, 1893

Dear Captain Mahan,

I greatly enjoyed the clipping from the *Tribune*. What a real donkey the *Evening Post* is! and what fearful mental degeneracy results from reading it, or the *Nation* as a steady thing—witness Judge Cooley. Well, I hate to have you abandon our own war-history, even temporarily; but you are the one man to write a history of Nelson, and such a history we ought to have.

Good luck go with you!

*Letters & Papers*, 2: 281
June 6, 1894

My dear Mr. Roosevelt:

By some unknown detention your letter of March 27 only reached me within the week. I hasten to assure you that I did not take in the least amiss what you said to me about extreme care. I fully recognize both the spirit and wisdom of your advice and have directed myself assiduously to carrying on duty thoroughly.

By this same mail I write to Mr. Lodge a letter he may probably show you. Being still in ignorance of the terms of Erben's indorsement, I can make no comment on it; but if it be as the press say, he has, so to say, introduced new matter in the cross-examination without allowing me the opportunity to rebut—which is contrary alike to justice and to reputations.

You will have seen how heartily we have been received over here. It has been a great pleasure, but has also involved a good deal of burden. Nevertheless, I confess to have derived great satisfaction from the lavish expressions of appreciation given to me personally—that is, to my work. To have an ex-first lord say he never understood how they downed Napoleon, and a veteran admiral that he had never before comprehended the first of June [battle], gave me ground to hope that I might yet be of some use to a navy, despite adverse reports. Still a clear writer may not be a first rate officer.

Rest assured I shall do my best to deserve the confidence you have so graciously expressed—and I believe I may truthfully say the *Chicago* is—and has always been—a well looked-after ship.

*Letters & Papers*, 2: 505–6
May 1, 1897

PERSONAL & PRIVATE

My dear Roosevelt:

You will I hope allow me at times to write to you on service matters, without thinking that I am doing more than throw out ideas for consideration. I had occasion to look over a file of the London *Times* yesterday, April 12–17, & there found a statement of the naval programme of Japan, which I think would be important to you to keep in mind. It is to be complete only in 1906, but you need not be told that one has to look far ahead now in building ships. That there is danger of trouble with her towards Hawaii, I think beyond doubt; if this administration is not able to put those islands under our wing, Mr. Cleveland's name will be immortalized a century hence by one thing only, that he refused them when he could have had them. Closely related to this is the need of strengthening our Pacific squadron. In my opinion, rendered decisive by the Venezuela affair, we have much more likelihood of trouble on that side than in the Atlantic. I don't know whether the battle ships we have can make the voyage—their coal endurance is small. Corollary: in building war ships, build on the Pacific side. Also, your best Admiral needs to be in the Pacific. Much more initiative *may* be thrown on him than *can* on the Atlantic man. I would suggest also, as bearing upon the general policy of the Administration, that the real significance of the Nicaragua canal now is that it advances our Atlantic frontier by so much to the Pacific, & that in Asia, not in Europe, is now the greatest danger to our proximate interests. It may be observed that it would suit Russia to see us in trouble with Japan, who is her own most knotty problem at present.

Of course Japan is a small and a poor state, as compared to ourselves; but the question is are we going to allow her to dominate the future of those most important islands because of our lethargy. It may very well happen, if we shut our eyes. I do not know your chief, but I fancy that at his age & having lived his life in what a clever Boston woman styled to me the "backwater" of Boston society, he regards the annexation of the islands, if offered, as an insoluble political problem. To this, in my mind, the only reply is: Do nothing unrighteous; but as regards the problem, take them first and solve

afterwards. Had Cleveland taken the islands, we would not be
threatened with the present mess. There is, in the same file of the
*Times*, a long letter, three or four columns, on Japan, Russia & Co-
rea. In it (I think) occurs the remark that the Japanese are devot-
edly friendly to the U.S. I am quite willing to hope it, & if so it will
much facilitate diplomacy; but withal there should be the most cour-
teous firmness in intimating that the propinquity of Hawaii makes
it our supreme concern. I remember when the Chilians would have
torn out their eyes for us—in 1866.

You will, I am sure, take this letter as it is meant, as a mere bun-
dle of thoughts.

(P.S.) I shall not mention my writing.

PSU - TR Papers, Series 2, Reel 313
May 3, 1897

*Personal and Private*

My dear Captain Mahan:

This letter must, of course, be considered as entirely confidential,
because in my position I am merely carrying out the policy of the
Secretary and the President. I suppose I need not tell you that as
regards Hawaii I take your views absolutely, as indeed I do on foreign policy generally. If I had my way we would annex those islands
tomorrow. If that is impossible I would establish a protectorate over
them. I believe we should build the Nicaraguan canal at once, and
in the meantime that we should build a dozen new battle ships, half
of them on the Pacific Coast; and these battle ships should have
large coal capacity and a consequent increased radius of action. I am
fully alive to the danger from Japan, and I know that it is idle to
rely on any sentimental good will towards us. I think President
Cleveland's action was a colossal crime, and we should be guilty of
aiding him after the fact if we do not reverse what he did. I earnestly hope we can make the President look at things our way. Last
Saturday night Lodge pressed his views upon him with all his
strength. I have been getting matters in shape on the Pacific coast
just as fast as I have been allowed. My own belief is that we should
act instantly before the two new Japanese warships leave England. I
would send the *Oregon* and, if necessary, also the *Monterrey* (either
with a deck load of coal or accompanied by a coaling ship) to Hawaii, and would hoist our flag over the island leaving all details for
after action. I shall press these views upon my chief just so far as he
will let me; more I cannot do.

As regards what you say in your letter, there is only one point to which I would take exception. I fully realize the immense importance of the Pacific coast. Strictly between ourselves, I do not think Admiral Beardslee quite the man for the situation out there, but Captain Barker, of the *Oregon*, is, I believe, excellent in point of decisions, willingness to accept responsibility, and thorough knowledge of the situation. But there are big problems in the West Indies also. Until we definitely turn Spain out of those islands (and if I had my way that would be done tomorrow), we will always be menaced by trouble there. We should acquire the Danish Islands, and by turning Spain out should serve notice that no strong European power, and especially not Germany, should be allowed to gain a foothold by supplanting some weak European power. I do not fear England; Canada is a hostage for her good behavior; but I do fear some of the other powers. I am extremely sorry to say that there is some slight appearance here of the desire to stop building up the Navy until our finances are better. Tom Reed, to my astonishment and indignation, takes this view, and even my chief, who is one of the most high-minded, honorable and upright gentlemen I have ever had the good fortune to serve under, is a little inclined toward it.

I need not say that this letter must be strictly private. I speak to you with the greatest freedom, for I sympathize with your views, and I have precisely the same idea of patriotism, and of belief in and love for our country. But to no one else excepting Lodge do I talk like this.

As regards Hawaii I am delighted to be able to tell you that Secretary Long shares our views. He believes we should take the islands, and I have just been preparing some memoranda for him to use at the Cabinet meeting tomorrow. If only we had some good man in the place of John Sherman as Secretary of State there would not be a hitch, and even as it is I hope for favorable action. I have been pressing upon the Secretary, and through him on the President, that we ought to act now without delay, before Japan gets her two new battle ships which are now ready for delivery to her in England. Even a fortnight may make a difference. With Hawaii once in our hands most of the danger of friction with Japan would disappear.

The Secretary also believes in building the Nicaraguan canal as a military measure, although I don't know that he is as decided on this point as you and I are; and he believes in building battle ships on the Pacific slope.

*Letters & Papers*, 2: 507
May 6, 1897

PERSONAL AND PRIVATE

My Dear Roosevelt:

Your letter has been read and destroyed. You will believe that
when I write to you it is only to suggest thoughts, or give information, not with any wish otherwise to influence action, or to ask information. I have known myself too long not to know that I am the
man of thought, not the man of action. Such an one may beneficially
throw out ideas, the practical effect of which can rest only, and be
duly shaped only, by practical men. The comparison may seem vain
but it may be questioned whether Adam Smith could have realised
upon his own ideas as Pitt did.

With reference to Barker, you have an admirable man—few more
so. He is extremely conscientious, and in such a case—and for officials generally—it is necessary that instructions be perfectly clear
on the view of the government. All other conscientious scruples in a
military mind disappear before the fundamental duty of obedience;
but government must speak clearly, without ifs and buts. Even Nelson asked this (Vol. II, p. 253). Miller is the same.

There are two things that may be interesting to you to recall now.
One—personal to myself—is that my article in the *Forum* on Hawaii, four years ago, was elicited by a previous letter of mine to the
*N.Y. Times*, pointing out that the question of the future of Hawaii
was rather Mongolian than European. Page, seeing this, asked for
the magazine article. The circumstance is of interest only as showing the crass blindness of the last administration, to which we now
owe a very real present danger of war, easily foreseen then. The second thing to recall is the anxiety we all felt at the time of the Chili
trouble over the progress of the *Prat*, we not then having any battleship. Today the same situation recurs; shall two Japanese battleships appear when we have but one and a Monitor? Armaments do
not in this day exist primarily to fight, but to avert war. Preparedness deters the foe, and right by show of superior force without use
of violence. It is lamentable to have to insist on such common-
places—more applications of the situation to which I call your attention may reinforce your argument; but at times I despair of our
country arousing until too late to avert prolonged and disastrous
conflict. In my last lecture to the Lowell Institute I said "The decision not to bring under the authority of one's own government some
external position, when just occasion offers, may by future generations be bewailed in tears of blood." God forbid.

PSU - TR Papers, Series 2, Reel 313
May 17, 1897

My dear Captain Mahan:

All I can do toward pressing our ideas into effect will be done, as I am sure you need not to be told. Do write me from time to time, because there are many, many points which you will see that I should miss.

Let me ask you a personal question. Have you finished your history of the Revolutionary War for Laird Clowes? I am going to send him in a fortnight my piece on the War of 1812. When do you intend to get out your book on the War of 1812? I take some interest in it because I rather hope they won't come out at the same time, not so much for my own sake as for Clowes; for what you say will be the final word on the subject, and will be rightfully so accepted.

PSU - TR Papers, Series 2, Reel 313
June 9, 1897

*PERSONAL*

My dear Mahan:

I have shown that very remarkable letter to the Secretary. Yesterday I urged immediate action by the President as regards Hawaii. Entirely between ourselves, I believe he will act very shortly. If we take Hawaii now, we shall avoid trouble with Japan, but I get very despondent at times over the blindness of our people, especially of the best educated classes.

In strict confidence I want to tell you that Secretary Long is only luke-warm about building up our Navy, at any rate as regards battleships. Indeed, he is against adding to our battleships. This is, to me, a matter of the most profound concern. I feel that you ought to write to him—not immediately, but some time not far in the future—at some length, explaining to him the vital need of continuity in our naval policy. [N.B.: "forces" changed to "policy".] Make the plea that this is a measure of peace and not of war. I cannot but think your words would carry weight with him.

He didn't like the address I made to the war college at Newport the other day. I shall send it to you when I get a copy.

I do not congratulate you upon the extraordinary compliment paid you by the Japanese, only because I know you care more for what we are doing with the Navy than for any compliment.
P.S. I reenclose that letter.

PSU - TR Papers, Series 2, Reel 314
August 30, 1897

My dear Captain Mahan:

Just a line to say what a noble article that was of yours in *Harper's*. It did me good to read it.

By the way, I was amused the other day to see in the *Popular Science Monthly* an article by an unknown person named Franklin Smith, in the course of which he attacked me as a "typical representative of modern barbarism," chiefly because of a review of mine of "one of Captain Mahan's laudations of naval barbarism". I wish very much I could get a chance to see you. There are a number of things about which I want to get your advice, and a number of other things I would like to talk over with you.

PSU - TR Papers, Series 2, Reel 315
December 9, 1897

My dear Captain Mahan:

I wish you could grant Mr. Hartwell's request. Senator Hoar is in doubt what to do about Hawaii. There is serious danger of Congress not backing up the President. It seems incredible that such short-sighted folly should obtain among our public men, but it does. If we refuse these islands, then I honestly hope England will take them if only to bring back to our people the knowledge of their folly.

P.S. I don't suppose that Mr. Hartwell needs to be introduced to you, but if you require anything more than the fact that he is my personal friend, I may mention that he is a great crony of Henry Adams and John LaFarge.

PSU - TR Papers, Series 2, Reel 315
December 11, 1897

My dear Captain Mahan:

I will try to persuade Hoar to read that book, but I earnestly hope you have written him personally. I agree with all you say as to what will be the result if we fail to take Hawaii. It will show that we either have lost, or else wholly lack, the masterful instinct which alone can make a race great. I feel so deeply about it I hardly dare express myself in full. The terrible part is to see that it is the men of education who take the lead in trying to make us prove traitors to our race.

PSU - TR Papers, Series 2, Reel 315
December 11, 1897

[Telegram]

Captain A. T. Mahan,

Think it very important you should write Hoar personally at once not mentioning me.

PSU - TR Papers, Series 2, Reel 315
December 13, 1897

My dear Captain Mahan:

I am exceedingly obliged for what you did about Hoar. My telegram was sent after consultation with Lodge and one or two others of the friends of Hawaii. It is bitter that there should be the necessity of taking action at all; but, as you say, it is due to the men of a by-gone age having to deal with facts of the present, complicated in this case with the further fact that we have in America among our educated men a kind of belated survivor of the little English movement among the Englishmen of thirty years back. They are provincials, and like all provincials, keep step with the previous generation of the metropolis. The American who are not provincials don't suffer from this trouble.

PSU - TR Papers, Series 2, Reel 315
December 14, 1897

My dear Captain Mahan:

I had seen those allusions in the papers. I am glad you liked the President's message. So did I, very much.

I share often the feelings you rather bitterly express in your letter; but I take a grim consolation in thinking that we have acted quite as foolishly during the past hundred years as we possibly can act now, and yet we have lived through trial after trial, and so we shall continue to do. At any rate your creed and mine is, and must be, resolute to do our best to stand by our country to the utmost of our power, and to accept whatever comes. I showed your letter to the President, who was much pleased with it.

PSU - TR Papers, Series 2, Reel 315
January 3, 1898

My dear Captain Mahan:

Having the historical 'sense', your project appeals to me and I shall see if it can't be put through.

I trust I shall have the pleasure of meeting you next Sunday. I think my sister has asked you to dinner. The Hawaiian matter is just touch-and-go, but I am inclined to think we shall get the republican party solid, and some democrats.

I shall speedily send you a copy of my report on the personnel bill.

PSU - TR Papers, Series 2, Reel 315
January 5, 1898

My dear Captain Mahan:

I send you herewith my report on the personnel bill. I have marked one or two sentences which I think embody really the most important part of what I have to say.

I shall look forward to seeing you next Sunday afternoon.

P.S. After consultation with the Bureau of Yards and Docks I have asked the Secretary to recommend that Congress should erect that memorial on the [balance is missing]

PSU - TR Papers, Series 2, Reel 315
January 8, 1898

My dear Captain Mahan:

Mrs. Roosevelt was suddenly taken with a very severe attack of grippe, and as her baby is very young it threatened serious complications, and I was unable to leave. I am exceedingly sorry. I will be in New York on Thursday or Friday, the 27th and 28th—certainly Friday. I earnestly hope that I can arrange to meet you then. What are your engagements at that time?

Present my regards and regrets to Mrs. Mahan.

PSU - TR Papers, Series 2, Reel 315
March 10, 1898

My dear Captain Mahan:

Your statement about the Hawaiians is literally correct. The statistics show a curiously steady diminution year by year. The original

Hawaiian blood will remain only [through?] [as?] the half-breeds [remain] between them [and] the intrusive white and yellow races.

Mrs. Roosevelt has been very sick. I think she is now a little better.

I earnestly wish that my chief would get you on here to consult in the present crisis.

PSU - TR Papers, Series 2, Reel 315
March 14, 1898

My dear Captain Mahan:

I entirely agree with you. A year ago, when we had seven armored ships against the Spanish fleet, I thought a flying squadron might be of use; at present we have six against eight, and I don't think so. We are taking the *Oregon* around, and I hope that she will be at Cuba by the time the *Pelayo* may be gotten out of Toulon and sent across. You know my opinion pretty well. We should have struck a year and a half ago, when our superiority of forces was great, and when we could have saved Cuba before it was ruined. Every month since the situation has changed slightly to our disadvantage, and it will continue so to change. It is the case of the sibylline books again. We should fight this minute in my opinion, before the torpedo-boats get over here. But we won't. We'll let them get over here and run the risk of serious damage from them, and very possibly we won't fight until the beginning of the rainy season, when to send an expeditionary force to Cuba means to see the men die like sheep.

I send you a copy of a letter I submitted to the Secretary two months ago. Will you please send it back to me? I agree with you that we should not try to do anything much with Porto Rico at present.

I think much better of the *Brooklyn* than you do, but quite as badly of the *Minneapolis* and *Columbia*. I further agree with you with all my heart about local coast defense. I shall urge, and have urged, the President and the Secretary to pay absolutely no heed to the outcries for protection from Spanish raids. Take the worst—a bombardment of New York. It would amount to absolutely nothing, as affecting the course of a war, or damaging permanently the prosperity of the country. I should not myself divert a ship from the Cuban waters for any threat against our coast, bar always that I should protect the battleships building at Newport News. However, I am afraid we shall have to make up our minds that a monitor will be sent to Boston, another to New York, and another to Newport News—of which last I should entirely approve.

I am going to show your letter to Captain Goodrich and also to the Secretary. I have Captain Goodrich at work on a plan of attack for we haven't a plan of any kind excepting that prepared last June.

PSU - TR Papers, Series 2, Reel 315
March 14, 1898

My dear Captain Mahan:

I have just seen the Secretary and he says by all means you ought to go. I showed him your confidential letter, as well as the other. In view of what he says I think you would be unwise to give up going; moreover, I fear the President does not intend that we shall have war if we can possibly avoid it. I read to him your typewritten letter, dwelling upon the first page, saying that the one important thing to my mind would be to disregard minor punishment, and devote our attention to smashing Spain in Cuba.
With warm regards to Mrs. Mahan,

PSU - TR Papers, Series 2, Reel 315
March 16, 1898

My dear Captain Mahan:

I send you a plan of campaign which we have developed. It is of course purely tentative until we know what we are to fight, and when. Will you send it back to me with any comments you see fit to make.

PSU - TR Papers, Series 2, Reel 315
March 21, 1898

My dear Captain Mahan:

There is no question that you stand head and shoulders above the rest of us! You have given us just the suggestions we want. I am going to show your letter to the Secretary first, and then get some members of the board to go over it.
Personally, I can hardly see how we can avoid intervening in Cuba if we are to retain our self-respect as a nation.
You probably don't know how much your letter has really helped me clearly to formulate certain things which I had only vaguely in mind. I think I have studied your books to pretty good purpose. If I can get the Secretary to enunciate just the policy about promotions

which you advocate, I am sure it will help us more than anything else.

I enclose the letter from the Italian Embassy.

Pray give my warm regards to Mrs. Mahan.

P.S. There are mines off Fort Monroe, and in the fort three modern 10-inch rifles, and a number of good mortars. These, with a couple of small harbor torpedo-boats, would I think be enough to prevent a raid on Hampton Roads by a hostile fleet.

PSU - TR Papers, Series 2, Reel 315
March 24, 1898

My dear Captain Mahan:

Again I thank you for suggestions that are very valuable. I need not tell you however—what I learned from your books long before I had any practical experience—that it is out of the question at the last moment to improvise efficient war vessels, small or great. All we can do is to get makeshifts capable of approximately decent service. Revenue cutters, lighthouse tenders, yachts and tugboats we are now getting. We are putting on them what guns we can scrape together and they will carry, and we will supply them with a view [obviously, "few" is meant here] regular officers and a few man-of-warsmen from the fleet, with a big lot of raw recruits, because we cannot denude the battleships of officers and men. These craft will be from one-half to two-thirds as fast as the torpedo-boats against which they will be pitted. They will not be as noiseless or as invisible, and they will have fewer guns, and only here and there a torpedo tube. It is not necessary to say that they will constitute far from an ideal flotilla, but it will be the best we can improvise.

We have at least got the right men as commander and second in command of the Key West fleet. I shall give Captain Evans all your letters to me to take down and show to Captain Sampson, and afterwards to return them to me.

I think I told you that I advised the President and the Secretary to treat the sailing of the torpedo flotilla from the Canaries for Porto Rico as an act of hostility. I have repeated the advice today. I do not think it will be regarded.

Your address will be kept, and I can assure you we will communicate with you at once in the event of need.

P.S. I quite agree with what you say as to administering this office. I have been under a great strain this winter owing to the long and critical sickness of both my wife and my oldest son.

PSU - TR Papers, Series 2, Reel 319
January 3, 1899

My dear Captain Mahan:

I have your letter of the first.

I have not been asked to attend the Colonial Club Dinner. I think
I can go to it. Where is it to be, what hour, etc.?

Shall I see you at the Century on Friday?


PSU - TR Papers, Series 2, Reel 322
January 17, 1900

My dear Captain Mahan:

My sister, Mrs. Douglas Robinson, No. 422 Madison Avenue,N.Y.
is going to ask you to lunch next Saturday, the 20th inst at one
oclock. Do come! I shall be so glad to see you.

Did you see my article in *The Independent* on Expansion and
Peace? I think you would like it.


*Letters & Papers*, 2: 676
January 18, 1900

My dear Governor:

I shall look forward with pleasure to meeting you at Mr. Robinson's on Saturday. I infer from the papers you have a very difficult
task in the Payn matter, but I am also confident that if you decide it
in utter disregard of the effect on your own future—which I am sure
you will—you will be guided aright. You won't mind my saying that
I hope the power of the Spirit may rest upon you in this.

I almost never see *The Independent*, but shall look up your article
at the Club.


PSU - TR Papers, Series 2, Reel 323
February 14th, 1900

My dear Captain Mahan:

I have yours of the 15th [13th?] and am very glad you approve of
my action about the Vice Presidency.

As you know, I am heartily friendly to England, but I cannot help
feeling that the State Department has made a great error in the
canal treaty. We really make not only England but all the great

continental powers our partners in the transaction, and I do not see why we should dig the canal if we are not to fortify it so as to insure its being used for ourselves and against our foes in time of war.

PSU - TR Papers, Series 2, Reel 324
June 16, 1900

My dear Captain:

I thank you heartily for your letter of the 12th inst. and agree with you absolutely about myself and the Governorship. I do not believe that White will be seriously considered as a vice-presidential candidate. Perhaps Frank Greene will be.

PSU - TR Papers, Series 2, Reel 324
August 2, 1900

My dear Captain Mahan:

This is to introduce to you Rev. Josiah Strong, the man for whom I have the very highest regard and the man who has consistently championed both manliness and morality—a combination which seems wholly uncomprehensible. I most cordially commend him to your consideration and courtesy.

PSU - TR Papers, Series 2, Reel 324
August 7, 1900

My dear Captain Mahan:

I thank you very much for your letter. I understand just how you feel. I am more than impatient with the machine myself. I turned down Mr. Platt and his followers at Philadelphia in great shape, but the demand in the West was very strong for me to be nominated and I could not without giving a black eye to the ticket well refuse. It seems to me that the crisis of this year is even more serious than in '96 and even of '64, and if I am able to be of assistance to the National ticket, why, I am entirely satisfied, though it was a great disappointment to me personally [not] to have the governorship in New York.

Now, as to voting the Democratic state ticket. That seems to me to be an extreme measure this year, so long as the Republicans put up an honest man. Men who run as a Democratic Governor must necessarily approve the Kansas City platform. I do not think that such a

man could be elected. Moreover, while it is entirely ... [proper] for
an intellectual man to vote against the [Republican candidate for]
Governor while supporting the presidential ticket, it is certain to
produce the effect of making some men vote the straight democratic
ticket. It does not seem to me that we can afford to sacrifice the
greater to the lesser need.

*Letters & Papers*, 2: 706–8
March 12, 1901

To Theodore Roosevelt

My dear Vice President:

It has been my purpose, somewhat vague I fear, to write you at
any time since election, congratulating you on the event; but I have
been busy, & I knew you had many to perform to you that function
of felicitation, & moreover I did not so wholly congratulate myself
upon the concomitant result of your removal from the Governorship
here. Truth to say, it seems to me I need not deny myself the deplor-
able satisfaction of feeling that my premonitions were correct. So far
as I can understand matters, it seems to me that your successor is
showing far less than the sound judgment & discretion which you,
despite a temper impetuous & not overcautious, appeared to me to
display in your general course.

I do, however, rejoice in one thing; and that is that you are with-
drawn perforce, & not by your own volition, for a prolonged rest
from the responsibilities and cares of office. ... Idle it is not in you to
be; but work is a very different thing from the grinding friction of
executive office on a large scale. A very sagacious clergyman once
remarked to me on the providential ordering in the life of St. Paul—
whose career, I think, you will agree was at the least strenuous—by
which in midcourse he was arrested, and spent two years of enforced
inactivity under Felix in Judaea, followed by two more in the Ro-
man captivity. The total, four, as you will observe, is just a Vice
Presidential term; & I trust this period may be to you, as it was to
him, a period of professional rest coupled with great intellectual advance and ripening.

As you were in Washington on the 3d., I propose to send you the
number of the *Sun* for that day, which has my paper on the development of naval material during the century. It is not amiss to observe
that it was sent in before the Spanish War, & never revised beyond
proofreading. I was satisfied to let my conclusions of 1897 stand.

I hope you may read—but I don't ask to know whether you do—

my *Problem of Asia*. It ought to be, & I intend it shall be, my swan's song on contemporary politics. I become continually more and more convinced that the average man can't tell—as years advance—when he has really got out of touch with the times, & becomes a mere "wind-jammer"—to use a naval expression for useless talk. Look at the eminently respectable Mr. Howe, and I fear Mr. Harrison also. If his present illness prove fatal, what a pity it will seem that he did not get out, or be silent, before he wrote his recent articles. I haven't read them, but have gathered their drift. I trust it may not be so with us, but I feel—itself perhaps an indication that I am dropping behind—that neither we nor Great Britain, separate or combined, can adequately check Russia by main force in Northern China; and that therefore naval power always at hand & available in the Yangtze valley—the heart of China in every sense of the word—is the true counter-check. It will work in two ways; (1) it will at once humanize and strengthen China, the surest element of resistance to Russian mastery, & to consequent brutalizing of Chinese develop-ment; & (2) its pressure will operate by force of moral assurance to Russia, that trespass as she will in our quarter, a solid core of resist-ance, invincible, is building up in the decisive field & will be per-fected before she can have strength to reach so far. If the Sea Powers,to reach [?] physical and moral support in the Yang Tse, will require of China simple, but entire, liberty of entrance for European thought, as well as European commerce, China will in my judgment be saved, or rather, & better, will save herself.

Such I say, & hope, is my swan song. After sixty, one can't tell how soon behindedness will be his lot; but I cannot but hope that this idea may enter, for whatever it is worth, into the grasp of one who by years has still much of activity & growth before him & by achievement & promise the reasonable prospect of affecting, for good or ill, the future course of a great Christian State.

*Letters & Papers*, 2: 708
March 12, 1901

My dear Mr. Roosevelt:

It has occurred to me that the enclosed might interest you as bear-ing on very current foreign politics. The writer is the Missionary Bishop of the Episcopal Church in the Yangtze valley—at Shang-hai—and is very highly esteemed by all who know him. I have never met him. Don't trouble to return the letter.

PSU - TR Papers, Series 2, Reel 325
March 18th, 1901

My dear Captain Mahan:

I have received both your letters. Yes, I have read with the greatest interest your Asiatic Problems, and in the main, with entire agreement. I feel that the United States and England should so far as possible work together in China, and that their co-operation and the effective use of sea power on behalf of civilization and progress which this co-operation would mean in the valley of the Yangtse Kiang, is of the utmost importance for the future of Asia, and therefore of the world. But I do not have to tell you, with your wide and profound historical research, that while something can be done by public mean[s] in leading the people, they cannot lead them much further than public opinion has prepared the way. They can lead them somewhat further, but not very much. Now, as yet our [public?] opinion is dull on the question of China, and moreover, we are all somewhat in the dark as to the true facts. For instance, take the letter of the Bishop, which I return. The best men from whom I have heard about China, including our officers, naval and military, and writers like Millard and Doyle (an American and an Englishman) take exactly the opposite view from that taken by the Bishop. Generals Chaffee and Wilson feel that the awful outrages committed by many of the European troops, notably by the Russians, French and even Japanese, and the wanton so-called punitive expeditions of the German troops, and indeed the original misconduct of some of the foreigners, notably the Germans and Russians, have left the count against us rather than against the Chinese. I wish you could see some of the reports of our officers as to the misconduct even of some of our missionaries. Did you read Millard's articles in the *Scribners*?

All this of course has nothing to do with the principles you lay down, which to my mind are eminently sound. I am very sorry that there should be any complexity caused by what I feel is England's unwisdom in refusing to accept what I again feel to be our entirely proper proposals about the Nicaragua Canal and the Alaskan boundary. From the standpoint of world interests, the questions are not nearly as important as what is happening in China. But our people feel much more keenly about them.

For Heaven's sake, my dear Captain, do not talk about your activities ending! We must rely upon you as one of the foremost educators of public thought, and I trust for many years to come. I agree with all you say as to [portion written is undecipherable] ex-Presi-

dent Harrison's later utterances. But he rendered great service in
his day, and now "peace to his ashes."

I greatly wish to see you and have a long talk with you.

PSU - TR Papers, Series 2, Reel 327
December 11, 1901

My dear Captain Mahan:

I thank you cordially for the book and for your letter. Most of the
chapters of the book I know, for I have read them as magazine articles. By the way, I believe you will like what I said of the Navy in
my message.

*Letters & Papers*, 3: 6–7
January 25, 1902

My dear Mr. Roosevelt:

That you should in the past, before you became President, have
given consideration to some of my opinions in matters upon which I
might be supposed to know something, is a poor excuse for intruding
where I cannot be thought to have particular knowledge. I hope,
however, that certain general considerations may make this step
less inexcusable than it might appear.

I have been, frankly, frightened by the very drastic recommendations of Judge Taft, foreshadowed in his free communications to the
Press, concerning the reduction of the force in the Philippines; and
my suggestion is this: Would it not be well to ask of the Philippine
Commission, and of the Commanding General in the Philippines,
separate estimates, itemized as an Appropriation Bill would be, of
the force necessary; not in general terms only, but by localities? The
total would be determined by the aggregate of the particular forces
thus calculated.

This would amount in effect to a kind of plan of campaign, con-
templating the possibility of a more or less extensive insurrection,
among a people naturally treacherous and so lately in general re-
volt. The distribution of force for such a contingency, its localization
in numbers, the capacity of localities for mutual support, all have to
enter into consideration. Upon these, too, there needs to be allowed
a margin of safety.

This of course is a calculation essentially military, while Judge
Taft's ideas proceed on his conceptions of the civil condition. He has,

however, in his reported interviews, committed himself to specification of numbers. Where does he get it?

I need not appeal to your historical knowledge of the disastrous effects of insufficient power at a needed point, as in British India in 1857. All would doubtless agree that it will be more economical for the United States to keep 20,000 men too many, five years longer than they are needed, than to remove the same number six months too soon. As for the islands themselves, and their welfare, even more is at stake in the alternative between internal quiet and intestine strife. Nor can a people that have endured Spanish soldiery three centuries feel ours as an indignity; however petty chiefs, impatient of restraint, may resent them.

*Letters & Papers*, 3: 38–40
October 16, 1902

To Theodore Roosevelt

There is much to be said on the side of individual power for battle ships, as well as on the side of numbers. Therefore, it is not an unqualified certainty, but only a preponderance of argument that can be adduced for limiting size in favor of numbers.

The primary consideration is that the battle ship is meant always to act with others, not alone. Strategically, and yet more tactically, this demands homogeneousness. In the battle ship, one is designing a class, not a unit. This imposes upon the designer conditions other than those of the single ship, especially in tactical qualities, such as dimensions, speed and turning power. These should be harmonized by an antecedent determination of a size, to which battle ships must conform during a measurable future. This object may be attained by designing a class, forming a tactical unit, to be completed simultaneously. This is the least demand; but I believe calculation could be pressed to the further extent of controlling shipbuilding hereafter; nearly as the recognized 74 once did, admitting variations in gun power, but not in nautical qualities.

In my *Lessons of the War with Spain*, pp. 36–42, I have stated, with detail and illustration, the argument for numbers against size—given the same aggregate tonnage—as clearly as I think I now can do. These are summarized in the words: "War depends largely upon combination, and facility of combination increases with numbers. Numbers therefore, mean increase of offensive power, other things remaining equal." By a comparison made by me when then writing, I found that from the 10,000 to the 15,000 ton ship (in the British Navy), there was, as my memory now serves me, little more broadside gain than one six-inch rapid fire gun. In conversation with the present Chief of the Bureau of Equipment—an extremely able officer—I understood him to admit this, but to advocate increase of size on account of coal endurance. This is a very important consideration; but to my mind, it can in no wise justify an increase of nearly fifty per cent in tonnage with less than ten per cent of offensive power. All questions of communications—which coal supply essentially is—are subordinate to the offensive power to which they minister. The inconvenience of coal renewal can be alleviated, but not obviated; and the extent of alleviation should not overpass absolute necessity, if offensive power thereby suffers.

The same remark applies to speed. Beyond a certain point not difficult of approximation, it should not be purchased by increase of size. Speed is under distinct limitations as a strategic quality, and as a tactical unit it can be sufficiently insured—for chase, for example—by the armored cruiser; that is, by a class of battle ship—relatively few—in which speed is purchased by some sacrifice of fighting strength;—an exception, for exceptional purposes.

The conflict of interest in the organs of administration, I believe to be the main cause of increasing size. The chief object appears to be to satisfy all demands. Here enters an underlying administrative defect. Professional opinion is not represented; and no conception of a standard battle ship is framed or even imagined. It cannot be, for a majority consensus does not exist, much less has received formulation. To illustrate: The old 74 represented a professional consensus, reached by long experience and accepted, if not formulated. It therefore controlled the ship building, intrusted to a civil administrative board. We have now neither the experience, nor the time, our predecessors had. We must therefore, be at pains to supply by reflection what they gained by experience. Size and other qualities are now determined by administrative officers. The sea-officer is not represented, except as he finds place in the administration proper. As soon as he does so, he represents a particular interest—speed, or armor, or coal endurance; what not. He becomes an advocate, on the board which decides qualities. What is needed supremely is an organ, wholly detached from administration, to evolve conclusions which shall stand for the professional opinion of the instructed sea-officer; of the man who cares nothing about the administrative processes, but simply for the fighting efficiency of the ship. Such an organ, be it one man or many, might conceivably realize—what a group of administrative officers never will—that a ship is not an aggregation of functions, each of which gets all it can—(in order to which, each ship must be bigger than the last)—but that it has, according to its class, one dominating object to which all others must be subordinated. Like war in general, a war ship is a work of art, a unit in conception; not an aggregation of incompatibilities.

A distinguished British Naval architect—Scott Russell, I think— once defined the relative function of the sea-officer and the naval architect, thus: Let the naval officer tell us what he wants—nautical qualities, guns, armor, coal endurance, etc., and then leave us to produce the article. The production of the article is the administrative function: for the function of conception, for ascertaining what the sea-officer needs, no provision exists, either in accepted professional opinion, or in such an organ as I suggest. Yet this is what the Navy requires. Needless to say, it is not to be attained by polling the service, or by promiscuous discussion. These may offer useful side lights; but decision can only be had by consultation among a very few really enlightened officers, the essence of whose position in this respect should be that they are entirely unconcerned in administration and look only to the purpose which the particular ship is to serve in the fleet in campaign. Let them define her qualities.

PSU - TR Papers, Series 2, Reel 329
October 25, 1902

My dear Captain Mahan:

I enclose Admiral Bowles's memorandum which please return to me. He seems to show that instead of an increase of 50 percent in tonnage, meaning an increase of less than 10 percent of offensive power, which you state seems to be the case in the English navy, there is in the American navy an increase of 50 percent in offensive power for an increase of 25 percent in tonnage. I have had up Admirals Taylor and Bowles and have gone over the matter with them and they are now going over the matter further with the Secretary.

*Letters & Papers*, 3: 73–74
September 7, 1903

My dear Mr. Roosevelt:

It gave me much pleasure to know that you had found my books worth rereading, and still more to know that you had found time for holiday. A man may damage his private work by overwork if he like; but public affairs demand that officials keep their brains and faculties unjaded.

I do not now recall particularly the DeRuyter letters you mention. The only life I had was Gerard Brandt's huge folio of the seventeenth century when men had time to build monuments. I wonder whether the one you mention has the curious incident that, at the beginning of one of his many collisions with the English, he felt so perturbed with fear that he was unable to command his faculties. Finally, he retired to the cabin and said his prayers; after which his customary composure returned.

I doubt whether full justice has ever been done, or will be done him. He was, I imagine, better appreciated in his own day than ever since. As regards our own two instances you mention, there cannot be the slightest doubt, what the verdict of naval history will be. The Schley Court settles that, even if the unsworn testimony before had been insufficient. What has amazed me most is that after the Court—Dewey included—had found his coal reports "inaccurate and misleading," men of intelligence and position have been found to give him open welcome; ignoring what those words mean, if put into plain English. One of Dewey's officers said to me, "Upon the whole, I think I would rather have been found guilty of cowardice; for that may be the result of uncontrollable constitutional infirmity."

As regards Miles I know the matter only superficially. An incident which occurred immediately after my recall to Washington, in 1898, shook my faith in him; and what little I saw afterwards confirmed the impression. After this began his singular semi-political actions. Concerning these, I need only to say that to my mind the end stamps the career. If Finis Coronat Opus, doubtless it may be that Finis discoronat opus. I daresay this Latin is impeachable, but you will know what I mean. I entirely went with you in your omission of words of commendation.

Your administration bids fair to have accomplished two fundamental successes on the military side—Root's reorganization and the Naval General Staff Bill. As regards the latter, which I hope will pass in principle, it appears to me of the utmost importance that the designing of ships—their classes, numbers, and qualities—should be brought into direct relation with the naval policy and strategy of the country. This can never—in my judgment—be the case while these decisions are left to Bureau Chiefs. The General Staff having digested what will need to be done in time of war, can best and can alone pronounce the relative importance of the several qualities; subject to the revision of the President and Secretary. This or that man's views may be more or less valuable; but an organized body can alone impart accuracy, clearness and fixity, lasting from administration to administration.

P.S. The kindest remembrances from Mrs. Mahan and myself to Mrs. Roosevelt.

PSU - TR Papers, Series 2, Reel 336
November 21, 1904

My dear Captain Mahan:

Your letter pleases me greatly. I thank you for it.
I wish you could get on here. There are so many things I should like to speak to you about.

*Letters & Papers,* 3: 112–114
December 27, 1904

My dear Mr. President:

I have seen with concern that in issuing the invitation to a second Hague Conference, the United States puts in the foreground of subjects for consideration, the exemption from capture at sea of "private property." This proposition was, it is true, advanced by us at the first conference; but we then were not the initiating power, nor was this the subject of the call. It was side-issue entirely, introduced by President McKinley as part of the traditional policy of the United States. This it is; and for the very reason that it is not traditional demands consideration, as to whether it may not have lost the fitness it possibly once had to national conditions.

That measures which tend to exempt commerce, finance, and, so far, the general community, from the sufferings of war, will not make for peace seems to me a proposition scarcely worth arguing. The furor of war needs all the chastening it can receive in the human heart, to still the mad impulses towards conflict.

I must not attempt, however, to occupy the time of so busy a man with general consideration. I take the liberty of enclosing a few pages from the introductory chapters to my forthcoming *War of 1812*, in which I have—not developed—but outlined the argument, which I conceive makes inexpedient and illogical such a change in the laws of war.

Should you find time to read these, I would like to add that the general situation of the United States, in the world policy of today, appears to me to make most impolitic this change. Circumstances almost irresistible are forcing us and Great Britain, not into alliance, but into a silent cooperation, dependent upon conditions probably irreversible in the next two generations. Our united naval strength can probably control the seas; but there is always a remaining chance of a combination in the East—the Western Pacific—which might approach an equilibrium. The future and policy of China remains uncertain. It may very well be that under such conditions the

power to control commerce,—the lawful right international precedent now confers,—may be of immense, of decisive, importance.
Also, this may not be; but what is there in the world to compel us to
a proposal, which in itself does not involve a moral issue. There is
no more moral wrong in taking "private" property than in taking
private lives; and I think my point incontestable, that property employed in commerce is no more private, in uses, than lives employed
on the firing line are private. One is at the communications in the
rear, the other at the front.

The question is one of expediency; and what was expedient to our
weakness of a century ago is not expedient to our strength today.
Rather should we seek to withdraw from our old position of the flag
covering the goods. We need to fasten our grip on the sea. I need
not, I suppose, assure you that all this in no wise changes my known
position about "commerce destroying". From the first, as now, I have
held it "a most important secondary operation, not likely to be aban-
doned till war itself shall cease"; but as a primary measure a delu-
sion (*Sea Power*, p. 539).

It has occurred to me, as an agreement tending to lessen the expense of armaments, that nations might agree on a limitation of the
tonnage of single ships. Doubtless this would be only an ameliora-
tion, but I think it would have a tendency to introduce a slight
brake, a little modification, which might eventually be felt as a relief all round. The question of limiting armaments is very thorny; it
will not be helped, I think, by allaying fears that commerce, men's
pockets, will suffer in war.

PSU - TR Papers, Series 2, Reel 336
December 29, 1904

My dear Captain Mahan:

I am interested in your letter and the enclosure, and shall take
them up with John Hay. You open a big subject for discussion.
There is a strong tendency to protect private property and private
life on sea and land. Of course the earlier races killed or enslaved
every private citizen of the hostile nation whom they could get at
and destroyed or took his property as a matter of course. I shall
have to think over the matter before I could answer you at all definitely on this last proposition.

*Letters & Papers*, 3:139
September 9, 1905

My dear Mr. President:

A few days ago I turned up, among my papers the enclosed clipping from the *Manchester Guardian*, towards the end of the Hague Conference. It is so interesting an indication of the extreme views that have been, and will be, advocated at the Peace Conference, believed to lie again in the near future, that I think it worth your attention.

Article 27 was distasteful to all the powers represented, except France, where I think it voiced the views only of a coterie. Yet it passed, though not without strong protest from small states—notably the Balkan.

It may interest you further to know that the enclosed clipping, coming under the eye of the American delegation, was the immediate cause of the Declaration attached to their signatures, saving the Monroe doctrine.

PSU - TR Papers, Series 2, Reel 339
September 21, 1905

My dear Captain Mahan:

That is an interesting clipping. I entirely agree with you as to the danger to which the extreme peace men expose not only their own cause but the cause of civilization. We have to watch them quite as much as the demagogues of war.

With warm regards,

*Letters & Papers*, 3: 164–165
July 20, 1906 [August 14, 1906?]

Dear Mr. President:

When at Oyster Bay, I mentioned to you my wish to be free to write for publication concerning matters that might come before the approaching Hague Conference; notably the question of exemption of private property, so called, from maritime capture.

A very proper and necessary regulation of the Navy forbids officers discussing publicly matters of policy on which the Government is embarked. The question arises, however, is the Hague Conference a body where measures are to be advocated as national policies; or whether they are to be advanced for discussion, with a view to reaching improved conditions of the code, common to all, which we call International Law.

It is by no means necessary that any Government should formally announce either of the above as its own attitude; but should the second construction be adopted by our own, there could be no impropriety in a public officer contributing a properly worded argument on either side. Taking the particular measure I mention, our Government, I understand, has advanced it; but, in so doing, is it as a matter of national advantage so pronounced that opposition is improper, or is the matter one so far open to consideration that light may be welcomed, whencever coming.

It must be obvious to you that the present prepossession of the public mind in most countries is such that the question of War itself, and of questions incidental to War, are in danger of being prejudged and "rushed." One side only is clamorous. A special element of danger in this direction is the present British Government, with its huge heterogeneous majority to keep placated. With a Conservative Government there, we might afford to be persistent in our old national policy, safe that it would not be accepted, but would go over to a further conference; with the present, you will on military questions be playing with fire. But especially to be considered is the popular attitude in Germany towards the English speaking communities, and the effect of the exemption of private property upon her ambitions at their expense. Maritime transportation, and commercial movement, which is what so-called "private property" really amounts to, is now one of her great interests, and is steadily growing. Great Britain, and the British Navy, lie right across Germany's carrying trade with the whole world. Exempt it, and you remove the strongest hook in the jaws of Germany that the English speaking peoples have; a principal gage for peace.

British interests are not American interests, no. But taking the constitution of the British Empire, and the trade interests of the British Islands, the United States has certainty of a very high order that the British Empire will stand substantially on the same lines of world policy as ourselves; that its strength will be our strength, and the weakening it injury to us. Germany is inevitably ambitious of trans-marine development. I dont grudge it her. As proof, after the Spanish War I refused a suggestion to use my supposed influence against her acquisition of the Carolines, etc.; but her ambitions threaten us as well as Great Britain, and I cannot but think that final action on the question of so called private property at sea would be better deferred, and the question be thrown into the arena of discussion, that action when taken may be in full light. As yet the public has heard but one side. The instance I quoted before to you is in clear point. No doubt our Government a century ago would have signed away the right of commercial blockade, which so helped us in the Civil War.

When to Germany are added the unsolved questions of the Pacific, it may be said truly that the political future is without form and void. Darkness is upon the face of the deep. We will have to walk very warily in matters affecting the future ability to employ national force.

PSU - TR Papers, Series 2, Reel 342
August 16, 1906

My dear Captain Mahan:

I have your letter of the 14th instant. Your position is a peculiar one, and without intending to treat this as a precedent, I desire you to have a free hand to discuss in any way you wish the so-called peace proposals. You have a deserved reputation as a publicist which makes this proper from the public standpoint. Indeed I think it important for you to write just what you think of the matter.

PSU - TR Papers, Series 4A, Reel 416
September 27, 1906

Strictly Personal

My dear Captain Mahan:

Will you treat the enclosed copy of a letter from Commander Sims to me as entirely confidential and return it to me when you have read it?

*Letters & Papers*, 3: 178–80
October 8, 1906

Dear Mr. President:

Your letter enclosing Sim's paper arrived on Saturday, at a moment most unhappy for me. Not only was I crowded with work promised for the next three months, which made even the reading of his 26 close-spaced pages a task, but I am moving my household hence to-morrow.

In these three working days left me this week, I tried to frame a short paper of comment. This I have done, but not in such shape as to submit. I must leave this till I am settled again.

Meantime I return his paper, with thanks for the opportunity to read it, and submit a brief of the general argument.

Three facts are obvious:

1. A 12 inch gun is vastly more powerful than, say, an 8 inch.
2. A fleet, A, composed of ships the force of which is 1, is weaker than a fleet, B, of the same numbers, whose force is 1-1/4.
3. A fleet, A, the fleet speed of which is three knots less than the fleet B, is at some disadvantage.

These things, as the French say, *sautent aux yeux*. They are the first broadside of an argument, and produce the proverbial effect of the first broadside. To them are to be added, less obvious at first, that the concentration of force under one hand in one ship is superior to the same force in two or three ships; while economically, the same tonnage in big ships is more economically built and maintained than in smaller.

This constitutes the main weight of the argument against those who, with me, advocate gun-power rather than speed; numbers against size; and an "intermediate" battery in part, instead of "primary" alone. I leave aside the "secondary" now so styled.

The argument above stated is very heavy, to first sight overpowering; and, for this reason, those with whom decision rests should the more gravely consider the less obvious points, urged on the other side. These are:

1. That there must be numbers to considerable extent; and that, while ten 1½ ships are cheaper than the same tonnage in—say 15—smaller vessels, each 1½ ship costs much more than a 1 ship. Consequently, some time numbers will compel a halt in size, or will themselves become utterly inadequate.
2. That, with numbers, the power of combination increases, and combined action is the particular force of fleets. The problem will not have been adequately handled until a competent, unbiased, tribunal shall have considered exhaustively the combinations open to fleets, engaging with numbers equal and unequal.
3. That speed confers the power of the offensive: yes; but, if used for long range action, it allows the defensive, inevitably, a wide field of action, with interior lines upon which to manoeuvre, in such mutual support as may be wished; and with abundant power to act at will, so long as a range of, say, 3 miles is maintained. An approach within that range will narrow the field, but bring the intermediaries into surer play.
4. It seems probable that the greatest development of fire, to a fleet acting on

an outer circle, is represented by the column, the full broadside effect. Greater numbers, acting within, can mass effectively against such a disposition.

The above, though longer than I hoped, is but a brief. I do not pretend to be fully equipped in tactical resource, and hold myself retired, as a rule from such discussion, though I present my views when asked. The Institute asked me for a paper. I have now neither time nor inclination for exhaustive study of tactics; and have besides full preoccupation in other more congenial matters. Still, as far as they go, I think my views sound; and if sound, they are pertinent.

In the relation of primary and intermediary guns to fire control, I cannot place my undigested knowledge against that of Mr. Sims. I think, however, that, like most specialists, he overvalues the extent of fire control in battle. I believe the present system, with its admirable results, will in the day of battle justify itself amply; yet not so much by its own particular action as by the habits it will breed in officers and men. The regularity of the drill ground is felt in the field, not in a similar regularity, but by the induced habit of looking to one another; each part duly remembering the other and the whole; not elbow touch but fire support.

When I am settled again, I will endeavor to send you the paper of comment.

P.S. I enclose a clipping, and will mention that *Blackwood's* for this month will have an article on speed by Vice Admiral Sir R. Custance. Bridge, lately commanding their China squadron, is of the like opinions.

*Letters & Papers*, 3: 182–89
October 22, 1906

My dear Mr. President:

I send herewith such comments as I have had time to make upon the general subject which elicited Sim's paper. I regret delay; but, even as it is, it is by sore sacrifice of other work that I have prepared this.

As regards the particular matter of the Battle of Tsushima, he accepts as decisive the testimony of the single witness cited by Lieut. White. Our old professor of astronomy, Chauvenet, a man of standing, used to say, "Never trust one sight, because you think it very good. Average several." I fancy most lawyers would say the same of a comparison of witnesses; as an historian, I certainly should. When

I wrote my account, I had Togo's official report, some others already published, and in addition the advance sheets of a work by Captain Klado of the Russian Navy, in which he had collated several, from Russian sources. It was from Togo's report that I assumed a Russian speed of 12 knots, against which Mr. White's witness says 9.

I presented, however, no account of the battle. I simply constructed, from the data, a plan of its probable opening scenes, in order from them to discuss the tactical question of speed. Mr. Sims's discussion begins by misunderstanding my statement, which he gives thus: "Shortly after the fleets sighted each other, the Japanese changed course from S.W. to East, while the Russians were steering N.E ; and the Japanese speed was slower than that of the Russians; 2 or 3 to the Russians 4." This assumption of mine, as to relative speeds, applied only (see my text, p. 449) to the time the Japanese, by Togo's report, were steering S.W.; not to their steering East—an entirely different condition. White's Russian witness says that, after the Japanese countermarched to East, both fleets were steering about N.N.E. My memory is that Togo makes no such statement; he gave no course, between East and the subsequent countermarch after the battle began. Indeed, as regards Japanese speed, after the first shot, I made no positive statements; only assumptions, for my argument on a general problem.

My impressions of "the nature of the action," (beyond the opening scene), had therefore nothing to do with the "reasoning by which Captain Mahan assumes Togo was influenced—in taking a position (across the head of the enemy's column) which he did not take." (Sims p. 4.) I do not believe the closest scanning of my article will detect an expression implying that Togo took a position across the head of the enemy's column; unless it be that I said that when first seen, the Japanese were ahead of the Russians; or, as White's witness says, "on the starboard bow." In this sense I did say "he had headed him," (p. 456); and had he not? But that is very different from taking a tactical order, for battle.

Deductions from the actual fighting of the battle, unless of a very technical character, e.g. the falling of funnels, are much vitiated by the Russian inefficiency. They did not enjoy, what Farragut called the best defense, "a rapid (and accurate) fire from our own guns." The Japanese in large measure had target practice of them. We therefore can scarcely be said to have a fair test of the battle efficiency of fire control. For this reason, while Mr. Sims is in some measure correct in saying that the three conclusions he attributes to me (p. 1) are, in my judgment, supported by the battle, he is mistaken in saying that they were derived from it. A careful reading of my article will show that the reasoning is largely a priori, supported only by inference from the occurrences of the battle. (See my page 451.) My reasoning far antedated the battle.

The view Mr. Sims attributes to me, (p. 1), that "in designing battleships of certain displacement we are never justified in increasing the speed, within reasonable limits, at the expense of gun power," is an exaggeration. See my pages 455, 456, 461, 469. Even at the expense of often seeming to hedge, I try to qualify my statements against exaggeration. Caricatures no man can avoid.

The opposite sides of the contention, on which Mr. Sims and I stand, are that one believes in size of ship, the other in numbers. The one believes in a few very heavy guns, the other prefers more numerous lighter ones. Let neither attribute extremes to the other. Mr. Sims does not believe in a navy of one huge ship, nor I in a thousand vessels of five hundred tons. Neither do I believe in ships of five knots speed; nor in a battery of smooth bore twenty-fours; nor yet in one primary battery of today. There must be adjustment.

Further, while I believe in volume of fire, I also believe in fewness of calibres. I would have one "primary" calibre, and one "intermediate"; being led thereto long ago by considerations, not of fire control, but of battery supply. Here, incidentally, let me remark that the several indexes of powder mentioned by Mr. Sims, (p. 10), if avoidable, would seem to call for simplification.

Also, while I deplore the present tendency, in size, as in speed, I admit that no one nation can wholly resist it. It compels by a power like gravitation; just as the stronger is in some measure compelled by a weaker enemy—unless hopelessly weak. It does not therefore follow, however, that no modification of a tendency, no brake, is possible; and it was to this I looked in the words that the "willful premature antiquating of good vessels is a growing and wanton evil." To an extent which might be lessened, nations are compelled to throw out of the line of battle ships otherwise good, which must be quickly replaced. The length of time, and the expense, required to build a battle-ship, are now the sole hindrance to the process of total discardment. In a measure Germany has just been compelled to such a discardment. (See article by "Excubitor" in one of the September British monthlies. Yet Brassey, in the passage I have marked in red, seems to show Great Britain suffers from the recoil of her own measures.) This harmful progress is possible only by bigness. Each step is by an increase of size, now that men have overcome the mechanical limits formerly imposed by their materials. There being now no limit to their wills, they exercise these, as most powerful persons do, indifferent to circumstances of reasonable consideration of the fact, that somewhere numbers and size must have a head-on collision.

For this reason I suggested, in an article in the *National Review*,

May, 1906, that in the approaching Hague Conference an artificial limit be attempted on the bigness of ships of war. Eliminate bigness beyond a certain tonnage, and men, having a limit in that direction, will turn their attention to the proper dispositions of the permitted tonnage, and to its tactical management. Bigness will no longer be a refuge from every difficulty, or a recourse from every embarrassment.

In matters of fire control, and reasonable deductions from practice in it, I must cede to the far greater familiarity of Mr. Sims. Of course, I do not mean by this that I unconditionally accept his inferences. For instance, Mr. White's calculation, which Mr. Sims makes much of, after giving the *Orel*'s injuries, goes on "the *Suavaroff* must have been struck, etc." "Allowing a little over thirty-five each for the *Alexander III*, etc." "It is hardly possible that these guns, etc." Such assumptions are perfectly permissible for making approximate inferences; but they remain assumptions, which qualify the conclusions. From such consideration as I have been able to give his paper, I cannot yet feel convinced as to the effect of volume of fire under battle conditions, as distinguished from target practice. That far better results will be achieved in battle, owing to the eminent work done by Mr. Sims and associates, I cannot doubt. I believe in it unconditionally. But I believe also in the probability that a fleet such as I would favor could, by dint of numbers, effect tactical combinations quite balancing mere weight of metal in the individual ship; could in the end enforce closing, when volume of fire would tell— probably tell also before.

In arguing, I have the right, within the limits of the possible, to choose the proportion of inferiority I accept for my battleship. I am on record as favoring in 1898 a maximum of 12,000 tons. It need not follow, if other nations now insist on 20,000, that I will deny that in measure we must follow—force of gravitation. I need not, however, accept a fleet double in number and half in individual size; nor yet dispositions putting half my fleet out of action.

To illustrate my views, as regards tactical combinations open to numbers, I present a diagram showing 12 ships, A, opposed to 8 B; the aggregate tonnage to be approximately the same. This would make each A ship two-thirds, or sixty-seven per cent, the size of each B. I give the A fleet three knots less speed—fleet speed—than the B; and I assume that, by this sacrifice of speed, and if necessary of some proportion of other qualities, the offensive gun power of A is three-fourths, 75 per cent, that of B. Whether this proportion can be reached, I do not know; but as I am informed by competent authority that the *Lord Nelson*, on one-eighths—twelve per cent—less tonnage, and three knots less speed, than the *Dreadnought*, carries an equal weight of battery, I presume my supposition may not overpass possibility. If it does, I would sacrifice something else to gun power. This would make the total gun power of A, to that of B, as 9 to 8.

The four rear ships of A are given two positions—blue and red. The interval between two adjacent blues, in the direction of the fleet's progress, is 250 yards; while in the line of bearing on which the blue are ranged the interval is 850 yards. For the red the distance 250 is doubled—500. Any interval intermediate between 250 and 500 is of course permissible. The nearest blue is 1.6 miles from the rear enemy; the nearest red 1.9 miles. The distance between the main bodies (1–8 inclusive) is 6,000 yards—three miles. The nearest red ship has to give most forward train to her guns; but the angle, 37°, is well within feasibility for a broadside.

The dotted lines show one method of concentration. By it the four rear B ships receive each the attack of two vessels, of .75 per cent their force, or a total against them of 1.5. The four leading A are pitted against a force which is to their own as 1.33 to 1.

It is to be observed that, if the B fleet mean to fight at the range of 6,000 yards—now apparently favored—it cannot prevent the A from assuming this formation; nor can it escape from the dilemma by its superior speed, except by making its four rear ships retire. It may retire altogether; but then that is not fighting. A moves on interior lines, with such an advantage of distance in its favor that B (granting the range) cannot control him, B, to maintain position and range, must accommodate himself to the speed A choses to observe. He can abandon position and range, and by virtue of speed bring A to action; but that presents another problem. If A has a speed of 15 knots, and chooses to steam at 12, or 10, B, to keep position, must do the same. A therefore can give his blue ships ample reserve of speed for manoeuvring. If B try to circle around A, A is master of that situation; for upon concentric arcs of small radii, three miles apart, a speed of at least 2 to 1 is necessary for the fleet on the outer circle. The radius of the inner circle is at the choice of A; and he can, if he choose, impose such a condition that B, to keep abeam, (or any fixed bearing), and the range, will need a speed of 3, or even 4, to 1. The blue ships of A, not to speak of their reserve of speed, also occupy inner position; and the advantage of their main body (1–8) remains with them in greater part, though diminished. The two fleets can circle indefinitely, keeping this formation. Any change must proceed from B, or from the accidents of battle.

I do not for a moment imply that B is tactically helpless; every thrust has its parry; but I conceive he is confronted "with a condition, not a theory." He cannot prevent A making the disposition; and if B wishes to engage at 3 miles he must accept it. Will B by steaming ahead, superior speed, withdraw his rear ships? Then he, in measure, takes his leaders out of position. Will he meet this by circling round A? But A can circle also, and on an inner circle. I subjoin a table, showing in three sets, five miles apart, the comparative diameters and circumferences of two concentric circles, the radii of which differs by 3 miles—the engaging range.

| | Radius | Diameter = 3.1 | Circumference | Speed needed |
|---|---|---|---|---|
| Inner: | 1 mile | 2 miles | 6 miles | 4:1 |
| Outer: | 4 " | 8 " | 25 " | |
| Inner: | 6 miles | 12 miles | 37 miles | |
| Outer: | 9 " | 18 " | 56 " | 2:1 |
| Inner: | 11 miles | 22 miles | 68 miles | 5:4 |
| Outer: | 14 " | 28 " | 87 " | 20:16 |

If A choses to circle with a radius of one mile, diameter two, he has a circumference of six against B's twenty-four; to keep abreast B must have four times the speed. Passing by the intermediate case it is plain that should A, being free to choose, choose even so large a circle as twenty-two miles diameter, B to keep abreast must steam as 5 to 4, or as twenty knots to sixteen. Now, without committing myself to any particular speed, I think I have never hinted at accepting this disparity. My argument has been: Where speed counts really for so little, why this mad race for speed? It has, for battleships, no reference to the great world of action, normally outside military matters, but which military control affects; it is little decisive in military matters; why maintain it?

The tactical advantage constituted by superior speed is this: it confers the offensive. A great advantage, admittedly; but the defensive is not made hopeless. Defensive campaigns are the highest test of merit. But, tactically, as shown by the table, if the offensive wishes long range, nothing can deprive the defensive of interior lines. He cannot prevent the assailant closing, nor taking short cuts; but, on the supposition of long range, he has tactical freedom and short lines for any combination or change he desires. If part of his battery is intermediate, he will wish closing; and it is thereby excluded to the offensive. Accepting the range, and the 3 knots difference of speed, the defensive has a circular area of not less than fifteen miles diameter within which he moves at will and compels the assailant—force of gravitation.

The second disposition of two A ships off the head of the column, I leave to speak for itself. It is a mere alternative suggestion.

The above has reference only to speed and a total weight of battery. The distribution of the latter, primary only, or primary and intermediate, is another, and to me more difficult, matter. I have presented certain argument on this; Mr. Sims others. Decision belongs elsewhere. If Mr. Sims is correct in his inferences as to the accuracy of intermediates, and the effect of funnel injuries, and of the gases from explosion, he has certainly damaged much of my argument in favor of more numerous lighter pieces. The enclosed clipping from the *N.Y. Sun* of October 19 seems, however, to leave still some hope for 6-inch intermediates at two miles.

As regards the comparative loss to a fleet by accident, coaling, etc. I suppose, in a matter of pure chance, the theory of probabilities would say that in twenty smaller vessels, the chance of an accident would be double that in ten larger. Yet I imagine that a careful investor, dealing with a hundred thousand dollars, would feel safer if he had placed it in ten companies than in two, or in five. The clipping I enclose seems to show this opinion in the present Lord Brassey; who is, I believe, conspicuous alike as a business man and as a lay expert in naval matters. In administrative processes, such as coaling, docking, etc., I cannot but think a real advantage obtains to numbers. Administration is not chance, and is largely combinative; combination proceeds with numbers; and I believe a good administrator would keep more force at the front with twenty ships than with ten. The question of numbers must also be considered with reference to the whole navy, not to a particular fleet only. If, for distribution of force in a fleet, twelve ships be only as good as eight, does it follow that for the general war forty-eight are not more advantageous than thirty-two? You have several stations, or you wish quickly to transfer a decisive detachment from one place to another. An instance in point was when we expected to detach Watson from before Santiago against Camara. From Sampson's seven armored ships we might send two; but suppose, with the same tonnage, he had had only five. Taking into consideration, coaling, accidents, etc., would three be sufficient to watch Cervera?

I have replied more at length than I could have wished, Mr. President; but I felt that when you had done me the honor of placing a paper before me, there was imposed upon me some recognition beyond mere acknowledgment. You will readily perceive that, in dealing with such questions, while engaged as I have been for years in work foreign to them, I am necessarily in the matter of details at a disadvantage, as towards men whose chief occupation is with present problems. The question may arise—it presents itself to me— whether under such circumstances it would be better for me to withdraw from discussions, in which I must limit myself chiefly to general principles. The only reply is that it is to be presumed that the men with whom executive decision lies will weigh all arguments, in the full light of all the evidence. This they are always able to command, from experts on all sides. The tactical diagram and explanation I present is cognate with my paper for the Institute, in that it represents one example of a use of numbers, familiar to my life-long line of thought; which, though unexpressed, underlay much of my argument. It is merely a specific instance of division, combination, and consequent "Grand Tactics," as the expression used to be. There cannot but be many dispositions similar in principle, and to be carried out more certainly than ever before, because of greater certainty of motive power, and, in measure at least, of clearer vision due to smokeless powder. The field is one which should be exhaustively explored by men younger and less occupied than I; by the coming men, in short, rather than by one of the past.

I will be permitted to guard myself against being understood to imply more than I say, The illustration given is assuredly one of many tactical expedients. Equally assuredly, there are tactical repartees to it and them; every thrust has its parry, and may be followed by a return; yet duels end in one winning. But will an exhaustive study of tactical situations place superiority of speed in so decisive a situation as to warrant sacrifice of gun power to it?

PSU - TR Papers, Series 2, Reel 343
October 22, 1906

Personal

My dear Captain Mahan:

In my message to Congress my present intention is to take the rather unusual course of commending your "War of 1812" for general reading. In any event I want to use several sentences that are contained in your book, weaving them in with my own in a way that would make it inadvisable to try to give credit for them to you. Do you object?

*Letters & Papers*, 3: 189–90
October 24, 1906

Mr dear Mr. President:

Owing to my change of address to this place for the winter, your letter was somewhat delayed in reaching me.

I shall be only too glad that you should use any of my writings in any manner that may be serviceable to you, or that you may think serviceable to the country. The question of credit in such connection is to me quite immaterial.

Judging by the sales, the book has not been very widely read in this country. Great Britain rather better.

*Letters & Papers*, 3: 202
January 10, 1907

Dear Mr. President:

I fear I may trespass on your indulgence, but the statement in the morning paper that four of our best battleships are to be sent to the Pacific has filled me with dismay.

In case of war with Japan what can four battleships do against their navy? In case of war with a European power, what would not the four battleships add to our fleet here?

I apprehend, should war with Japan come before the Panama Canal is finished, the Philippines and Hawaii might fall before we could get there; but, had we our whole fleet in hand, all could be retrieved. Between us and Japan any hostilities must depend on sea power. Invasion in force is possible to neither.

I had inferred from the recent sustained withdrawals of our battleships from Eastern waters, that this was the policy of our Government; and it may be I should at once apologize for writing upon a mere newspaper statement.

Have you chanced to see in the *Athenaeum*, December 22, (p. 799) some comments attributed to Sir George Clark, Secretary of the British Defence Committee, sustaining the opinion advanced by me concerning the 8 in. and 6 in. guns at Tsushima?

PSU - TR Papers, Series 2, Reel 344
January 12, 1907

Personal

My dear Captain Mahan:

I have your letter of the 10th instant. Haven't you gone far enough with newspapers to understand a matter like this, and a statement made as that statement was made? It isn't worth a second thought; and don't you know me well enough to believe that I am quite incapable of such an act of utter folly as dividing our fighting fleet? I have no more thought of sending four [more?] battle ships to the Pacific while there is the least possible friction with Japan than I have of going thither in a rowboat myself On the contrary, if there should come the most remote danger of war I should at once with-draw every fighting craft from the Pacific until our whole navy could be gathered and sent there in a body. Last year, as soon as the trouble about the poaching sealers occurred, I immediately got in touch with the Department so as to order the instant leaving of the Pacific waters by every one of our war vessels if the trouble developed. I have taken all our battleships away from the Asiatic Station. We have a squadron of cruisers out there. No battleship is to go there.

With great regard,

PSU - TR Papers, Series 2, Reel 345
May 24, 1907

My dear Captain Mahan:

I have your letter of the 13th instant. I am concerned to learn of your sickness and hope you will soon be all right. I shall read your articles with interest. A good many of the people of that peace conference by their utterances made it rather hard for anyone to continue being a real and sane advocate of peace.

PSU - TR Papers, Series 2, Reel 348
March 27, 1908

My dear Captain Mahan:

I do not know whether there is any chance to put your son into the office of Assistant District Attorney. I do not know whether there is any vacancy, or whether there have been any contingent promises; but it is a really great pleasure to send the enclosed, which I hope your son will present in person to my friend Stimson.

Hon. Henry L. Stimson,
United States Attorney,
New York

My dear Stimson:

This will be presented to you by Lyle Evans Mahan, the son of Captain A. T. Mahan, whose services to the navy, and therefore to the country, have been such as to make us all his debtors. Young Mahan wants to be an assistant attorney under you. Is there a chance for him? If so I should be glad indeed to have him appointed.

PSU - TR Papers, Series 2, Reel 349
May 25, 1908

To Rear Admiral A. T. Mahan

You are hereby directed to proceed to Washington, D.C., on temporary special duty, and on its completion to return to your home at
Quogue, N.Y.

PSU - TR Papers, Series 2, Reel 349
June 7, 1908

My dear Admiral:

Your letter of the 6th instant has been received, and I send you
herewith the President's order directing you to proceed to Washington, D.C., for special temporary duty and on its completion to return
to your home.

[signed] William Loeb
Secretary to the President

PSU - TR Papers, Series 2, Reel 349
June 8, 1908

My dear Captain Mahan:

I shall read those notes with great interest. By all means get the
information from Evans that you desire, and I shall see that you are
given authority.

What a ridiculous creature Dicey is! He knows no more about the
alleged "brutal discipline" in the navy than he does about our motive in sending the fleet abroad. I am not sure I ever heard of him
before; but I have a vague recollection of seeing his name. I should
say he corresponded to the solemn mugwumps who write articles, in
the *Nation* and *Atlantic Monthly* here, on subjects of which they
know nothing.

I have asked Metcalf to forward to you a very interesting letter
from Admiral Sperry about the effects of the cruise.

PSU - TR Papers, Series 2, Reel 350
July 10, 1908

Personal

My dear Admiral:

I can not see any objection to the publication of those pages, which I reenclose to you. In especial I think what you say about the misconduct of the press in that very delicate matter may be of real interest.

With hearty regard, believe me,


PSU - TR Papers, Series 2, Reel 351
October 1, 1908

My dear Admiral Mahan:

Mr. Loeb has placed before me your letter and enclosures of the 30th. It certainly seems to me that unless Admiral Goodrich produces the clear, precise and definite evidence for publication, or otherwise does just what he refuses to do, you are under no obligation whatever to take further action. Incidentally I may add that the reports from Sperry and the reports from the officers under Sperry, as to what Sperry has done on the voyage to Australia, show a constant and steady improvement in the fleet and warrant us in taking as accurate Sperry's original statements. You are probably aware that Admiral Goodrich was from the first opposed to the voyage around the world of the fleet, and has criticised it in every way. I return the enclosures.

With great regard, believe me.


PSU - TR Papers, Series 2, Reel 353
January 8, 1909

Personal

My dear Captain Mahan:

I have received the enclosed criticism as to Mr. Newberry's plan for the reorganization of the Navy Department. When we have the conference, will you give me your views about it?

*Letters & Papers*, 3: 275–77
January 13, 1909

My dear Mr. President:

Your letter of January 8, with enclosure, reached me only yesterday.

I have not yet learned Mr. Newberry's plan, and therefore cannot antecendently busy my mind as I could wish in considering the criticism.

Your letter does not require of me any opinion before the Conference; yet it may save time in ultimate expression to say at once that, as far as I have yet gone, I have never found fault with the Bureau organization, in itself, regarded as a civil administrative system. The failure is in the fact that the Secretary, the coordinating factor, as a rule comes to a big business not only without military conceptions, but without that antecedent practical experience of the civil side, which almost in every case the head of the great civil business has gained in subordinate functions. He is therefore, as usually appointed, quite unacquainted with the details, or the general ideas, that underlie his duties.

The only corrective has been the bureaus. They are essentially and almost purely civil offices; with the one possible exception of Navigation. At present, five of the eight are held by persons essentially civil in profession. That is the influence, and the sole influence, officially bearing upon the Secretary from below.

Ideally, the President does, and the Secretary as his lieutenant should, hold in his hands a complete mastery of the diplomatic, military and naval considerations, home and foreign, which for the time being at any moment affect the policy of the Country. Actually, neither the President nor the Secretary ordinarily can thus do, because usually they come new to the military considerations, afloat and ashore. The only means by which such consecutive knowledge can be maintained is by a corporate body, continuous in existence and gradual in change. That we call a General Staff. In my conception, the Chief of Staff can scarcely, with our institutions, hold certainly for as long as, say, ten years. The knowledge, therefore, must be in the general staff at large; but, and here perhaps is my particular point, he should be solely responsible for information, and for advice, given the Secretary. He should be compelled to act as President of a Board, composed of his chief subordinates; but the advice he gives must be his, not theirs. The advice must be single, not corporate.

I raised this point the instant I joined the War Board in 1898; and my experience then convinced me that some men will easily roll off personal responsibility; the result being that one man practically decides, but without individual responsibility for the advice. If I rightly read the English press, this is the case now in the Board of Admiralty. We only advised; but with many secretaries advice will practically be decision. Therefore, responsibility for advice should be individual.

For best results, the Chief of Staff should so possess the confidence of the Administration, as to be aware of the relations existing between our own Government and the various states interested in a possible theatre of war; and also of the attitude these states bear to one another, and hence their possible action in case of hostilities. All these are military factors. Thus equipped, the two Chiefs of Staff, Army and Navy, would be invaluable understudies to their respective Chiefs and to the President.

Have you read Corbett's *Seven Years War*? It is a good book. He brings out clearly that Pitt, besides eminent ability, had control of all three threads—diplomatic, military, and naval—and that in this, concentrated in one efficient man, consisted his great advantage. Jomini taught me from the first to scorn the sharp distinction so often asserted between diplomatic and military considerations. Corbett simply gives the help of putting the same idea into other words. Diplomatic conditions affect military action, the military considerations diplomatic measures. They are inseparable parts of a whole; and as such those responsible for military measures should understand the diplomatic factors, and vice versa. No man is fit for Chief of Staff who cannot be intrusted with knowledge of a diplomatic situation. The naval man also should understand the military conditions, and the military the naval.

Corbett makes another excellent point: that for a military establishment the distinction between a state of war and a state of peace is one of words, not of fact. Nothing so readily as a general staff will insure this. They, or a body like them, should in my opinion decide what the leading features of a ship of war and her armament should be. I would not have a bureau officer have a vote on such a question. I would compel the Staff—or Board—to hear the Bureaus in extenso, as expert witnesses, and their testimony should be recorded, to emphasize the responsibility of the Board; but the decision should be that of a body, or an individual, purely military. No one civil by profession, or by office, should control here, severally or collectively; except, of course, the Secretary or the President.

Do you remember how delightfully Nelson phrased all this in his last order. "The order of sailing is the order of battle." Every day ready for action. I should like to see that framed and hung up before the desk of every secretary who had wit enough to comprehend.

I am sure you understand my general position sufficiently to know that I would neither advocate nor countenance any measure tending to weaken the ultimate power of the Secretary. He should be able to overrule and upset, if necessary, every one beneath him, from Chief of Staff down.

PSU - TR Papers, Series 2, Reel 353
January 27, 1909

My dear Sir:

I have appointed you as a member of a commission to consider certain needs of the navy. The organization of the Department is now not such as to bring the best results, and there is a failure to co-ordinate the work of the Bureaus and to make the Department serve the one end for which it was created, that is, the development and handling of a first class fighting fleet. With this proposition in view I will ask you to consider:

1. All defects in the law under which the Navy Department is now organized, including especially the defects by which the authority of Chiefs of Bureaus is made in certain respects practically equal to that of the Secretary or the President.

2. The division of responsibility and consequent lack of coordination in the preparation for war and conduct of war.

3. The functions of certain Bureaus, so as to see whether it is not possible to consolidate them.

4. The necessity of providing the Secretary of the Navy with military advisers, who are responsible to him for co-ordinating the work of the Bureaus and for preparation for war.

5. The necessity for economical allotment and disbursement of appropriations and for a system which will secure strict accountability.

6. Finally, I want your views as to how best to reorganize and emphasize the strictly military character of the navy, so that preparation for war shall be controlled under the Secretary by the military branch of the navy, which bears the responsibility for the successful conduct of war operations.

I wish to have the above subjects considered under two general heads:

First, as to the fundamental principles of an organization that will insure an efficient preparation for war in time of peace, a separate report under this head to be submitted at the earliest practicable date.

Second, specific recommendations as to the changes in the present organization that will accomplish this result, the report under this head to be submitted later.

In addition to the above reports I desire your recommendation as to the number, location and general facilities of the navy yards which are required by strategic considerations in time of war and for maintaining the fleet in constant readiness for war in time of peace.

[Also on the commission were: Rear Admiral William M. Folger, ret.; Hon. A. G. Dayton, Judge, U.S. District Court, Philippi, West Virginia; Hon. Paul Morton; Rear Admiral Robley D. Evans; Hon. W. H. Moody, Associate Justice, Supreme Court of the United States; Rear Admiral William S. Cowles, Chief of the Bureau of Equipment; Rear Admiral (Ret.) Stephen B. Luce.]

PSU - TR Papers, Series 2, Reel 353
January 29, 1909

My dear Sir:

I hereby appoint Friday next, February 5th, at 2:30 p.m., for the first meeting of our Commission and request that the Commission meet at this hour in the office of the Secretary of the Navy.

*Letters & Papers*, 3: 279–80
February 1, 1909

My Dear Mr. President:

You will recall Dicey's article [see letter of June 8, 1908]. The English friend who sent it to me has sent me also the enclosed, London *Times*, Jan. 21, which I think will interest you; both in itself, and as showing that, despite proverbs to the contrary, Truth sometimes catches up with falsehood.

PSU - TR Papers, Series 2, Reel 353
February 3, 1909

My dear Admiral:

Yes, for both reasons that is an interesting clipping. I thank you for having sent it to me, and appreciate it.

PSU - TR Papers, Series 2, Reel 354
February 25, 1909

Rear Admiral A. T. Mahan, U.S.N. retired
Care Navy Department

Sir:

I desire to appoint you as Chairman of a Commission for the purposes indicated in my message to Congress of which I send you herewith a copy.

I also send you herewith a copy of a memorandum prepared for me by a naval officer of high rank, to which I invite your attention in connection with your work.

*Letters & Papers*, 3: 290
March 2, 1909

Dear Mr. President:

Will it be in any sense improper that you should give a last earnest recommendation to Mr. Taft on no account to divide the battleship force between the two coasts?

As a matter of popular outcry, this is a nightmare to me. With all his peculiarly eminent qualification for the Presidency, I do not know whether Mr. Taft has a strong military sense; and, as I see it, this is one of the most evident external dangers threatening the country.

Pardon the intrusion.

PSU - TR Papers, Series 2, Reel 354
March 3, 1909

My dear Admiral:

I had already warned Mr. Taft on the subject of dividing the battle fleet, and had shown him my letter to Mr. Foss of the House Naval Committee, the paragraph of which that deals with the subject I enclose for your information. I shall send him in writing one final protest. I am sure the fleet will never be divided. We got the mischievous proposition struck out of the bill.

P.S. I enclose you a copy of my final letter to Taft.

PSU - TR Papers, Series 2, Reel 367
June 8, 1911

Dear Captain Mahan:

A couple of days ago Mrs. Roosevelt showed me with triumph your letter to *The Times*, which I need hardly say I greatly appreciate; and immediately afterwards I picked up *The Century* and read your admirable piece on the Panama Canal. I do wish our authorities would consult you before committing themselves to foolish propositions which it would be dishonorable either to carry out, or to refuse to carry out, when once they had been made into solemn agreements. Any man who knows you knows that you are incapable of advocating national wrongdoing. But it is not virtue—it is mere weakness of the kind that ultimately leads to wickedness—to refuse to look facts in the face, and to take a position which implies the abandonment of national self-respect. With Great Britain, I firmly believe, no difficulty can rise which we cannot solve by arbitration. But if Great Britain claimed as regards us what not many years ago the British Government claimed as regards their own South African possessions, that is, the right to permit an unlimited coolie emigration to the United States, this country would not arbitrate the question and would no more admit the coolies than South Africa and Australia and British Columbia would do so. I had to refuse point blank to arbitrate the Alaskan boundary matter, and we got a settlement of that case only because I was forced to explain that if the commission could not agree, I would have no alternative but myself to reduce to possession the disputed territory. The settlement of the Alaskan boundary settled the last serious trouble between the British Empire and ourselves, as everything else could be arbitrated, but neither England nor the United States should agree to do something that they could not live up to. If we repeat with an English vessel the experiment Captain Wilkes tried in '61, England would not arbitrate the matter; she would say that we had to do as we did in '61, that is, express regret and undo the wrong we had done; and England would be quite right in taking such a position. I feel very differently toward England than I feel toward Germany, and still more differently from the way I feel toward Japan; but surely we must consider before making a treaty whether we could then refuse to make such a treaty with Germany or Japan. I do not believe this nation is prepared to arbitrate such questions as to whether it shall fortify the canal, as to whether it shall retain Hawaii, nor yet to arbitrate the Monroe Doctrine, nor the right to exclude immigrants if it thinks it wise to do so.

*Letters & Papers*, 3: 411–12
June 19, 1911

Dear Colonel Roosevelt:

Your letter of June 8 came just as I was leaving home for Newport for lectures at the War College, and I was there too heavily engrossed to allow a reply. On my return Saturday I found the *Outlook* of June 17, for which I imagine I am indebted to you, and in any case am much obliged by receiving.

Curiously enough, the night before your letter I had been reading John Hay's letters touching the Alaskan boundary question; in which he comments that Lord H_____ [Herschel] conducted the British case in the spirit of a lawyer trying to win a case, not in that of a statesman endeavoring to reach an equitable solution. "If a much less able lawyer had been sent, a man of diplomatic habit of mind, he might have been able to come to an arrangement." (Vol. III, p. 142).

This is to me the case in a nutshell. I had used equivalent words in the May *North American*, p. 650. Government everywhere is largely in the hands of lawyers; and, like the proverbial leather of the shoemaker, in their eyes there is "nothing like law." This is singular in this country; for admirable as the ideal of law is, here the delays and subterfuges of law have brought it into much disrepute, regarded as an instrument for working purposes. And when a decision of the Supreme Court is by five to four, what moral or intellectual demand is satisfied? We rightly submit, but we are not convinced; and an unconvinced nation is in a dangerous moral frame of mind in an international contention.

As regards Asiatic immigration, has your attention been called to a new British Quarterly, the *Round Table*? The third number has just reached me. It contains an article on the Emigration question in Japan. I have not had time to read thoroughly; but the gist is that neither in Manchuria nor Korea can the Japanese immigrants (there are already 15 to the square mile in Korea) contend economically with the native. What remains? Australia and America; where their economical advantage over the present occupants is greater even than their disadvantage in Asia. I presume you have noted the undercurrent of Japanese discontent with the latest treaty, indications of which have reached the surface amid all the jubilation over our concessions. This, and the huge strides of the German Navy, should be considered seriously by all as they are considered by you.

In one particular Sir E. Grey has helped us by enabling our government to insist upon a recognition of the Monroe Doctrine as antecedent to a Treaty of General Arbitration with any Power.

*Letters & Papers*, 3: 412–13
June 24, 1911

My dear Colonel Roosevelt:

At the wish of the President of the War College, I am revising the publication of my lectures there on Naval Strategy. I find in them the statement that in the early stages of the War with Spain "the Flying Squadron was kept in Hampton Roads mainly to assure our northern coast that nothing disagreeable should occur." As that squadron left for Key West within a week of my joining the Board, I had not personal knowledge of the previous deliberations of the Department; and I have thought best, before committing myself to print, to ask you whether the statement is substantially correct.

PSU - TR Papers, Series 2, Reel 367
June 27, 1911

My dear Captain Mahan:

You are entirely right. The flying squad was looked upon with hysterical anxiety by the Northeast and its representatives in Congress. If you can get in to see me, or motor over to take lunch with me at Oyster Bay, I should really like to tell you about some of the requests made to me for ships to protect Portland, Maine, Jekyl Island, Narragansett Pier, and other points of like vast strategic importance! Hale and Tom Reed actually made the President say that he would send a ship to Portland. I arranged to send them a Civil War monitor with 21 New Jersey Militia aboard, which satisfied Portland entirely!

*Letters & Papers*, 3: 414
July 1, 1911

My dear Colonel Roosevelt:

I am greatly indebted for your reply to my letter; with which I was loath to trouble you, but the information which it gives was as essential to me as it is satisfactory.

I should greatly like to talk the matter over with you, but I am tied down by the necessity of reading some 150,000 words of galleys, besides the same amount in subsequent page proof; the whole complicated by some promised magazine writing. It is due the publishers that they be able to get the book out in October. I myself am adequately remunerated by being kept on duty for the particular work.

I wonder whether you ever experience the feeling I from time to time do; a tremor of responsibility for what I have done in supporting naval development and fortification of the Canal. This comes when I reflect that all will be only half done, and therefore perhaps worse than not done at all. The Democratic party in foreign relations still dwells in Jefferson's tomb; and the chairman of the House Naval Committee is a one battleship man from Tennessee, sixty years old; without antecedents and too old to change. I had the satisfaction of telling the Committee that the size of the battle fleet was not a naval question, but an international.

*Letters & Papers*, 3: 420–421
August 11, 1911

My dear Colonel Roosevelt:

I have read very carefully, though without the advantage of legal training, the articles of the Treaty of General Arbitration with Great Britain.

1. If the Senate confirm the Treaty, it retains control in any future case only over the special agreement; and, as to that, not as to its being made at all, but as to its terms. The Editorial of the *New York Times* of August 8, favorable to the Treaty, shows the cloudiness of its terms.

As I read them the Senate parts forever with its power of advice and consent as to the determination whether a particular question is "justiciable." This power is by the terms of the Treaty transferred to the Joint High Commission of Inquiry. I doubt whether the Senate has the constitutional right thus to limit constitutional powers over international agreements, even its own: but in any event ought its decision to be rushed by popular demand for immediate action, which if in the present session, cannot but be precipitate?

2. Great Britain reserves the right to obtain the concurrence of any self-govering dominion whose interests are involved. The cases of a self-governing dominion and of a group of our states are not on all fours. Nevertheless, as the protection to a minority, ought there not to be some security that a strong sectional interest, such as that of the Pacific Coast as to Asiatic immigration, should be safeguarded. Article II provides that the Joint High Commission shall be six, Americans three. The Pacific coast could hardly have more than one; while, if all but one of the six decided that the question is justiciable, the decision stands. The Senate is impotent over this decision.

3. These considerations do not affect greatly, if at all, the pending

treaty, because with Great Britain we have so much in common. But the question arises whether we can refuse a treaty in similar terms with another country, without making an invidious distinction. In view of Germany's recent action in Africa, could we risk the Monroe Doctrine to a treaty of General Arbitration with her? Sir Edward Grey has already endorsed the Doctrine in words that should be noted, but which are not in the treaty. "It is a postulate of any successful arbitration treaty of an extended kind that there should be no possibility of conflict between the national policies of the nations which are party to it." Asiatic immigration seems to me much less probably justiciable than the Doctrine. The latter to my mind is right, in policy and in morals, but without a shred of legal right.

4. What I particularly deplore is the attempt to press the Senate to hasty action; for that not only fetters its due regard to its own responsibility, emasculating its functions, but precludes national discussion. All responsibility and power is thus placed in the hands of the negotiators of the Treaty, and taken away from Senate and people.

Obstruction on the part of the Senate is one thing, reasonable deliberation another. Few now regret the Senate's rejection of the first Hay-Pauncefote Treaty.

PSU - TR Papers, Series 2, Reel 368<br>August 15, 1911

My dear Admiral Mahan:

I absolutely agree with you. I think that these arbitration treaties are hopelessly wrong, and I am extremely sorry. As you say, I should not object if only Great Britain were concerned, simply because I am quite prepared to have a far closer relationship with the British Empire even than the one involved. But the evident purpose is to treat this as something which is to be an example for other nations, and as such it is atrocious.

PSU - TR Papers, Series 2, Reel 368<br>August 21, 1911

My dear Admiral Mahan:

Dr. Abbott and my other colleagues are pretty doubtful about these peace treaties. I very much wish you would write a letter to *The Outlook* on the subject. I would back it up by an article of mine. Cannot you do this? I think it would be a genuine service.

*Letters & Papers*, 3: 422
August 25, 1911

My dear Colonel Roosevelt:

I cannot very well write on the subject of the Treaties to the *Outlook*, because I am under an engagement to furnish a half-dozen articles to the *North American*. the third of which, Navies as a Diplomatic Factor, appears in September. It is true, I have much liberty in the choice of my subjects, but there was an express wish that I should consider Arbitration, and therefore, while I may not touch upon the treaties at all, if I do the *N.A.* has a mortgage upon me.

Moreover, I am getting out a book upon Naval Strategy which will probably be my last magmum opus, and which therefore requires so much of my time that I have with difficulty met the promise to the *N.A.*

Curiously, I find more satisfactory accounts of the attitude towards the treaties in the London *Times* than in my own paper—the N.Y. *Times*.

May I make a suggestion? The Senate is spoken of as clinging to its "privileges," "prerogatives," "rights." Is not duty the same word? The Senators may be wrongheaded, but surely they have a duty.

*Letters & Papers*, 3: 435–36
December 2, 1911

My dear Colonel Roosevelt:

I send you the clipping from the *Globe* of which I spoke to you last night. It came to me through Romeike enclosing it, with a request for my custom (I had not seen it myself); and it would have gone to Mr. Lodge three days ago, but that I had mislaid it for the moment. I hope therefore its history is providentially ordered to draw your attention to what in my mind is one of the worst and most dangerous features of the approaching organized agitation, viz: the attempt to coerce the Senate into acting in accordance with popular demonstration, irrespective of their convictions.

The *Globe*, as you know, favors the treaties as they stand, and with somewhat brutal candor states the object of agitation. But while the representative body exists to carry out the matured will of its constituency in matters, legally proper, it ceases to be truly representative when it neglects to give to matters of public right the close attention which individual citizens cannot give; and which they therefore perforce turn over to representative agents. If the

Senate without conviction, or against conviction, yields in such a matter to popular pressure, it is false to its representative duty.

The more I think, the more certain I am that the Monroe Doctrine is " justiciable," that is that there are settled principles and precedents in international law which apply; and they apply against the Doctrine. If this be so, the Commission of Inquiry must so decide, if honest; and equally arbitrators when it comes before them must decide against the U.S. This alone, if correct, condemns the treaty as it stands.

I purpose asking your acceptance of a copy of my last book *Naval Strategy*. I don't bank on the strategic part particularly but there are obiter dicta which I do value. Chiefly that Asiatic immigration is against the spirit of the Monroe D.; because, as they don't assimilate, they colonize, and virtually annex. Permitted, the Pacific slope would be an Asiatic territory in twenty years.

PSU - TR Papers, Series 2, Reel 370
December 5, 1911

My Dear Admiral:

I absolutely agree with you. It is a mere question with me as to how I can do good, whether by silence or otherwise. Did you see the *Times* editorial this morning in which it announced that we must not arbitrate the treaty with Russia to find out what is meant? This is really the most extraordinary bit of insincerity yet. The *Times* has been rabidly for the treaties, but the minute it comes to applying the principles and arbitrate in a case where it could be applied, but where Jewish sensitiveness is at stake, the *Times* positively refuses to apply it. Indeed I should greatly value receiving, with an inscription from you, the *Naval Strategy*.

PSU - TR Papers, Series 2, Reel 370
December 9, 1911

My dear Sir:

Mr. Roosevelt has asked me to forward you a copy of a letter which he received from Mr. Low, and which he thought you might like to see. This is a letter written by Mr. Low to Mr. Choate. Mr. Roosevelt does not wish to receive the copy of the letter back again.

[Secretary]

*Letters & Papers*, 3: 438
December 13, 1911

My dear Col. Roosevelt:

I am much obliged for the copy of Low's letter which you have been kind enough to send me. It happened that he had himself sent me a copy, but I am none the less obliged for your thoughtfulness in the matter. It is to be regretted that it did not find more place in the *daily* Press, for the people, at least the loudest talkers, seem bent upon going it blind in this matter. I was glad to see in the list of intending speakers last night fewer "eminent citizens" than I had feared might show up on the platform.

PSU - TR Papers, Series 2, Reel 371
December 21, 1911

My dear Admiral Mahan:

I have been reading your book with the utmost pleasure. When was it that the Senate passed that resolution about dividing the fleet? If it was in my term, I simply paid no earthly heed to it; but it is astounding and appalling that it should have been possible for them to pass such a resolution. Next week I have in *The Outlook* an article calling attention to the extraordinary hypocrisy of abrogating the Russian Treaty at the very time they are talking of entering into these general [and?] fool arbitration treaties. I can stand pretty much anything except a sham, and pretty much any man except a hypocrite.

*Letters & Papers*, 3: 439–40
December 23, 1911

My dear Colonel Roosevelt:

The Senate passed the resolution during the last month or six weeks of your second term. My impression is that it was a joint resolution, and that you procured its suppression in the House by omission. I was much concerned and wrote to Sperry, who was just back, suggesting that his reputation as commander of the fleet would weigh heavily in such a matter, and that he be prepared to express his opinion—which I knew—very clearly, if opportunity required.

I also wrote you, suggesting a recommendation to Mr. Taft on the subject. You wrote a letter to him in consequence; and sent a copy of it to me.

The treaties I imagine would die a natural death but for the organized agitation, which cannot last, I think, because it has no strong popular feeling behind it. Root's amendment will take the worst out of them; but then, as Olney says, with that attachment there is not much treaty left.

I am glad you find the book interesting, the more so that I have never been so sick of anything I have written as I was of this before ending it. I hear from the College that they like it there.

Permit me to congratulate you on Sheldon's letter. It was needed for some persons, though not for me as I never doubted. The *Times* seems engaging in the profitable task of proving evident truth to be falsehood; a very dangerous occupation for the soul.

(P.S.) I have just ascertained that at the bottom of p. 395, two or more lines have been left out, so that the first lines of 396 are, so to say, in the air. No serious difficulty is occasioned but it looks very queer.

PSU - TR Papers, Series 2, Reel 383<br>July 9, 1913

Dear Admiral Mahan:

Mr. Roosevelt is at present in the West, but I will certainly see that he gets your letter and the clippings from the London *Times*. As he is in the desert he may not be able to write you about them, but I know he will be pleased to read what you have written. As a matter of fact, I believe he has already seen it, as he receives the *Times* at Oyster Bay.

[Secretary]

[Copies of the following correspondence between Assistant Secretary of the Navy Franklin Delano Roosevelt and Alfred Thayer Mahan during the spring and summer of 1914 were provided to the author by Naval War College archivist Anthony Nicolosi. They had been obtained originally from the FDR library in Hyde Park, N.Y.]

May 28, 1914

My dear Admiral Mahan:

I want to make a suggestion to you which [is] of some importance at the present time. When the canal is finally opened next winter there will undoubtedly be a great deal of pressure brought to bear—

political and sectional—to have the Fleet divided, and to have one half kept in the Pacific and one half in the Atlantic. I am just back from a trip to the Pacific Coast and was struck by the total lack of any correct conception of fleet operations. The people can be educated, but only if we all get together ahead of time and try to show the average "man in the street" the military necessity of keeping the Fleet intact. Your voice will carry more conviction than that of anybody else, and if you could publish an article or articles this summer or autumn it would be a true service. I realize that this would mean in large part a repetition, but it would be particularly timely & effective.

I have been doing all I could officially & unofficially to keep the danger of a divided fleet from becoming imminent.

Very sincerely yours,
Franklin D. Roosevelt

June 2, 1914

My dear Mr. Roosevelt:

Your letter of May 28 arrived here only yesterday. I am sorry to learn that there is danger of that old fallacy being seriously revived and pressed. I shall of course be ready to do what I can to resist and disprove it, but for the moment am at a loss as to the most advantageous manner. What part of the country is it most essential to convert? The Pacific, I presume, is for the most part hopelessly irrational on this subject; and any stand against the idea, taking in the Atlantic and Gulf states, will be attributed to sectional, non-national, points of view. The central states will be hard to interest.

Altogether the question of strategy in such a campaign is important, most important. What class of periodicals—daily, weekly, or monthly? In what section of the country published? What periodical—other than the illustrated, which will not care for such a subject—will reach the greatest number—or, rather, the most widely diffused of readers?

Possibly all these points have engaged your attention. Possibly, also, your letter to me is only one among several, to other persons, for one man will scarcely suffice. You will not have overlooked the influence of ex-President Roosevelt in the West. I fancy he is the heaviest weight to be had in this contest, and his views are known.

For the present I can only take the whole matter into consideration, for it seems to me that the best means of compassing the visceral cut will require much deliberations.

June 16, 1914

My dear Admiral Mahan:

The only other person I have written to in regard to the possible division of the Fleet is my cousin, the ex-President, and I feel sure that when he gets back he will do all he can, especially in the West. Personally, I do not think it would be wise to have it appear that a regular campaign is being started. This would almost inevitably lead to opposition, and my own feeling was that the opinion of yourself and the ex-President would, if given a very wide range of circulation, carry the greatest possible amount of weight.

As to the means of carrying the news, I suppose that the *Saturday Evening Post* has the greatest circulation and reaches the greatest number of persons throughout the country. I do not know whether you have ever written anything for them, but without question they would be more than glad to have an article or a series of articles from your pen.

When I was on the Pacific Coast in April I took every occasion, both in public speeches and in private conversation, to emphasize the fact that the main Fleet will, when it goes to the Pacific Coast, proceed in a body. I was surprised to find very little opposition to this view and the people out there were quick to grasp the idea that if the whole Fleet goes to the Pacific Coast the facilities on that coast for taking care of the Fleet would have to be greatly increased. I have recently suggested a plan to the General Board for their consideration. This involves the creation of a cruiser squadron to consist of practically all the armored cruisers, such squadron to be based on the Pacific Coast and to visit the Atlantic Coast during the times the main Fleet is in the Pacific. This exchange of fleets between the two coasts will, I think, be highly popular on the Pacific Coast as it will give the enlisted personnel of the cruiser squadron, who come almost entirely from the Pacific and Mountain States, an opportunity to visit the West Indies and the Atlantic seaboard. I am telling you all this merely to give you my thought that the West Coast people can be easily reconciled to the maintenance of a single main fleet if we go about it in the right way. During the Summer I expect to write an article on the result of the opening of the Canal for one of the popular weeklies, probably *Collier's*, but you and the ex-President can do more effective work than all the rest of us combined. I wish I could see you personally to tell you all the reasons I have for believing that there is a real danger of a division of the main Fleet. All I can tell you is that I believe such a danger to exist and that the only two ways to combat it will be, first, to have the Navy itself take a very definite and unanimous stand; and secondly, to bring the attention of the public at large to the opinions of two or three very big men whose views will be respected.

You probably know the incident of our ships at Shanghai last Summer; if not, I want to relate it to you very briefly and in confidence. At the time last year when the Japanese immigration question became really acute four of our ships, the *Saratoga*, *Cincinnati*, *Albany* and *Rainbow*, I think, were at the mouth of the Yangtze river on their Summer cruise north of the Philippines. I did all in my power to have them return nearer their base, but the President and Secretary of State felt that the chief danger to the negotiations lay in a possible explosion of the Japanese populace and that any movement on the part of our ships which might be considered as hostile might help to cause such an explosion. Orders were therefore sent against my protest to Admiral Nicholson, telling him not to move out of the Yangtze river. Of course, if hostilities had developed these ships would have been interned or overwhelmed by a superior force without difficulty. This to my mind is an excellent example of what might happen in case half our battleships were at San Francisco and the other half at New York. To bring the two fleets together during critical diplomatic negotiations would be almost impossible and if the negotiations failed the time for a possible junction of the fleets would be gone.

June 26, 1914

My dear Mr. Roosevelt:

Your letter of June 16, postmarked 22, reached me on the 23d Since your former letter I have not lost sight of the matter, but have felt, and still feel, a little perplexed just where and how to take hold. Last night it occurred to me that perhaps an historical retrospect of the disastrous results of division, with direct, yet incidental, application to Panama, might be a good form to take.

Your project of a cruiser squadron and a battleship squadron, to interchange biennially—as I understand it—between the two coasts, strikes me very favorably. It would insure the constant concentration of the main fleet, with regular practice in shifting from one coast to the other, and consequently familiarity with the passage of the Canal. In an article written in 1907, when the fleet went round, I advocated an occasional repetition.

Personally, I feel that our danger in the Pacific much exceeds that in the Atlantic. The Mexican imbroglio gives good assurance that the European Powers are disposed not to interfere with us. It has made large demands upon their patience, and yielded good demonstrations of it. They have too much of a crisis on their hands in the Near Eastern conditions, and, what to my mind is still more important, the only possible questions between them and us concern interests only, not national sentiment, a much more explosive factor. With Japan it is different. She feels as an insult what we regard as essential to national security in forestalling and avoiding a race problem.

From this view of the danger, I have necessarily felt the need of developing the resources of the West Coast for maintenance and repair. The shifting of the two squadrons would show and emphasize this need. I note your persuasion that in this view the Pacific slope might be reconciled to the concentration, when handled in the two squadron method, and will bear this in mind in anything I may write.

August 3, 1914

My dear Mr. Roosevelt:

May I take the liberty of suggesting that the war fever now in the air is extremely contagious, and likely to affect diplomatic transactions in unexpected ways. It may very well extend to Japan, and impart acerbity and danger to the questions pending. For this, as well as for general reasons—not least the languor which midsummer brings to people in Washington—I venture to submit that the fleet should be brought into immediate readiness and so disposed as to permit of very rapid concentration, ready to proceed when desired.

I do not know whether operations at Panama can be expedited; but in my judgment the officials there should be instructed to do their utmost, and also that it be ascertained whether a sufficient number of battleships could even now be passed through on occasion.

August 4, 1914

My dear Mr. Roosevelt:

I fear you may think I abound too much in suggestions, but a telephonic inquiry that came to me last night caused me to think that in the proclamation of neutrality which I suppose must soon issue, it would be politic for us to declare that *no coal* would be permitted to any belligerent vessel entering our ports.

The formula hitherto has been "coal only enough to reach the nearest national port." For Germany, at least, that would mean a run across the Atlantic, doing whatsoever belligerent work offered. Moreover, it might facilitate hovering near our own coasts as German vessels are now reported; injuring, more by fear than by act, the belligerent merchant carriers upon whom our own neutral trade depends. The effect of refusal of coal would be to eliminate some troublesome questions as to neutral and belligerent rights, most apt to arise from occurrences near our shores; into this I need not enter. The *Evening Post* of last night has an interview from me in which I analyzed the general past, present, and immediate future, as I see it. You can read these, if you desire, without my enlarging here. I haven't yet seen it, but presume it is correctly given.

[P.S.] Refusal of coal would prevent a merchant vessel, transformed (or thought probably to be transformed) into a commerce destroyer, from getting out. I fear Germany is already at this.

August 18, 1914

My dear Mr. Roosevelt:

Forgive my intruding again. The sudden and ill-conceived action of Japan raises some questions for us, in which Great Britain will be greatly involved, partly from the military side.

1. First, from the first article of the Treaty between Great Britain and Japan, it would appear that Japan could not have taken this step, on the ground alleged in the 'Ultimatum', without consulting Great Britain. Under this understanding, the utterly inadequate grounds alleged for the action cannot but rouse sympathy for Germany, militating against the pretty general feeling heretofore testified against her by our people. It seems to me our Government, in its neutral impartiality, should represent this to Great Britain; with the frank acknowledgment that, while it can answer for its own fairness, it cannot control the sympathies of the people, which are almost sure to swing around; for the ultimatum of Austria was reason itself compared with the reasons advanced by Japan.

2. Japan, going to war with Germany, will be at liberty to take the German Islands, Pelew, Marianne, Caroline, and Samoa. The first three flank our Mercator course to the Philippines; and it is one thing to have them in the hands of a Power whose main strength is in Europe, and quite another that they should pass into the hands of one so near as Japan. The question is pertinent to Great Britain, "If these islands are seized, will they henceforth be considered among those territorial possessions of Japan which the Treaty of Alliance guarantees?" Let Great Britain be brought at once to face the fact

that the action of her ally thus seriously affects her relations to us, because of this military contingency; and also that the infallible effect of Japan's action will be to transfer popular sympathy in the present war from Great Britain to Germany, because the latter, in a moment of extreme embarrassment and danger, has been wantonly and needlessly assailed, on a trumpery pretext. If action goes beyond Kiao-Chau, to the above named German islands, Australia, New Zealand, and Canada will be offended equally with ourselves.

3. These considerations are so obvious, that I doubt if Great Britain was consulted; but, which I bring as it stands, she will be believed to have been, which amounts to the same thing.

The seizure of the islands can better be forestalled through Great Britain than by direct representation to Japan, because of the delicate state of our present relations, the existing halted negotiations, and because the war spirit once aroused, as by the ultimatum, will be little amenable, and very resentful of what may seem interference. I believe the moment very critical, and one in which we might well desire the services of a highly trained diplomatist.

My own sympathies have been strongly against Germany, because I have believed her ultimately the state responsible for the general war; but I love fair play, and I hate disingenuousness, which is written all over the Japanese ultimatum.

[P.S.] I write to you because I know no one else in the Administration to whom I should care to write. If the letter approves itself to you, you may show it to whom you will.

LC - Mahan MSS<br>
2025 Hillyer Place<br>
Jan. 9, 1915

My dear Mr. Roosevelt:

I have just received your note of Jan. 6—enclosing the resolution, passed by the British Navy Records Society of their sympathy with us at this time, for which I thank you.

Will you convey to the Society our grateful appreciation of their thought of us, but especially for the tribute paid my husband.

Sincerely Yours<br>
(signed) Ellen Lyle Mahan

[P.S.] Shortly after his arrival in Washington my husband went to the Department to pay his respects to you—he told me that he had not seen you and that his card had been returned to him. I mention this as I would like you to know that he tried to see you and was disappointed.

# Selected Bibliography

## PRIMARY SOURCES

### Official Records

Naval War College, Newport, R.I.: RG 8 - Intelligence and Technological Archives

### Manuscript Collections

Houghton Library, Harvard University, Cambridge, Mass.: Theodore Roosevelt Collection

Library of Congress, Washington, D.C.: Stephen B. Luce Papers, Alfred Thayer Mahan Papers, Theodore Roosevelt Papers, William S. Sims Papers

Penn State University Libraries, State College, Pa.: Theodore Roosevelt Papers, Series 2, Correspondence

Massachusetts Historical Society, Boston, Mass.: Henry Cabot Lodge Papers, John D. Long Papers

Naval War College, Newport, R.I.: Stephen B. Luce Papers, Alfred Thayer Mahan Papers

### Collected Works, Memoirs, and Contemporary Accounts

Butt, Archie. *The Letters of Archie Butt*. Edited by Lawrence F. Abbott. Garden City, N.Y.: Doubleday, 1924.

Evans, Robley D. *An Admiral's Log: Being Continued Recollections of Naval Life*. New York: Appleton, 1910.

————. *A Sailor's Log: Recollections of Forty Years of Naval Life*. New York: Appleton, 1901.

Fiske, Bradley A. *From Midshipman to Rear-Admiral*. New York: Century, 1919.

Hay, John. *Life and Letters of John Hay*. Edited by William R. Thayer. 2 vols. Boston: Houghton Mifflin, 1916.

Lodge, Henry Cabot, ed. *Selections from the Correspondence of Theodore Roosevelt and Henry Cabot Lodge, 1884–1918*. 2 vols. New York: Charles Scribner's Sons, 1925.

Long, John Davis. *America of Yesterday, as Reflected in the Journal of John Davis Long*. Edited by Lawrence S. Mayo. Boston: Atlantic Monthly Press, 1923.

————. *The New American Navy*. 2 vols. New York: Outlook, 1903.

————. *The Papers of John Davis Long, 1897–1904*. Edited by Gardner Weld Allen. Boston: Massachusetts Historical Society, 1939.

Luce, Stephen B. *The Writings of Stephen B. Luce*. Edited by John D. Hayes and John B. Hattendorf. Newport: Naval War College Press, 1975.

Mahan, Alfred Thayer. *Armaments and Arbitration, or the Place of Force in the International Relations of States*. New York: Harper & Brothers, 1912.

————. *From Sail to Steam: Recollections of Naval Life*. New York: Harper & Brothers, 1907.

————. *The Influence of Sea Power Upon History: 1660–1783*. Boston: Little, Brown, 1890.

————. *The Influence of Sea Power Upon the French Revolution and Empire: 1793–1812*. 2 vols. Boston: Little, Brown, 1892.

————. *The Interest of America in International Conditions*. Boston: Little, Brown, 1910.

————. *The Interest of America in Sea Power, Present and Future*. Port Washington, N.Y.: Kennikat Press, 1970, o.d. 1897.

————. *Lessons of the War with Spain and Other Articles*. Boston: Little, Brown, 1899.

————. *The Letters and Papers of Alfred Thayer Mahan*. Edited by Robert Seager II and Doris D. Maguire. 3 vols. Annapolis, Md.: U.S. Naval Institute Press, 1975.

————. *Naval Administration and Warfare: Some General Principles*. Boston: Little, Brown, 1908.

————. *The Problem of Asia and Its Effect upon International Policies*. Boston: Little, Brown, 1900.

————. *Retrospect and Prospect: Studies in International Relations Naval and Political*. Boston: Little, Brown, 1903.

————. *Sea Power in Its Relation to the War of 1812*. 2 vols. Boston: Little, Brown, 1905.

————. *Some Neglected Aspects of War*. Boston: Little, Brown, 1907.

Robinson, Corinne Roosevelt. *My Brother Theodore Roosevelt*. New York: Charles Scribner's Sons, 1929.

Roosevelt, Nicholas. *Theodore Roosevelt: The Man As I Knew Him*. New York: Dodd, Mead and Co., 1967.

Roosevelt, Theodore. *An Autobiography*. New York: Macmillan, 1913.
_____. "Expansion and Peace." The *Independent* 51 (21 December 1899).
_____. "A Great Public Servant." The *Outlook*, 109 (13 January 1915), pp. 85–86.
_____. *Letters from Theodore Roosevelt to Anna Roosevelt, 1870–1918*. Edited by Anna Roosevelt Cowles. New York: Charles Scribner's Sons, 1924.
_____. *Letters of Theodore Roosevelt*. Edited by Elting E. Morison and John M. Blum. 8 vols. Cambridge: Harvard University Press, 1951–1954.
_____. Review of *The Influence of Sea Power Upon History, 1660–1783*, by Alfred Thayer Mahan. The *Atlantic Monthly* 66 (October 1890).
_____. Review of *The Influence of Sea Power Upon the French Revolution and Empire, 1793–1812*, by Alfred Thayer Mahan. The *Atlantic Monthly* 71 (April 1893).
_____. Review of *The Influence of Sea Power Upon History, 1660–1783*, and *The Influence of Sea Power Upon the French Revolution and Empire, 1793–1812*, by Alfred Thayer Mahan. *Political Science Quarterly* 9 (December 1893): 171.
_____. "The War with the United States, 1812–15." In *The Royal Navy: A History from the Earliest Times to the Present*, edited by William Laird Clowes. 7 vols. London: Sampson Low, Marston, 1901. vol. 6.
_____. *The Works of Theodore Roosevelt*. Edited by Hermann Hagedorn. 20 vols. National Edition. New York: Charles Scribner's Sons, 1926.
Wister, Owen. *Roosevelt: The Story of a Friendship, 1880–1919*. New York: MacMillan, 1930.

## SECONDARY SOURCES

### Books

Beale, Howard K. *Theodore Roosevelt and the Rise of America to World Power*. Baltimore: Johns Hopkins University Press, 1956
Braisted, William R. *The United States Navy in the Pacific, 1897–1909*. Austin: University of Texas Press, 1958.
_____. *The United States Navy in the Pacific, 1909–1922*. Austin: University of Texas Press, 1971.
Campbell, Alexander E. *Great Britain and the United States, 1895–1903*. London: Longmans, 1960.
Campbell, Charles S., Jr. *Anglo-American Understanding, 1898–1903*. Baltimore: Johns Hopkins Press, 1957.
Challener, Richard. *Admirals, Generals, and American Foreign Policy, 1898–1914*. Princeton: Princeton University Press, 1973.
Coletta, Paolo. *Admiral Bradley A. Fiske and the American Navy*. Lawrence: Regents Press of Kansas, 1979.
_____. *French Ensor Chadwick: Scholarly Warrior*. Washington: University Press of America, 1980.

Coletta, Paolo, K. Jack Bauer and Robert G. Albion. *American Secretaries of the Navy*. 2 vols. Annapolis: U.S. Naval Institute Press, 1980.

Cooling, Benjamin F. *Benjamin Franklin Tracy: Father of the Modern American Fighting Navy*. Hamden, Conn.: Shoe String, 1973.

Davis, Calvin DeArmond. *The United States and the First Hague Peace Conference*. Ithaca: Cornell University Press, 1962.

————. *The United States and the Second Hague Peace Conference*. Durham: Duke University Press, 1976.

Esthus, Raymond A. *Theodore Roosevelt and Japan*. Seattle: University of Washington Press, 1967.

Gleaves, Albert. *Life and Letters of Rear-Admiral Stephen B. Luce, U.S. Navy: Founder of the Naval War College*. New York: Putnam, 1925.

Hagan, Kenneth J. *American Gunboat Diplomacy and the Old Navy, 1877–1889*. Westport, Conn.: Greenwood Press, 1978.

————. *In Peace and War: Interpretations of American Naval History, 1775–1978*. Westport, Conn.: Greenwood Press, 1978.

Harbaugh, William H. *Power and Responsibility: The Life and Times of Theodore Roosevelt*. New York: Farrar, Straus and Cudahy, 1961.

Hart, Robert A. *The Great White Fleet: Its Voyage Around the World, 1907–1909*. Boston: Little, Brown, 1965.

Herrick, Walter R. *The American Naval Revolution*. Baton Rouge: Louisiana State University Press, 1967.

Herwig, Holger. *Politics of Frustration: The United States in German Naval Planning, 1889–1941*. Boston: Little, Brown, 1976.

Karsten, Peter. *The Naval Aristocracy: The Golden Age of Annapolis and the Emergence of Modern American Navalism*. New York: Free Press, 1972.

Knox, Dudley W. *A History of the United States Navy*. New York: G. P. Putnam's Sons, 1936.

LaFeber, Walter. *The New Empire: An Interpretation of American Expansion, 1860–1898*. Ithaca: Cornell University Press, 1963.

————. *The Panama Canal*. New York: Oxford University Press, 1977.

Langley, Lester D. *The Struggle for the American Mediterranean: United States–European Rivalry in the Gulf-Caribbean, 1776–1904*. Athens: University of Georgia Press, 1975.

————. *The United States and the Caribbean, 1900–1970*. Athens: University of Georgia Press, 1980.

Livezey, William E. *Mahan on Sea Power*. Norman: University of Oklahoma Press, 1947.

Long, David F. *Sailor-Diplomat: A Biography of Commodore James Biddle, 1783–1848*. Boston: Northeastern University Press, 1983.

McCullough, David. *Mornings on Horseback*. New York: Simon & Schuster, 1981.

————. *The Path Between the Seas: The Creation of the Panama Canal, 1870–1914*, New York: Simon & Schuster, 1977.

Marder, Arthur. *The Anatomy of British Sea Power: A History of British Naval Policy in the Pre-Dreadnought Era, 1880–1905*. New York: Knopf, 1940.

————. *From the Dreadnought to Scapa Flow: The Royal Navy in the Fisher Era, 1904–1919*. 5 vols. New York: Oxford Press, 1961–1970.

Marks, Frederick W. III. *Velvet on Iron: The Diplomacy of Theodore Roosevelt.* Lincoln: University of Nebraska Press, 1979.

Mitchell, Donald W. *History of the Modern American Navy.* New York: Alfred A. Knopf. 1946.

Morison, Elting E. *Admiral Sims and the Modern American Navy.* Boston: Houghton Mifflin, 1942.

Morris, Edmund. *The Rise of Theodore Roosevelt.* New York: Coward, McCann & Geoghegan, 1979.

Mowry, George W. *The Era of Theodore Roosevelt.* New York: Harper & Row, 1962.

Munro, Dana G. *Intervention and Dollar Diplomacy in the Caribbean, 1900–1921.* Princeton: Princeton University Press, 1964.

Neu, Charles. *An Uncertain Friendship: Theodore Roosevelt and Japan, 1906–1909.* Cambridge: Harvard University Press, 1967.

O'Gara, Gordon C. *Theodore Roosevelt and the Rise of the Modern Navy.* Princeton: Princeton University Press, 1943.

Perkins, Bradford. *The Great Rapprochement.* New York: Atheneum, 1968.

Pringle, Henry F. *Theodore Roosevelt: A Biography.* New York: Harcourt, Brace, 1931.

Puleston, William D. *Mahan: The Life and Work of Captain Alfred Thayer Mahan.* New Haven: Yale University Press, 1939.

Putnam, Carleton. *Theodore Roosevelt: The Formative Years, 1858–1886.* New York: Charles Scribner's Sons, 1958.

Seager, Robert II. *Alfred Thayer Mahan: The Man and His Letters.* Annapolis: U.S. Naval Institute Press, 1977.

Spector, Ronald. *Admiral of the New Empire: The Life and Career of George Dewey.* Baton Rouge: Louisiana State University Press, 1974.

————. *Professors of War: The Naval War College and the Development of the Profession.* Newport, R.I.: Naval War College Press, 1977.

Sprout, Harold, and Margaret Sprout. *The Rise of American Naval Power, 1776–1938.* Princeton: Princeton University Press, 1939.

Trask, David F. *The War with Spain in 1898.* New York: Macmillan, 1981.

Weigley, Russell. *The American Way of War: A History of United States Military Strategy and Policy.* Bloomington: Indiana University Press, 1977.

Widenor, William C. *Henry Cabot Lodge and the Search for an American Foreign Policy.* Berkeley: University of California Press, 1980.

## Articles

Allin, Lawrence C. "The Naval Institute, Mahan, and the Naval Profession." *Naval War College Review* 31 (Summer 1978): 29–48.

Ashe, Samuel A. "Memories of Annapolis." *South Atlantic Quarterly* 17 (July 1919).

Cane, Guy. "Sea Power—Teddy's 'Big Stick.' " *U.S. Naval Institute Proceedings* 102 (August 1976): 40–48.

Corgan, Michael T. "Mahan and Theodore Roosevelt: The Assessment of Influence." *Naval War College Review* 33 (November 1980): 89–97.

Johnson, Arthur M. "Theodore Roosevelt and the Navy." *U.S. Naval Institute Proceedings* 84 (October 1958): 76–82.
Karsten, Peter. "The Nature of 'Influence': Roosevelt, Mahan and the Concept of Sea Power." *American Quarterly* 23 (October 1971): 585–600.
Turk, Richard W. "The United States Navy and the 'Taking' of Panama, 1901–1903." *Military Affairs* 38 (October 1974): 92–96.

# Index

Train, Charles J., 29
Tsushima, battle of, 57, 59

Venezuelan crisis (1902–1903), 41, 49–51, 103

*Wachusett, U.S.S.*, 10–11, 21 n.16
Wainwright, Richard, 30, 33
Walker, John Grimes, 30

War of 1812, 13, 22 n.28, 44, 63–69, 104–105
"The War With the United States, 1812–15," 64–66
*Wasp, U.S.S.*, 9
Wilhelm, Kaiser, II, 3, 18. *See also* Germany
Windward Passage, 30
*The Winning of the West*, 15
World War I, 2, 4

## About the Author

RICHARD W. TURK, Professor of History, Allegheny College, is the author of contributed chapters, journal articles, and scholarly papers on a variety of topics dealing with American diplomatic and naval history.